SWAMI [illegible]

[illegible]DOM

Edited and with an Introduction by
SWAMI CHETANANANDA

Foreword by
CHRISTOPHER ISHERWOOD

Preface by
HUSTON SMITH

Advaita Ashrama
(Publication Department)
5 Dehi Entally Road
Kolkata 700 014

Published by
Swami Mumukshananda
President, Advaita Ashrama
Mayavati, Champawat, Himalayas
from its Publication Department, Kolkata
Email: advaita@vsnl.com
Website: www.advaitaonline.com

First Indian Edition, January 1987
Seventh Impression, April 2005
3M3C

ISBN 81-85301-23-9

Printed in India at
Trio Process
Kolkata 700 014

PUBLISHER'S NOTE

It gives us great pleasure in placing this first Indian edition of *Vedanta : Voice of Freedom* in the hands of the students and researchers of the Vivekananda literature. This book is a compilation in the Swami's own words on the subject from *The Complete Works of Swami Vivekananda* (in eight volumes) by Swami Chetanananda of the Vedanta Society of St. Louis, U.S.A., who has accomplished this difficult task in a remarkable manner.

There is an ever-increasing demand for books on the Vedanta and on and by Swami Vivekananda from all over the world. This book, we are sure, will be a useful addition to that class of literature. Swami Vivekananda carried the message of Vedanta to the West in the last century and raised his powerful voice in defence of India and her people, when they were subject to a foreign rule. In fulfilment of a prophecy he made, as it were, India attained political freedom in 1947.

According to Swami Vivekananda, the message of Vedanta consists in unfolding the potential divinity of man, developing an unshakable faith in oneself, manifesting absolute fearlessness of any kind, and attaining complete freedom of the Spirit now enmeshed in this body-mind complex. To attain to that total freedom even while living is the ultimate goal of human beings. Such is the voice of freedom found in the pages of the book.

We take this opportunity to express our deep sense of gratitude to the Vedanta Society of St. Louis, U.S.A., for preserving the copyright of this excellent compilation an passing it on to us formally for publication and circulation only in India.

This book is merely a reproduction in a smaller format of the original one published by Philosophical Library, New York, to which our sincere thanks are due.

Advaita Ashrama
Mayavati, Pithoragarh, Himalayas
12 January 1987

PUBLISHER

Swami Vivekananda at the Parliament of Religions, Chicago, September 1893

THE VOICE OF VIVEKANANDA

A FOREWORD

By compiling this selection from the eight volumes of Swami Vivekananda's lectures, writings, and letters, Swami Chetanananda has performed a most valuable task. This task must have been extraordinarily difficult because it required a firm intellectual grasp of Vivekananda's message to his hearers or readers—a message which had to be delivered in Vivekananda's own words. Paraphrase would have been out of the question—however convenient that might have sometimes been—lest Vivekananda's voice—his way of expressing himself, his vivid phraseology, his humor, the passion of his faith and the shock of his frankness—should be lost for the sake of mere clarity.

It must be remembered that much of this material was first spoken to audiences—sometimes extemporary, without even a rough draft of what Vivekananda wished to say. In such cases, it was taken down in shorthand by his devotees—to whom we can never be sufficiently grateful. Thus we experience the freshness of the Swami's unedited live speech.

Vivekananda's living presence often becomes powerfully evident behind his words. Like all others, no doubt, who have read them aloud in public, I have often felt aware that I was sharing that presence with my listeners. Even if you try reading Vivekananda aloud to yourself, alone in your room, you will probably have an experience of the same kind.

Christopher Isherwood

PREFACE

I know of no better way to preface this useful book than through the three key words around which its editor has woven its title, *Vedanta: Voice of Freedom*.

In reverse order, first, *freedom*. I happen to be writing these lines on the day* in history when human astronauts have achieved their first untethered walk in space. To float as they are floating, like birds with the whole sky to fly in, may seem at first like the ultimate freedom, but we know of course that their floating only tokens the spiritual freedom we truly seek. For our desire for freedom is, above all, our desire for God, absolute freedom being an aspect of divinity. Thus it is that Hinduism speaks of the final freedom that marks the end of the mystic path as liberation (*moksha*), for it is the state of union (*yoga*) with the Absolute, the Infinite, and the Eternal, and therefore of freedom from all the bonds of relativity. It was to this freedom above all that Christ referred when he said, "the truth shall make you free."

Second, *voice*. Until we are free, we need voices to witness to its possibility and point us toward its light. But voices imply vocalists, which in the context of this book introduces something interesting. For the voice of freedom that resounds through its pages has no identifiable source; if we hear it

* February 7, 1984.

aright, we see that from the world's perspective it issues from nowhere. This is not, of course, to deny that an identifiable human being, a very great one, uttered or penned the words that fill these pages. But if we listen through the words to the thoughts they express, we know that Vivekananda is their conduit only, not their author. Etymologically *Vedanta* means "the culmination of the Vedas," but the Vedas themselves are no more than channels of the *sanatana dharma*, that "wisdom uncreate" or "breath of the eternal" that ever was and always shall be.

So our outreach for freedom carries us, via a lesser disembodied voice, Vivekananda's, to the larger disembodied voice, the *Vedanta*, that tokens freedom's reality. Of this larger voice, one of the most discerning comparative philosophers alive has written: "The Vedanta appears among explicit doctrines as one of the most direct formulations possible of what makes the very essence of our spiritual reality."[1]

What needs to be added? Only appreciation. Appreciation, first, to Swami Chetanananda of the Vedanta Society of St. Louis, successor to my own beloved teacher, Swami Satprakashananda, for distilling the voluminous writings of Swami Vivekananda into these manageable proportions. And beyond the book's editor, appreciation to Vivekananda himself.

It is said that when Vivekananda arrived, uninvited and unannounced, at the Chicago Parliament of Religions, he took that Parliament by storm. The year was 1893, and it has become a symbol for the harmony of faiths which its conveners hoped it would inaugurate. As we approach the centenary of that historic event it is appropriate that these key passages from Vivekananda's writings be reissued, for though our century has brought progress in interfaith understanding, much remains to be done. Attentiveness to the voice of freedom that sounds through these pages can help us get on with the job.

Huston Smith
Hanna Professor of Philosophy
Hamline University

[1] Schuon, Frithjof, *The Language of the Self* (Madras: Ganesh & Co., Pvt. Ltd., 1959), 15.

CONTENTS

LIST OF ILLUSTRATIONS

EDITOR'S NOTE

When a person asks me, "What is *Vedanta*?" it reminds me of a story. Once a great teacher of Vedanta was invited by a group of people to give a talk on Vedanta. When he arrived at the lecture hall he asked the audience, "Do you know what I am going to tell you?" The people all said, "No." "Then I shall not say anything to you, because you have no background." Saying this, the teacher left the hall. The following week he was again invited by the people, but the leaders of the group planned in advance. They told the audience to say yes if the teacher asked them the same question. The teacher was escorted to the hall, and sure enough, he asked the same question. This time the audience replied, "Yes." Immediately the teacher said, "You know everything then, so I have nothing to say," and he left. Again the leaders made a plan for the teacher's next visit and asked half of the audience to say yes and the other half to say no. When the teacher came for the third time he repeated the same question, "Do you know what I am going to tell you?" and the audience responded as they had been instructed. Then the teacher said, "Those who have said no, please learn from those who have said yes." Without another word he left. The people were puzzled and did not know what to do. They finally decided that the next time they would simply remain silent. After repeated requests the teacher came once more and asked the same question. This time he did not get any answer. He noticed that the whole audience was absorbed in deep silence, and he knew that this was the right time to talk to them about Vedanta.

This is the age of the jet, the rocket, and the satellite. People want to move speedily and expect to achieve everything fast, if not instantly. People unfamiliar with Vedanta do not realize that they are trying to know in five minutes about a spiritual tradition that has been handed down to us for the last five thousand years. I know I am not doing proper justice to Vedanta by trying to describe it in this short note, but nevertheless I shall try to answer the question, "What is *Vedanta*?"

Vedanta is the culmination of knowledge, the sacred wisdom of the Hindu sages, the transcendental experience of the seers of Truth. It is the essence, or conclusion, of the Vedas. As the Upanishads come at the end of the Vedas, so it is called *Vedanta*. Literally, *Veda* means knowledge and *anta* means end.

The main tenets of Vedanta are: (1) *Brahman* is the ultimate reality, the one without a second. It is Existence-Consciousness-Bliss Absolute. It is beyond name and form, devoid of qualities, without beginning or end. It is the unchanging Truth, beyond space, time, and causation. But this vast, infinite Brahman manifests itself as the universe and the individual beings through its inscrutable power of *maya*. Thus the one becomes many. When Brahman is associated with its maya, it is called God, or *Ishvara*.

(2) The universe is apparent, like water in a mirage, and is continuously changing. We perceive the universe through space, time, and causation. Space begins when one gets a body, time begins when one starts thinking, and causation begins when one becomes limited. This beautiful, tangible universe disappears from one's awareness when one enters into the sleep state or merges into *samadhi*, and again it reappears in the waking state. So this world is in the mind.

(3) Human beings are divine. Their real nature is the *Atman*,

which is infinite, eternal, pure, luminous, ever free, blissful, and identical with Brahman. They are not sinners. They make mistakes and suffer because of ignorance. As darkness disappears when light dawns, so ignorance goes away with the advent of knowledge. Bondage and freedom are in the mind. Thinking of weakness and bondage, one becomes weak and bound. Thinking of strength and freedom, one becomes strong and free. No human being wants slavery, because it is painful. Joy is only in freedom, which is, as Vedanta declares, the inherent nature of all beings. The goal of human life is to realize God, and the purpose of religion is to teach one how to manifest the divinity within.

(4) How does one manifest the divinity within? Vedanta suggests four *yogas*: (a) *karma yoga*, the path of unselfish action, (b) *jnana yoga*, the path of knowledge, (c) *raja yoga*, the path of meditation, and (d) *bhakti yoga*, the path of devotion. The word *yoga* signifies the union of the individual soul with the Cosmic Soul.

(5) Truth is one and universal. It cannot be limited to any country or race or individual. All religions of the world express the same Truth in different languages and in various ways. Just as the sun is no one's property, so also Truth is not confined to one particular religion or philosophy. No one can say that the sun is a Christian sun or a Hindu sun or a Buddhist sun or a Jewish sun or an Islamic sun. Vedanta, rather, promulgates the harmony of religions. As different rivers originate from different sources but mingle in the ocean, losing their names and forms, so all the various religious paths that human beings take, through different tendencies, lead to God, or the Truth.

Now if a person would ask me, "What do you suggest that I read to know about Vedanta?" it would be hard for me to give an answer. Vedanta is a vast subject. Its scriptures have been evolving for the last five thousand years. The three basic scriptures of Vedanta are the Upanishads (the revealed truths), the Brahma Sutras (the reasoned truths), and the Bhagavad Gita (the practical truths). But it is hard for someone to get the essence of these scriptures without the help of a teacher and without going through the commentaries. Sometimes we suggest that a person read *Sri Ramakrishna: The Great Master* and *The Gospel of Sri Ramakrishna*, because Sri

Ramakrishna's life and teachings were saturated with Vedanta. Or we suggest *The Complete Works of Swami Vivekananda*, because it was Swami Vivekananda who brought the message of Vedanta to the West. But invariably we have noticed that the inquirer is dismayed, seeing the huge volumes of the *Great Master*, the *Gospel*, and the *Complete Works*, which consist of 1081, 1063, and 4363 pages respectively. Of course, many swamis of the Ramakrishna Order have written excellent shorter books on Vedanta and yoga, and these undoubtedly are very helpful.

Once, however, a prophetic saying of Swami Vivekananda's flashed through my mind: "I have a message to the West, as Buddha had a message to the East." What was his message? It was Vedanta. And it is this message that I have put together for the readers in Vivekananda's own words from his *Complete Works*.

I have supplied a title for each selection, and definitions for some less familiar Sanskrit terms are given in a glossary at the end of the book. Also, for the sake of clarity and readability, I have occasionally cut one or more sentences or introductory phrases and modernized the punctuation without indicating these deletions or variations from the original. In a few places I compared the version of *The Complete Works of Swami Vivekananda* with Swami Nikhilananda's *Vivekananda: The Yogas and Other Works*, and accepted that version which would be more clear to Western readers. At the end of each selection, a reference is given to the volume and page number of the *Complete Works* from which that section has been taken. The volume numbers are indicated in Roman numerals and the page numbers are indicated in Arabic numerals. The following are references to the editions used for each of the eight volumes:

Volume I	13th ed., 1970
Volume II	12th ed., 1971
Volume III	10th ed., 1970
Volume IV	10th ed., 1972
Volume V	9th ed., 1970
Volume VI	9th ed., 1972
Volume VII	7th ed., 1969
Volume VIII	5th ed., 1971

My special thanks to Christopher Isherwood, who read the manuscript, gave many valuable suggestions, and wrote an inspiring foreword. My heartfelt gratitude to Huston Smith, who contributed an illuminating preface and also gave many valuable suggestions. I am indebted to Advaita Ashrama, Mayavati, Himalayas, for giving me permission to reproduce these selections from *The Complete Works of Swami Vivekananda*.

St. Louis

Chetanananda

INTRODUCTION

Temple Garden of Dakshineswar

VEDANTA AND VIVEKANANDA

The river does not drink its own water, nor does the tree eat its own fruit. They live for others. Similarly, from time to time, great souls are born whose lives are lived for the good of others. They bring peace and happiness to mankind. Having themselves crossed the dreadful ocean of maya (relative existence), they help others to cross without any selfish motive. It does not matter when and where a great soul is born or how long he lives; his life and message are a source of inspiration to all people in all ages.

In the later part of the nineteenth century, Swami Vivekananda brought the eternal message of Vedanta to the Western world. His teacher, Sri Ramakrishna, had commissioned him to convey to mankind the sublime teachings of Vedanta—the oneness of Truth, the divinity of man, and the harmony of religions. But even from his early youth the Swami had had an intuitive knowledge of his destiny, and he later declared, like a prophet at the dawn of his mission, "I have a message to the West as Buddha had a message to the East."[1]

Sri Ramakrishna had several visions about Vivekananda before he ever met him. Once, in a state of samadhi, Sri Ramakrishna's mind soared higher and higher, transcending the realm of the gods and goddesses, until it reached the transcendental realm. There he found seven venerable sages seated in samadhi. He felt that those sages had surpassed not only men, but even the gods, in knowledge and holiness, in renunciation and love. He then saw a divine child move toward one of the sages, put his arms around his neck, and, addressing him in a sweet voice, try to drag his mind down from samadhi. When the magic touch had roused the sage, the child said to him: "I am going down to earth. Won't you come with me?" With a benign look the sage gave his tacit consent and again became immersed in samadhi. "No sooner had I seen Naren [Vivekananda] than I recognized him to be that sage," said Sri Ramakrishna. And he later disclosed, on inquiry, that the divine child was none other than himself.[2]

In another vision, Sri Ramakrishna saw a streak of light flash across the sky from Varanasi toward Calcutta. "My prayer has been answered," he exclaimed, "and *my man* must come to me one day."[3]

Bhuvaneshwari Devi, the mother of Vivekananda, also had a vision about her son before his birth. Hoping that the Lord would bless her with a male child, she asked one of her relatives in Varanasi to pray and make some offerings at the shrine of Vireshwar Shiva on her behalf. Meanwhile she spent her days in fasting and meditation. Soon after, in a dream, she saw the Lord Shiva arouse Himself out of His meditation and take the form of a child who was to be her son.

Vivekananda was born in Calcutta on January 12, 1863, and was given the name Narendranath Datta. Many years later he wrote in a letter to Mary Hale of Chicago about his premonastic name: "It is a very poetic name. Narendra meaning the 'Chief of men' (*nara* means man, and *indra* stands for ruler or chief)—very ludicrous, isn't it? But such are the names in our country; we cannot help it, but I am glad that I have given that up."[4]

It is the ancient tradition of India that men of renunciation, and not men of wealth, lead society and the nation. We observe the tremendous influence such spiritual giants as Buddha, Shankara, Chaitanya, and Nanaka have over millions of people. Their impact on the minds of the masses is deeper and more lasting than that of kings and emperors. Even as a boy Vivekananda had an inclination to become a wandering monk. Pointing to a line on his palm, he would say to his young friends: "I shall certainly become a monk. A palmist has predicted it."[5] Another time he said to them: "At best you will be lawyers or doctors or judges. Wait, I shall chalk out a path for myself."[6]

Vivekananda was a precocious boy of indomitable energy. Yet his innate tendency toward meditation showed itself even in his early life. Meditation was one of his childhood games. Once he was meditating with his friends when a cobra appeared. The other boys became frightened, shouted a warning to him, and ran away; but he remained motionless. Later he told his parents: "I knew nothing of the snake or anything else. I was feeling inexpressible joy."[7]

Brought up and educated in nineteenth-century Calcutta, Vivekananda was introduced at an early age to the principles of Western thinking, which taught that one should not accept anything without evidence. Although he was a brilliant student and was well-versed in history, philosophy, literature, and contemporary Western thought, he held firmly to the idea: "Do not believe a thing because you read it in a book. Do not believe a thing because another has said it is so. Find out the truth for yourself. That is realization."[8]

In his intense desire to realize the truth, Vivekananda practiced meditation; he studied different religious and philosophical systems of the East and the West; he met different religious leaders, but nothing was of any avail. Nothing could satisfy his all-devouring hunger for truth. At last he met Sri Ramakrishna at the Dakshineswar temple garden near Calcutta and asked this simple question, "Sir, have you seen God?" Without a moment's hesitation Sri Ramakrishna replied: "Yes, I have seen God. I see Him as I see you here, only more clearly. God can be seen. One can talk to Him. But who cares for God? People shed torrents of tears for their wives, children, wealth, and property, but who weeps for the vision of God? If one cries sincerely for God, one can surely see Him."[9]

Sri Ramakrishna's reply was the turning point of Vivekananda's life. But he tested Sri Ramakrishna in many ways before he finally accepted him as his teacher. Later he said, "I fought my Master for six long years, with the result that I know every inch of the way!"[10]

During Vivekananda's first visit, Sri Ramakrishna said to him in an ecstatic mood: "Ah! You have come so late. How unkind of you to keep me waiting so long! My ears are nearly burnt from listening to the rubbish talk of worldly people. Oh, how I have been yearning to unburden my mind to one who will understand my thoughts!" Then with folded hands he addressed the astonished young man: "Lord! I know you are the ancient sage, Nara—the incarnation of Narayana—born on earth to remove the miseries of mankind."[11]

Sri Ramakrishna's overwhelming love and concern made Vivekananda his own forever. He trained Vivekananda in a number of disciplines and at last transmitted his own spiritual power to him before his death. Sri Ramakrishna knew Vivekananda's mind was naturally inclined to the path of knowledge, so he initiated him into the teachings of nondualistic Vedanta. Sometimes he asked Vivekananda to read aloud passages from the Ashtavakra Samhita and other Vedanta treatises so that he could grasp the essence of the Vedanta philosophy.

In nondualistic Vedanta, Brahman is the Ultimate Reality, Existence-Knowledge-Bliss Absolute. The world is shown to be nothing but name and form, all of which is apparent, not real, having only a relative existence. But from the absolute standpoint, everything is Brahman—one without a second. The individual soul is nothing but Brahman. Name and form evolve and dissolve, but the Self, the real nature of every being, is immortal and unchanging. After realizing one's identity with Brahman through meditation, a person then sees Brahman, or God, in everything.

In the beginning it was hard for Vivekananda to accept the nondualistic view that 'everything is really Brahman', because he was then a staunch follower of the Brahmo Samaj, which taught a theistic philosophy. As he said to Sri Ramakrishna: "It is blasphemous, for there is no difference between such philosophy and atheism. There is no greater sin in the world than to think of oneself as identical with the Creator. I am God, you are God, these created things are God—what can be more absurd! The sages who wrote such things must have been insane." Because Sri Ramakrishna knew how to train a mind, the young man's outspokenness did not deter him. Smiling, he said: "You may not accept the views of these seers. But how can you abuse them or limit God's infinitude? Go on praying to the God of Truth and believe in any aspect of His that He reveals to you."[12]

According to the Vedantic tradition, one must reach an understanding of the philosophy with the help of *shruti* (the scriptures), *yukti* (reason), and *anubhava* (experience). Vivekananda's rebellious nature did not surrender easily. He was a votary of Truth. Whatever did not tally with reason and experience, he considered false, and it was his nature to stand against falsehood.

One day at Dakshineswar, while chatting with one of his friends, Vivekananda sarcastically remarked concerning the Vedantic experience of oneness: "How can this be? This jug is God, this cup is God, and we too are God! Nothing can be more preposterous!" Sri Ramakrishna heard Vivekananda's laughter from his room. He came out and inquired: "Hello! What are you talking about?" He then touched Vivekananda and entered into samadhi.[13] Preachers merely talk about religion, but Incarnations like Buddha, Christ, and Ramakrishna can transmit religion through a glance or by a touch. Vivekananda graphically described the effect of that touch:

> The magic touch of the Master that day immediately brought a wonderful change over my mind. I was stupefied to find that there was really nothing in the universe but God! I saw it quite clearly but kept silent, to see if the idea would last. But the impression did not abate in the course of the day. I returned home, but there too, everything I saw appeared to be Brahman. I sat down to take my meal, but found that everything—the food, the plate, the person who served, and even myself—was nothing but That. I ate a morsel or two and sat still. I was startled by my mother's words: "Why do you sit still? Finish your meal," and began to eat again. But all the while, whether eating or lying down, or going to college, I had the same experience and felt myself always in a sort of comatose state. While walking in the streets, I noticed cabs plying, but I did not feel inclined to move out of the way. I felt that the cabs and myself were of one stuff. There was no sensation in my limbs, which, I thought, were getting paralyzed. I did not relish eating, and felt as if somebody else were eating. Sometimes I lay down during a

> meal and, after a few minutes, got up and again began to eat. The result would be that on some days I would take too much, but it did no harm. My mother became alarmed and said that there must be something wrong with me. She was afraid that I might not live long. When the above state altered a little, the world began to appear to me as a dream. While walking in Cornwallis Square, I would strike my head against the iron railings to see if they were real or only a dream. This state of things continued for some days. When I became normal again, I realized that I must have had a glimpse of the Advaita state. Then it struck me that the words of the scriptures were not false. Thenceforth I could not deny the conclusions of the Advaita philosophy.[14]

As time passed and Vivekananda went through various kinds of experiences, his rebellious attitude, intellectual skepticism, and argumentative nature were gradually transformed into self-surrender, faith, and devotion. Brajendra Nath Seal, one of his friends who later became a well-known professor, watched this change and remarked: "A born iconoclast and free thinker like Vivekananda, a creative and dominating intelligence, a tamer of souls, himself caught in the meshes of what appeared to me an uncouth, supernatural mysticism, was a riddle that my philosophy of Pure Reason could scarcely read at the time."[15]

In the early part of 1884, Vivekananda's father died unexpectedly of a heart attack. Unfortunately he left behind many unsettled debts, and the once well-to-do family was suddenly thrust into acute poverty. To add to their troubles, some relatives filed a lawsuit with a view to depriving them of their home. Since Vivekananda was the eldest son, the responsibility for the family's welfare fell upon his shoulders. He had just passed his B.A. examination and had been admitted to law school. He had no job and, moreover, no previous practical experience. But forced by circumstances, he began visiting offices, barefoot and shabbily dressed, looking for a job. Many times he attended classes without having eaten and was often faint with hunger and weakness. The only one of his friends who knew the gravity of the situation would occasionally send a little money to Vivekananda's mother anonymously so that they could survive. His friends invited him now and then to their houses and offered him food, but the thought of his starving mother and brothers at home prevented him from eating. At home he would eat as little as possible in order that the others might have enough. This first contact with the harsh sufferings of life convinced Vivekananda that unselfish sympathy is a rarity in the world. There is no place here for the weak, the poor, and the destitute.

Misfortune does not come alone. Vivekananda related: "Various temptations came my way. A rich woman sent me an ugly proposal to end my days of penury, which I sternly rejected with scorn. Another woman also made similar overtures to me. I said to her: 'You have wasted your life seeking the pleasures of the flesh. The dark shadows of death are before you. Have you done anything to face that? Give up all these filthy desires and remember God.' "[16]

Unable to find a permanent solution to the financial problems of his family, Vivekananda came to Sri Ramakrishna one day and asked him to pray to God on his behalf. The Master told him to go to the temple and pray himself for help to the Divine Mother, assuring him that his prayer would be granted. Vivekananda went to the temple with great expectation. But as soon as he came before the image of the Divine Mother, he saw that She was living and conscious. He forgot the world. He forgot the pitiable condition of his mother and brothers. In ecstatic joy he prostrated before Her and prayed: "Mother, give me discrimination! Give me renunciation! Give me knowledge and devotion! Grant that I may have an uninterrupted vision of Thee!" He came back to Sri Ramakrishna and told him what had happened. Sri Ramakrishna sent Vivekananda back to the temple to pray again, but the same thing happened. The third time he remembered his intention, but he felt ashamed to ask for something so small from the Mother of the Universe. At last, at Vivekananda's request, Sri Ramakrishna blessed him: "All right, your people at home will never be in want of plain food and clothing."[17]

Vivekananda learned from his Master the synthesis of knowledge and devotion, the harmony of religions, the true purport of the scriptures, and the worship of God in man. When Sri Ramakrishna was on his deathbed at the Cossipore garden house, Vivekananda requested a boon from him that he could remain immersed in *nirvikalpa samadhi*, the culmination of Vedantic experience, for three or four days at a time.

In that state, knower, knowledge, and knowable become one. But Sri Ramakrishna reprimanded him: "Shame on you! You are asking for such an insignificant thing. I thought that you would be like a big banyan tree and that thousands of people would rest in your shade. But now I see that you are seeking your own liberation."[18] Sri Ramakrishna knew the future mission of Vivekananda, which was service to humanity, so he guided him in that direction.

Nevertheless, Vivekananda persuaded his Master to give him the realization of the great Vedic dictum *Aham Brahmasmi* (I am Brahman). One evening, when he was meditating with one of his brother disciples at Cossipore, he suddenly became aware of a light at the back of his head, as if a lamp had been placed there. It gradually became more brilliant until finally it seemed to burst. He was engulfed by that light and lost body-consciousness. After some time, when he started to regain normal consciousness, he cried out, "Where is my body?" The amazed brother disciple assured him: "It is there. Don't you feel it?" He then rushed to Sri Ramakrishna's room upstairs and told him of Vivekananda's condition. "Let him stay in that state for a while," remarked Sri Ramakrishna. "He has pestered me long enough for it."[19]

After Sri Ramakrishna passed away on August 16, 1886, some of the young disciples, under the leadership of Swami Vivekananda, established a monastery at nearby Baranagore. There they embraced the life of renunciation and took final monastic vows, as Sri Ramakrishna had done, according to the Order of Shankara, the great teacher of nondualistic Vedanta. Thus the Ramakrishna Order came into existence, taking for its motto: "To work for one's own liberation and to dedicate oneself to do good to the world."

There is a saying, "The monk is pure who goes and the river is pure which flows." After some time Vivekananda left the monastery to live as a wandering monk. He traveled almost all over India, mostly on foot, visiting places of pilgrimage. He was thus able to have firsthand experience of the lives of the people. Seeing the pitiable living conditions of the masses, he was at times moved to tears. Only one who has suffered can understand the sufferings of others. Once he remarked, with his usual vigor, that a God who could not in this life give a crust of bread was not to be trusted in the next for the kingdom of heaven. He observed that religion was not the crying need of India, and recalled Sri Ramakrishna's pithy saying, "Religion is not for an empty stomach." He tried to draw the attention of local rulers to the pitiable conditions of the masses, but he could not get much response. Later, he expressed his feelings: "May I be born again and again, and suffer thousands of miseries so that I may worship the only God that exists, the only God I believe in, the sum total of all souls—and above all, my God the wicked, my God the miserable, my God the poor of all races, of all species, is the special object of my worship."[20]

While Vivekananda was traveling in India, he heard about the Parliament of Religions which was to be held in Chicago in September 1893. Many Indian rulers and influential people asked him to attend and represent Hinduism (the religion of Vedanta), but he refused. While at Madras he had a symbolic dream in which he saw Sri Ramakrishna walking over the ocean and beckoning him to follow. He also heard the Master's voice saying, "Go." At last, Vivekananda agreed.

While arrangements were being made for his departure, Raja Ajit Singh of Khetri, who was a disciple of Vivekananda, requested him to come and bless his newborn son, and also offered to provide the ticket for his passage to America. Vivekananda consented and went to Khetri for the birthday function. One evening while he was there, the Maharaja invited Vivekananda to attend a musical performance by a dancing girl, but the Swami sent word in return that, as he was a monk, he was not permitted to enjoy secular pleasures. The girl was hurt when she heard the message and sang this plaintive song, which reached the Swami's ears:

> Look not, O Lord, upon my sins!
> Is not Same-sightedness Thy name?
> One piece of iron is in the image in the temple,
> And another, the knife in the hand of the butcher;
> Yet both of these are turned to gold
> When touched by the philosophers' stone.
> So, Lord, look not upon my evil qualities....

Vivekananda was deeply moved. This dancing girl, whom society condemned as impure, had taught him a great lesson: Brahman, the ever-pure, ever-free, ever-illumined, is the essence of all beings. He immediately understood his mistake and came out of his room and joined the party. He later said: "That incident removed the scales from my eyes. Seeing that all are indeed the manifestation of the One, I could no longer condemn anybody."[21]

Vivekananda left Bombay for Chicago on May 31, 1893, traveling via Japan and the Pacific. The World's Parliament of Religions of Chicago was one of the significant events in the history of the world. In the opening session of that Parliament, Vivekananda reiterated the eternal message of Vedanta: "As the different streams having their sources in different places all mingle their water in the sea, so, O Lord, the different paths which men take, through different tendencies, various though they may appear, crooked or straight, all lead to Thee!"[22]

Mrs. S.K. Blodgett, an American woman, said later: "I was at the Parliament of Religions at Chicago in 1893, and when that young man [Vivekananda] got up and said, 'Sisters and Brothers of America,' seven thousand people rose to their feet as a tribute to something, they knew not what; and when it was over, and I saw scores of women walking over the benches to get near him, I said to myself, 'Well, my lad, if you can resist that onslaught, you are indeed a god.' "[23]

The newspapers of America gave Vivekananda much publicity, and he became widely known. The homes of some of the wealthiest people of American society were open to him, and there he was received as an honored guest. But he never swayed from his monastic ideals or from the service he had set out to perform. He started lecturing all over the Midwest as well as on the East Coast and in some southern states of the U.S.A. He founded the Vedanta Society in New York and trained some sincere students at Thousand Island Park. Both through lectures and through personal contacts, Vivekananda unveiled the spiritual treasures of Vedanta to the Western world. As Sister Nivedita (Margaret Noble) wrote: "Where others would talk of ways and means he knew how to light a fire. Where others gave directions, he would show the thing itself."[24] He was "an orator by divine right,"[25] as one American newspaper reporter described him.

Truth is always simple, as the teachings of all great teachers of the world demonstrate. Since Vivekananda had himself experienced the Ultimate Reality, he could make the truths of

Vedanta understandable to all. He wrote to one of his disciples: "To put the Hindu ideas into English and then make out of dry philosophy and intricate mythology and queer, startling psychology, a religion which shall be easy, simple, popular, and at the same time meet the requirements of the highest minds—is a task only those can understand who have attempted it. The dry, abstract Advaita must become living—poetic—in everyday life; out of hopelessly intricate mythology must come concrete moral forms; and out of bewildering yogi-ism must come the most scientific and practical psychology—and all this must be put in a form so that a child may grasp it. That is my life's work."[26]

Vivekananda came in contact with many outstanding figures of the Western world, such as Max Müller, Paul Deussen, William James, Robert Ingersoll, Nikola Tesla, Sarah Bernhardt, and Madame Emma Calvé. Madame Calvé, the famous opera singer, wrote in her autobiography that she was indebted to Vivekananda for her peace and prosperity. She also related an interesting story about the meeting of John D. Rockefeller with Vivekananda at Chicago. The Swami made Rockefeller understand that God had given him wealth so that he might have an opportunity to help and do good to others. Rockefeller was annoyed that anyone would dare talk to him that way, telling him what to do. He left the room without even saying good-bye. But about a week later he came again to see the Swami with a paper which set forth his plans to donate an enormous sum of money to a public institution.

"Well, there you are," he said. "You must be satisfied now, and you can thank me for it."

Vivekananda quietly read it and said: "It is for you to thank me." This was Rockefeller's first large donation to public welfare.[27]

Vivekananda returned to India in 1897 after visiting and lecturing in some European countries. The triumphal reception of Vivekananda in India was phenomenal. Millions of people paid homage to the Swami, and even rajas prostrated themselves before him. He traveled and lectured all over India, this time as a national hero. He began to awaken the sleeping, subjugated nation with the clarion call of Vedanta:

> Awake! Arise! And stop not till the goal is reached.[28]

> Strength, strength is what the Upanishads speak to me from every page. Be not weak. Will sin cure sin, weakness cure weakness? Stand up and be strong.[29]

> The first step in getting strength is to uphold the Upanishads, and believe: "I am the Soul." "Me the sword cannot cut; nor weapons pierce; me the fire cannot burn; me the air cannot dry; I am the Omnipotent, I am the Omniscient." So repeat these blessed, saving words. Do not say we are weak; we can do anything and everything. We all have the same glorious soul. Let us believe in it.[30]

> These conceptions of Vedanta must come out, must not remain only in the forest, not only in the cave, but they must come out to work at the bar and the bench, in the pulpit, and in the cottage of the poor man.[31]

> Carry the light and the life of Vedanta to every door, and rouse up the divinity that is hidden within every soul.[32]

In 1897, Vivekananda founded the Ramakrishna Math and Mission and framed its rules and regulations. He delineated the aims and ideals of the Ramakrishna Order, which are purely spiritual and humanitarian in nature. Property was purchased at Belur, across the river from Calcutta, which became the headquarters of the Order. There Vivekananda installed the relics of Sri Ramakrishna. "The Master once told me," said Vivekananda, " 'I will go and live wherever you take me, carrying me on your shoulder, be it under a tree or in the humblest cottage.' "[33] Two days before his passing away Vivekananda made this prophetic statement: "The spiritual impact that has come here to Belur will last fifteen hundred years—and this will be a great university. Do not think I imagine it—I see it."[34]

Two other centers were started by Vivekananda—one at Mayavati in the Himalayas, where westerners could practice nondualistic Vedanta, and the other in Madras. He also started three magazines to propagate the ideas and ideals of Vedanta. But soon his health began to fail because of constant work. He badly needed rest. His American disciples and friends wanted him to come back to America, and his brother disciples also felt that a sea voyage would do him good.

Thus on June 20, 1899, Vivekananda left for the West for a second time, accompanied by Swami Turiyananda and Sister Nivedita. During this voyage the Swami said to Nivedita: "The older I grow, the more everything seems to me to lie in manliness. This is my new gospel."[35] He stopped a few days in London and then proceeded to America. "I love the Yankee land," he wrote to an American woman. "I like to see new things. I do not care a fig to loaf about old ruins and mope a life out about old histories and keep sighing about the ancients. I have too much vigor in my blood for that. In America is the place, the people, the opportunity, for everything new. I have become horribly radical."[36]

As he continued his travels, his teaching, his observations, writing, and meditation, Vivekananda's belief in the effectiveness of Vedanta grew. He saw it not as a mere religion or philosophy, but rather as a means by which science and religion could become reconciled, and material prosperity and spirituality blended. He noticed how the East was strong in noble religious and spiritual traditions even though it suffered from grinding poverty, while the West, for all its technological advancements and affluence, suffered from spiritual poverty. There was no reason, he thought, why East and West could not profit from each other's strengths by removing each other's weaknesses. And in his teachings, writings, and lectures, Vivekananda expressed his belief that the strength-giving, rational, and practical principles of Vedanta could help mankind advance in mind, spirit, and science.

"By preaching the profound secrets of Vedanta in the Western world," he said, "we shall attract the sympathy and regard of these mighty nations, maintaining for ourselves the position of their teachers in spiritual matters; let them remain our teachers in all material concerns. Nothing will come of crying day and night before them, 'Give me this!' or 'Give me that!' When there grows a link of sympathy and regard between both nations by this give-and-take intercourse, there will be then no need for these noisy cries. They will do everything of their own accord. I believe that by this cultivation of religion and the wider diffusion of Vedanta, both our country and the West will gain enormously."[37]

This time Vivekananda stayed in the West a year and a half. He preached mainly in New York and on the West Coast.

Typically he paid no heed to the continued strain his workload placed on his health. He was burning up his energy in ceaseless service to mankind. In San Francisco he said to a woman disciple: "You know, I may have to be born again. You see, I have fallen in love with man."[38]

In July 1900, he left New York to attend the Congress of the History of Religions in Paris, where he spoke twice. He then traveled to Vienna, Constantinople, Athens, and Cairo accompanied by Madame Calvé and Miss Josephine MacLeod. After returning to India in December 1900, Swami Vivekananda concentrated on giving final shape to his "man-making religion." It was his experience that an ideal character could be formed by combining the four yogas—the paths of action, knowledge, devotion, and meditation—and he trained the monks accordingly. But, as he knew he was coming to the end of his mission, he guided and inspired his brother monks and his own disciples so that they could relieve him of his responsibilities. Once he said to Miss MacLeod: "I shall never see forty. I delivered my message and I must go." When she asked, "Why go?" he replied: "The shadow of a big tree will not let the smaller trees grow up. I must go to make room."[39] He consulted the Bengali almanac and, unknown to anyone else, chose a date for his final departure: July 4, 1902.

Sister Nivedita left this graphic account: "He had spent hours of that day in formal meditation. Then he had given a long Sanskrit lesson. Finally he had taken a walk from the monastery gates to the distant highroad. On his return from this walk, the bell was ringing for evensong, and he went to his own room and sat down, facing towards the Ganges, to meditate. It was the last time. The moment was come that had been foretold by his Master from the beginning. Half an hour went by, and then, on the wings of that meditation, his spirit soared whence there could be no return, and the body was left, like a folded vesture, on the earth."[40]

Once, toward the end of his mission, he said to a Western audience: "It may be that I shall find it good to get outside of my body—to cast it off like a disused garment. But I shall not cease to work! I shall inspire men everywhere, until the world shall know that it is one with God."[41]

Notes

[1] *The Complete Works of Swami Vivekananda* (Mayavati Memorial Edition) (Calcutta: Advaita Ashrama, 1969-72), Vol. V, 314.
[2] *Vivekananda: The Yogas and Other Works*, ed. by Swami Nikhilananda (New York: Ramakrishna-Vivekananda Center, 1953), 14.
[3] *The Life of Swami Vivekananda*, by His Eastern and Western Disciples (Calcutta: Advaita Ashrama, 1979-81), Vol. I, 81.
[4] *Complete Works*, VIII, 304.
[5] *Vivekananda: The Yogas*, 5.
[6] *Life*, I, 143.
[7] *Life*, I, 19.
[8] *Life*, I, 31.
[9] *Vivekananda: The Yogas*, 13.
[10] Nivedita, Sister, *The Master As I Saw Him* (Calcutta: Udbodhan Office, 1977), 10-11.
[11] *Vivekananda: The Yogas*, 13.
[12] *Life*, I, 96.
[13] *Life*, I, 96.
[14] *Life*, I, 96-97.
[15] *Life*, I, 111.
[16] *Life*, I, 124.
[17] *Life*, I, 128.
[18] *Vivekananda: The Yogas*, 31.
[19] *Life*, I, 178.
[20] *Complete Works*, V, 137.
[21] *Life*, I, 286.
[22] *Complete Works*, I, 4.
[23] *Life*, I, 418.
[24] Nivedita, 82.
[25] Burke, Marie Louise, *Swami Vivekananda In America: New Discoveries* (Calcutta: Advaita Ashrama, 1958), 85.
[26] *Complete Works*, V, 104-5.
[27] Burke, 113-114.
[28] *Complete Works*, III, 193.
[29] *Complete Works*, III, 237.
[30] *Complete Works*, III, 244.
[31] *Complete Works*, III, 245.
[32] *Complete Works*, III, 199.
[33] *Vivekananda: The Yogas*, 146.
[34] *Reminiscences of Swami Vivekananda*, by His Eastern and Western Admirers (Calcutta: Advaita Ashrama, 1964), 249.
[35] Nivedita, 145.
[36] *Complete Works*, VII, 495-6.
[37] *Complete Works*, VI, 448-9.

[38] Ashokananda, Swami, *Swami Vivekananda In San Francisco* (San Francisco: Vedanta Society of Northern California, 1969), 13.
[39] *Reminiscences*, 248.
[40] Nivedita, 331-2.
[41] *Complete Works*, V, 414.

I

WHAT IS VEDANTA?

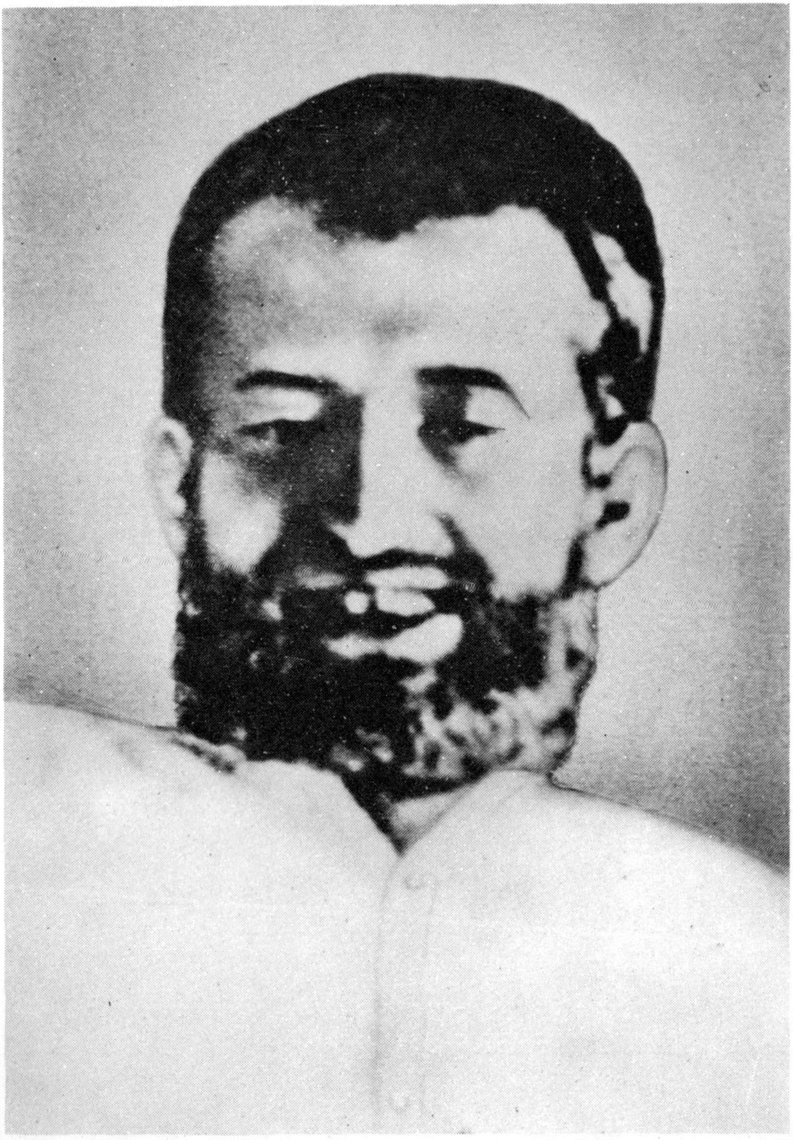

Sri Ramakrishna (1836-1886)
"As many faiths, so many paths."

VEDANTA: THE CULMINATION OF THE VEDAS

The word *Hindu*, by which it is the fashion nowadays to style ourselves, has lost all its meaning, for this word merely meant those who lived on the other side of the river Indus (in Sanskrit, Sindhu). This name was murdered into *Hindu* by the ancient Persians, and all people living on the other side of the river Sindhu were called by them *Hindus*. Thus this word has come down to us, and during the Mohammedan rule we took up the word ourselves. There may not be any harm in using the word of course, but, as I have said, it has lost its significance, for you may mark that all the people who live on this side of the Indus in modern times do not follow the same religion as they did in ancient times. The word, therefore, covers not only Hindus proper, but Mohammedans, Christians, Jains, and other people who live in India. I, therefore, would not use the word *Hindu*. What word should we use then? The other words which alone we can use are either the *Vaidikas*, followers of the Vedas, or better still, the *Vedantists*, followers of Vedanta. Most of the great religions of the world owe allegiance to certain books which they believe are the words of God or some other supernatural beings, and which are the basis of their religion. Now, of all these books, according to the modern savants of the West, the oldest are the Vedas of the Hindus. A little understanding, therefore, is necessary about the Vedas.

This mass of writing called the Vedas is not the utterance of persons. Its date has never been fixed, can never be fixed, and, according to us, the Vedas are eternal. There is one salient point I want you to remember, that all the other religions of the world claim their authority as being delivered by a Personal God or a number of personal beings, angels, or special messengers of God, unto certain persons, while the claim of the Hindus is that the Vedas do not owe their authority to anybody. They are themselves the authority, being eternal—the knowledge of God. They were never written, never created. They have existed throughout time. Just as creation is infinite and eternal, without beginning and without end, so is the knowledge of God without beginning and without end. And this knowledge is what is meant by the Vedas (*Vid* to know). The mass of knowledge called Vedanta was discovered by personages called *rishis*, and the *rishi* is defined as a *mantra-drashta*, a seer of thought—not that the thought was his own. Whenever you hear that a certain passage of the Vedas came from a certain rishi, never think that he wrote it or created it out of his mind. He was the seer of the thought which already existed—it existed in the universe eternally. This sage was the discoverer—the rishis were spiritual discoverers.

This mass of writing, the Vedas, is divided principally into two parts, the *karma kanda* and the *jnana kanda*—the work portion and the knowledge portion, the ceremonial and the spiritual. The work portion consists of various sacrifices. Most of them of late have been given up as not practicable under present circumstances, but others remain to the present day in some shape or other. The main ideas of the karma kanda, which consists of the duties of man, the duties of the student, of the householder, of the recluse, and the various duties of the different stations of life, are followed more or less down to the present day. But the spiritual portion of our religion is in the second part, the jnana kanda, the Vedanta, the end of the Vedas—the gist, the goal of the Vedas. The essence of the knowledge of the Vedas was called by the name *Vedanta*, which comprises the Upanishads. And all the sects of India—Dualists, Qualified-Monists, Monists, or the Shaivites, Vaishnavites, Shaktas, Sauras, Ganapatyas, each one that dares to come within the fold of Hinduism—must acknowledge the Upanishads of the Vedas. They can have their own interpretations and can interpret them in their own way, but they must obey the authority. That is why we want to use the word *Vedantist* instead of *Hindu*. All the philosophers of India who are orthodox have to acknowledge the authority of Vedanta. (III. 118-120)

THE VEDAS: WITHOUT BEGINNING OR END

The Hindus have received their religion through revelation, the Vedas. They hold that the Vedas are without beginning and without end. It may sound ludicrous to this audience, how a book can be without beginning or end. But by the Vedas no books are meant. They mean the accumulated treasury of spiritual laws discovered by different persons in different times. Just as the law of gravitation existed before its discovery and would exist if all humanity forgot it, so is it with the laws that govern the spiritual world. The moral, ethical, and spiritual relations between soul and soul and between individual spirits and the Father of all spirits were there before their discovery and would remain even if we forgot them.

The discoverers of these laws are called *rishis*, and we honor them as perfected beings. I am glad to tell this audience that some of the very greatest of them were women. Here it may be said that these laws, as laws, may be without end, but they must have had a beginning. The Vedas teach us that creation is without beginning or end. Science is said to have proved that the sum total of cosmic energy is always the same. Then, if there was a time when nothing existed, where was all this manifested energy? Some say it was in a potential form in God. In that case God is sometimes potential and sometimes kinetic, which would make Him mutable. Everything mutable is a compound, and every compound must undergo that change which is called destruction. So God would die—which is absurd. Therefore there never was a time when there was no creation.

If I may be allowed to use a simile, creation and Creator are two lines, without beginning and without end, running parallel to each other. God is the ever active providence, by whose power systems after systems are being evolved out of chaos, made to run for a time, and again destroyed. This is what the brahmin boy repeats every day: "The sun and the moon, the Lord created like the suns and moons of previous cycles." (I. 6-7)

THOUGHTS ON THE VEDAS AND UPANISHADS

The Vedic sacrificial altar was the origin of geometry.

The invocation of the *devas*, or bright ones, was the basis of worship. The idea is that the one invoked is helped and helps.

Hymns are not only words of praise but words of power, being pronounced with the right attitude of mind.

Heavens are only other states of existence with added senses and heightened powers.

All higher bodies also are subject to disintegration, as is the physical. Death comes to all forms of bodies in this and other lives. Devas are also mortal and can only give enjoyment.

Behind all devas there is the Unit Being—God—as behind this body there is something higher that feels and sees.

The powers of creation, preservation, and destruction of the universe, and the attributes, such as omnipresence, omniscience, and omnipotence, make God of gods.

On earth we die. In heaven we die. In the highest heaven we die. It is only when we reach God that we attain life and become immortal.

The Upanishads treat of this alone. The path of the Upanishads is the pure path. Many manners, customs, and local allusions cannot be understood today. Through them, however, truth becomes clear. Heavens and earth are all thrown off in order to come to Light.

The Upanishads declare: "He, the Lord, has interpenetrated the universe. It is all His."

"He, the Omnipresent, the One without a second, the One without a body, pure, the great Poet of the universe, whose meter is the suns and stars, is giving to each what he deserves."[1]

"They are groping in utter darkness who try to reach the Light by ceremonials. And they who think this nature is all are in darkness. They who wish to come out of nature through this thought are groping in still deeper darkness."[2]

Are then ceremonials bad? No, they will benefit those who are coming on.

In one of the Upanishads [i.e., Katha] this question is asked by Nachiketa, a youth: "Some say of a dead man, 'He is gone'; others, 'He is still living.' You are Yama, Death. You know the truth. Do answer me." Yama replies: "Even the devas, many of them, know not—much less men. Boy, do not ask of me this answer." But Nachiketa persists. Yama again replies: "The enjoyments of the gods, even these I offer you. Do not insist upon your query." But Nachiketa was firm as a rock. Then the god of death said: "My boy, you have declined, for the third time, wealth, power, long life, fame, family. You are brave enough to ask the highest truth. I will teach you. There are two ways: one of truth, one of enjoyment. You have chosen the former."

Now note here the conditions of imparting the truth. First, purity—a boy, a pure, unclouded soul, asking the secret of the universe. Second, that he must take truth for truth's sake alone.

Until the truth has come through one who has had realization, from one who has perceived it himself, it cannot become fruitful. Books cannot give it. Argument cannot establish it. Truth comes unto him who knows the secret of it.

After you have received it, be quiet. Be not ruffled by vain argument. Come to your own realization. You alone can do it.

Neither happiness nor misery, vice nor virtue, knowledge nor nonknowledge is it [Truth]. You must realize it. How can I describe it to you?

He who cries out with his whole heart, "O Lord, I want but Thee"—to him the Lord reveals Himself. Be pure, be calm. The mind when ruffled cannot reflect the Lord.

"He whom the Vedas declare, He, to reach whom, we serve with prayer and sacrifice, Om is the sacred name of that indescribable One. This word is the holiest of all words. He who knows the secret of this word receives that which he desires."[3] Take refuge in this word. Who so takes refuge in this word, to him the way opens. (VI. 86-88)

"CHILDREN OF IMMORTAL BLISS"

The human soul is eternal and immortal, perfect and infinite, and death means only a change of center from one body to another. The present is determined by our past actions, and the future by the present. The soul will go on evolving up or reverting back, from birth to birth and death to death. But here is another question: Is man a tiny boat in a tempest, raised one moment on the foamy crest of a billow and dashed down into a yawning chasm the next, rolling to and fro at the mercy of good and bad actions—a powerless, helpless wreck in an ever-raging, ever-rushing, uncompromising current of cause and effect—a little moth placed under the wheel of causation, which rolls on crushing everything in its way and waits not for the widow's tears or the orphan's cry? The heart sinks at the idea. Yet this is the law of nature.

Is there no hope? Is there no escape?—was the cry that went up from the bottom of the heart of despair. It reached the throne of mercy, and words of hope and consolation came down and inspired a Vedic sage, and he stood up before the world and in trumpet voice proclaimed the glad tidings: "Hear, ye children of immortal bliss, even ye that reside in higher spheres! I have found the Ancient One, who is beyond all darkness, all delusion. By knowing Him alone will you be saved from death over again."[4] "Children of immortal bliss—what a sweet, what a hopeful name! Allow me to call you, brethren, by that sweet name—heirs of immortal bliss. Yea, the Hindu refuses to call you sinners. Ye are the children of God, the sharers of immortal bliss, holy and perfect beings. Ye divinities on earth—sinners! It is a sin to call a man so; it is a standing libel on human nature. Come up, O lions, and shake off the delusion that you are sheep. You are souls immortal, spirits free, blest, and eternal. You are not matter, you are not bodies. Matter is your servant, not you the servant of matter.

Thus it is that the Vedas proclaim not a dreadful combination of unforgiving laws, not an endless prison of cause and effect, but that at the head of all these laws, in and through every particle of matter and force, stands One "by whose command the wind blows, the fire burns, the clouds rain, and death stalks upon the earth."

And what is His nature?

He is everywhere, the pure and formless One, the Almighty and the All-merciful. "Thou art our father, Thou art our mother, Thou art our beloved friend. Thou art the source of all strength: give us strength. Thou art He that beareth the burdens of the universe: help me bear the little burden of this life."[5] Thus sang the rishis of the Vedas. And how to worship Him? Through love. "He is to be worshipped as the one Beloved, dearer than everything in this and the next life." (I. 10-11)

FREEDOM IS THE SONG OF THE SOUL

A huge locomotive has rushed on over the line, and a small worm that was creeping upon one of the rails saved its life by crawling out of the path of the locomotive. Yet this little worm, so insignificant that it can be crushed in a moment, is a living something, while this locomotive, so huge, so immense, is only an engine, a machine. You say the one has life and the other is only dead matter, and all its powers and strength and speed are only those of a dead machine, a mechanical contrivance. Yet the poor little worm which moved upon the rail and which the least touch of the engine would have deprived of its life is a majestic being compared to that huge locomotive. It is a small part of the Infinite, and therefore it is greater than this powerful engine. Why should that be so? How do we know the living from the dead? The machine mechanically performs all the movements its maker made it to perform; its movements are not those of life. How can we make the distinction between the living and the dead, then? In the living there is freedom, there is intelligence. In the dead, all is bound and no freedom is possible, because there is no intelligence. This freedom that distinguishes us from mere machines is what we are all striving for. To be more free is the goal of all our efforts, for only in perfect freedom can there be perfection. This effort to attain freedom underlies all forms of worship, whether we know it or not.

The child rebels against law as soon as it is born. Its first utterance is a cry, a protest against the bondage in which it finds itself. This longing for freedom produces the idea of a Being who is absolutely free. The concept of God is a fundamental element in the human constitution. In Vedanta, *Sat-Chit-Ananda* (Existence-Knowledge-Bliss) is the highest concept of God possible to the mind. It is the essence of knowledge and is, by its nature, the essence of bliss. We have been stifling that inner voice long enough, seeking to follow law and quiet the human nature, but there is that human instinct to rebel against nature's laws. We may not understand what the meaning is, but there is that unconscious struggle of the human with the spiritual, of the lower with the higher mind, and the struggle attempts to preserve one's separate life, what we call our "individuality."

Even hells stand out with this miraculous fact that we are born rebels. And the first fact of life—the inrushing of life itself—against this we rebel and cry out, "No law for us." As long as we obey the laws we are like machines, and the universe goes on and we cannot break it. Laws, as laws, become man's nature. The first inkling of life on its higher level is in seeing this struggle within us to break the bonds of nature and to be free. "Freedom, oh, freedom! Freedom, oh, freedom!" is the song of the soul. (I. 333-35)

DEHYPNOTIZE YOURSELF

Shall we advise men to kneel down and cry, "O miserable sinners that we are!" No. Rather let us remind them of their divine nature. I will tell you a story. A lioness in search of prey came upon a flock of sheep, and as she jumped at one of them, she gave birth to a cub and died on the spot. The young lion was brought up in the flock, ate grass, and bleated like a sheep, and it never knew that it was a lion. One day another lion came across this flock and was astonished to see in it a huge lion eating grass and bleating like a sheep. At the sight of him the flock fled and the lion-sheep with them. But the lion watched his opportunity and one day found the lion-sheep asleep. He woke him up and said, "You are a lion." The other said, "No," and began to bleat like a sheep. But the stranger-lion took him to a lake and asked him to look in the water at his own image and see if it did not resemble him, the stranger-lion. He looked and acknowledged that it did. Then the stranger-lion began to roar and asked him to do the same. The lion-sheep tried his voice and was soon roaring as grandly as the other. And he was a sheep no longer.

That is it. We are lions in sheep's clothing of habit. We are hypnotized into weakness by our surroundings. And the province of Vedanta is the self-dehypnotization.

If the room is dark, do you go about beating your chest and crying, "It is dark, dark, dark!" No. The only way to get light is to strike a light, and then the darkness goes. The only way to realize the light above you is to strike the spiritual light within you, and the darkness of sin and impurity will flee away. Think of your higher self, not of your lower. (I. 326-27, VIII. 257)

THE GOSPEL OF STRENGTH

Men, men, these are wanted—everything else will be ready, but strong, vigorous, believing young men, sincere to the backbone, are wanted. A hundred such and the world becomes revolutionized. The will is stronger than anything else. Everything must go down before the will, for that comes from God and God Himself. A pure and strong will is omnipotent. What we want is strength, so believe in yourselves. We have become weak, and that is why occultism and mysticism come to us—these creepy things. There may be great truths in them, but they have nearly destroyed us. Make your nerves strong. What we want is muscles of iron and nerves of steel. We have wept long enough. No more weeping, but stand on your feet and be men. It is a man-making religion that we want. It is man-making theories that we want. It is man-making education all round that we want. And here is the test of truth: Anything that makes you weak physically, intellectually, and spiritually, reject as poison. There is no life in it; it cannot be true. Truth is strengthening. Truth is purity; truth is all-knowledge. Truth must be strengthening, must be enlightening, must be invigorating. Go back to your Upanishads—the shining, the strengthening, the bright philosophy—and part from all these mysterious things, all these weakening things. Take up this philosophy. The greatest truths are the simplest things in the world, simple as your own existence. The truths of the Upanishads are before you. Take them up; live up to them.

Strength, strength is what the Upanishads speak to me from every page. This is the one great thing to remember. It has been the one great lesson I have been taught in my life. Strength, it says, strength, O man, be not weak. Are there no human weaknesses?—says man. There are, say the Upanishads, but will more weakness heal them? Would you try to wash dirt with dirt? Will sin cure sin, weakness cure weakness? Strength, O man, strength, say the Upanishads. Stand up and be strong. Ay, it is the only literature in the world where you find the word *abhih*, "fearless", used again and again. In no other scripture in the world is this adjective applied either to God or to man. Abhih, [be] fearless! And in my mind rises from the past the vision of the great emperor of the West, Alexander the Great, and I see, as it were, in a picture, the great monarch standing on the bank of the Indus, talking to one of our *sannyasins* [monks] in the forest—the old man he was talking to, perhaps naked, stark naked, sitting upon a block of stone, and the emperor, astonished at his wisdom, tempting him with gold and honor to come over to Greece. And this man smiles at his gold, and smiles at his temptations, and refuses. Then the emperor, standing on his authority as an emperor, says, "I will kill you if you do not come," and the man bursts into a laugh and says: "You never told such a falsehood in your life as you tell just now. Who can kill me? Me you kill, emperor of the material world! Never! For I am Spirit, unborn and undecaying. Never was I born and never do I die. I am the Infinite, the Omnipresent, the Omniscient. And you kill me, child that you are!"

The Upanishads are the great mine of strength. Therein lies strength enough to invigorate the whole world. The whole world can be vivified, made strong, energized, through them. They will call with trumpet voice upon the weak, the miserable, and the downtrodden of all races, all creeds, and all sects to stand on their feet and be free. Freedom—physical freedom, mental freedom, and spiritual freedom are the watchwords of the Upanishads. (III. 223-25, 237-38)

THE BOLD MESSAGE OF THE EAST

About fourteen hundred years before Christ, there flourished in India a great philosopher, Patanjali by name. He collected all the facts, evidences, and researches in psychology and took advantage of all experiences accumulated in the past. Remember, this world is very old. It was not created only two or three thousand years ago. It is taught here in the West that society began eighteen hundred years ago, with the New Testament. Before that there was no society. That may be true with regard to the West, but it is not true for the whole world. Often, while I was lecturing in London, a very intellectual and intelligent friend of mine would argue with me, and one day after using all his weapons against me, he suddenly exclaimed, "But why did your rishis not come to England to teach us?" I replied: "Because there was no England to come to. Would they preach to the forests?"

"Fifty years ago," said Ingersoll[6] to me, "you would have been hanged in this country if you had come to preach. You would have been burnt alive or you would have been stoned out of the villages."

On some other occasions, I told you the definition of God and man. Man is an infinite circle whose circumference is nowhere, but whose center is located in one spot; and God is an infinite circle whose circumference is nowhere, but whose center is everywhere. He works through all hands, sees through all eyes, walks on all feet, breathes through all bodies, lives in all life, speaks through every mouth and thinks through every brain. Man can become like God and acquire control over the whole universe if he multiplies infinitely his center of self-consciousness.

The great error in all ethical systems, without exception, has been the failure of teaching the means by which man could refrain from doing evil. All the systems of ethics teach, "Do not steal!" Very good. But why does a man steal? Because all stealing, robbing, and other evil actions, as a rule, have become automatic. The systematic robber, thief, liar, unjust man and woman, are all these in spite of themselves! It is really a tremendous psychological problem. We should look upon man in the most charitable light. It is not so easy to be good. What are you but mere machines until you are free? Should you be proud because you are good? Certainly not. You are good because you cannot help it. Another is bad because he cannot help it. If you were in his position, who knows what you would have been? The woman in the street, or the thief in the jail, is the Christ that is being sacrificed that you may be a good man. Such is the law of balance. All the thieves and the murderers, all the unjust, the weakest, the wickedest, the devils, they all are my Christ! I owe a worship to the God Christ and to the demon Christ! That is my doctrine—I cannot help it. My salutation goes to the feet of the good, the saintly, and to the feet of the wicked and the devilish! They are all my teachers, all are my spiritual fathers, all are my saviors. I may curse one and yet benefit by his failings; I may bless another and benefit by his good deeds. This is as true as that I stand here. I have to sneer at the woman walking in the street because society wants it! She, my savior, she, whose street-walking is the cause of the chastity of other women! Think of that. Think, men and women, of this question in your mind. It is a truth—a bare, bold truth! As I see more of the world, see more of men and women, this conviction grows stronger. Whom shall I blame? Whom shall I praise? Both sides of the shield must be seen. (II. 27, 33-34)

Notes

[1] Isha Upanishad, 8, adapted.
[2] Isha Upanishad, 9.
[3] Katha Upanishad, 1.2.15-16.
[4] Shvetashvatara Upanishad, 2.5, 3.8.
[5] Pandava Gita, adapted.
[6] Robert Ingersoll, a well-known American lecturer and agnostic of the nineteenth century.

II

THE PHILOSOPHY OF VEDANTA

Swami Vivekananda as an itinerant monk, Belgaum, India, October 1892

THE SPIRIT AND INFLUENCE OF VEDANTA

I came here to represent a philosophy of India, which is called the Vedanta philosophy. This philosophy is very, very ancient. It is the outcome of that mass of ancient Aryan literature known by the name of the Vedas. It is, as it were, the very flower of all the speculations and experiences and analyses embodied in that mass of literature collected and culled through centuries. This Vedanta philosophy has certain peculiarities. In the first place, it is perfectly impersonal. It does not owe its origin to any person or prophet. It does not build itself around one man as a center. Yet it has nothing to say against philosophies which do build themselves around certain persons. In later days in India, other philosophies and systems arose, built around certain persons—such as Buddhism, or many of our present sects. They each have a certain leader to whom they owe allegiance, just as the Christians and Mohammedans have. But the Vedanta philosophy stands at the background of all these various sects, and there is no fight and no antagonism between Vedanta and any other system in the world.

Vedanta claims that man is divine, that all this which we see around us is the outcome of that consciousness of the divine. Everything that is strong and good and powerful in human nature is the outcome of that divinity, and though potential in many, there is no difference between man and man essentially, all being alike divine. There is, as it were, an infinite ocean behind, and you and I are so many waves, coming out of that infinite ocean. And each one of us is trying his best to manifest that infinite outside. So, potentially, each one of us has that infinite ocean of Existence, Knowledge, and Bliss as our birthright, our real nature, and the difference between us is caused by the greater or lesser power to manifest that divinity. Therefore Vedanta lays down that each man should be treated, not as what he manifests, but as what he stands for. Each human being stands for the divine, and therefore every teacher should be helpful, not by condemning man, but by helping him to call forth the divinity that is within him.

It also teaches that all the vast mass of energy that we see displayed in society and in every plane of action is really from inside out, and, therefore, what is called inspiration by other sects, the Vedantist begs the liberty to call the *expiration* of man. At the same time it does not quarrel with other sects. Vedanta has no quarrel with those who do not understand this divinity of man. Consciously or unconsciously, every man is trying to unfold that divinity.

Man is like an infinite spring, coiled up in a small box, and that spring is trying to unfold itself. And all the social phenomena that we see are the result of this trying to unfold. All the competitions and struggles and evils that we see around us are neither the causes of these unfoldments nor the effects. As one of our great philosophers says—in the case of the irrigation of a field, the tank is somewhere upon a higher level, and the water is trying to rush into the field and is barred by a gate. But as soon as the gate is opened, the water rushes in by its own nature, and if there is dust and dirt in the way, the water rolls over them. But dust and dirt are neither the result nor the cause of this unfolding of the divine nature of man. They are coexistent circumstances, and, therefore, can be remedied.

Now this idea, claims Vedanta, is to be found in all religions, whether in India or outside of it. Only in some of them, the idea is expressed through mythology, and in others, through symbology. Vedanta claims that there has not been one religious inspiration, one manifestation of the divine man, however great, but it has been the expression of that infinite oneness in human nature. And all that we call ethics and morality and doing good to others is also but the manifestation of this oneness. There are moments when every man feels that he is one with the universe, and he rushes forth to express it, whether he knows it or not. This expression of oneness is what we call love and sympathy, and it is the basis of all our ethics and morality. This is summed up in the Vedanta philosophy by the celebrated aphorism, *Tat Tvam Asi*, "Thou art That."

To every man this is taught: Thou art one with this Universal Being, and, as such, every soul that exists is your soul, and every body that exists is your body. And in hurting anyone, you hurt yourself. In loving anyone, you love yourself. As soon as a current of hatred is thrown outside, whomsoever else it hurts, it also hurts yourself. And if love comes out from you, it is bound to come back to you. For I am the universe. This universe is my body. I am the Infinite, only I am not conscious of it now. But I am struggling to get this consciousness of the Infinite, and perfection will be reached when full consciousness of this Infinite comes.

Another peculiar idea of Vedanta is that we must allow this infinite variation in religious thought and not try to bring everybody to the same opinion, because the goal is the same. As the Vedantist says in his poetical language, "As so many rivers, having their sources in different mountains, roll down, crooked or straight, and at last come into the ocean—so, all these various creeds and religions, taking their start from different standpoints and running through crooked or straight courses, at last come unto Thee."[1]

As a manifestation of that, we find that this most ancient philosophy has, through its influence, directly inspired Buddhism, the first missionary religion of the world, and indirectly it has also influenced Christianity through the Alexandrians, the Gnostics, and the European philosophers of the Middle Ages. And later, influencing German thought, it has produced almost a revolution in the regions of philosophy and psychology. Yet all this mass of influence has been given to the world almost unperceived. As the gentle falling of the dew at night brings support to all vegetable life, so, slowly and imperceptibly, this divine philosophy has been spread through the world for the good of mankind. No march of armies has been used to preach this religion.

Thus in India there never was any religious persecution by the Hindus, but only that wonderful reverence which they have for all religions of the world. They sheltered a portion of the Hebrews when they were driven out of their own country, and the Malabar Jews remain as a result. They received at another time the remnant of the Persians when they were almost annihilated, and they remain to this day, as a part of us and loved by us, as the modern Parsees of Bombay. There were Christians who claimed to have come with St. Thomas, the disciple of Jesus Christ, and they were allowed to settle in India and hold their own opinions. A colony of them is even now in existence in India. And this spirit of toleration has not died out. It will not and cannot die there.

This is one of the great lessons that Vedanta has to teach. Knowing that consciously or unconsciously we are struggling to reach the same goal, why should we be impatient? If one man is slower than another, we need not be impatient. We need not curse him or revile him. When our eyes are opened and the heart is purified, the work of the same divine influence, the unfolding of the same divinity in every human heart, will become manifest, and then alone we shall be in a position to claim the brotherhood of man.

When a man has reached the highest, when he sees neither man nor woman, neither sect nor creed nor color nor birth nor any of these differentiations, but goes beyond and finds that divinity which is the real man behind every human being—then alone has he reached the universal brotherhood, and that man alone is a Vedantist.

Such are some of the practical historical results of Vedanta. (I. 387-92)

PRINCIPLES OF VEDANTA

The Vedantist says that a man neither is born nor dies nor goes to heaven, and that reincarnation is really a myth with regard to the soul. The example is given of a book being turned over. It is the book that evolves, not the man. Every soul is omnipresent, so where can it come or go? These births and deaths are changes in nature which we are mistaking for changes in us.

Reincarnation is the evolution of nature and the manifestation of the God within.

Vedanta says that each life is built upon the past, and that when we can look back over the whole past we are free. The desire to be free will take the form of a religious disposition from childhood. A few years will, as it were, make all truth clear to one. After leaving this life, and while waiting for the next, a man is still in the phenomenal.

We would describe the soul in these words: This soul the sword cannot cut nor the spear pierce. The fire cannot burn nor water melt it. Indestructible, omnipresent is this soul. Therefore weep not for it.

If it has been very bad, we believe that it will become good in the time to come. The fundamental principle is that there is eternal freedom for everyone. Everyone must come to it. We have to struggle, impelled by our desire to be free. Every other desire but that to be free is illusive. Every good action, the Vedantist says, is a manifestation of that freedom.

I do not believe that there will come a time when all the evil in the world will vanish. How could that be? This stream goes on. Masses of water go out at one end, but masses are coming in at the other end.

Vedanta says that you are pure and perfect, and that there is a state beyond good and evil, and that is your own nature. It is higher even than good. Good is only a lesser differentiation than evil.

We have no theory of evil. We call it ignorance.

So far as it goes, all dealing with other people, all ethics, is in the phenomenal world. As a most complete statement of truth, we would not think of applying such things as ignorance to God. Of Him we say that He is Existence, Knowledge, and Bliss Absolute. Every effort of thought and speech will make the Absolute phenomenal and break Its character.

There is one thing to be remembered: that the assertion, "I am God," cannot be made with regard to the sense world. If you say in the sense world that you are God, what is to prevent your doing wrong? So the affirmation of your divinity applies only to the noumenal. If I am God, I am beyond the tendencies of the senses and will not do evil. Morality, of course, is not the goal of man but the means through which this freedom is attained. Vedanta says that yoga is one way that makes men realize this divinity. Vedanta says this is done by the realization of the freedom within and that everything will give way to that. Morality and ethics will all range themselves in their proper places.

All the criticism against the Advaita philosophy can be summed up in this, that it does not conduce to sense enjoyments. And we are glad to admit that.

The Vedanta system begins with tremendous pessimism and ends with real optimism. We deny the optimism of the senses but assert the real optimism of the supersensuous. That real happiness is not in the senses but above the senses, and it is in every man. The sort of optimism which we see in the world is what will lead to ruin through the senses.

Abnegation has the greatest importance in our philosophy. Negation implies affirmation of the real Self. Vedanta is pessimistic insofar as it negates the world of the senses, but it is optimistic in its assertion of the real world.

Vedanta recognizes the reasoning power of man a good deal, although it says there is something higher than intellect. But the road lies through intellect.

We need reason to drive out all the old superstitions, and what remains is Vedantism. There is a beautiful Sanskrit poem in which the sage says to himself: "Why weepest thou, my friend? There is no fear nor death for thee. Why weepest thou? There is no misery for thee, for thou art like the infinite blue sky, unchangeable in thy nature. Clouds of all colors come before it, play for a moment, and pass away. It is the same sky. Thou hast only to drive away the clouds."[2]

We have to open the gates and clear the way. The water will rush in and fill in by its own nature, because it is there already.

Vedanta teaches that *nirvana* can be attained here and now, that we do not have to wait for death to reach it. Nirvana is the realization of the Self. And after having once known that, if only for an instant, never again can one be deluded by the mirage of personality. Having eyes, we must see the apparent, but all the time we know what it is. We have found out its true nature. It is the screen that hides the Self, which is unchanging. The screen opens and we find the Self behind it. All change is in the screen. In the saint the screen is thin and the reality can almost shine through. In the sinner the screen is thick, and we are liable to lose sight of the truth that the Atman is there as well as behind the saint's screen. When the screen is wholly removed, we find it really never existed—that we were the Atman and nothing else. Even the screen is forgotten.

The two phases of this distinction in life are: first, that the man who knows the real Self will not be affected by anything; secondly, that that man alone can do good to the world. That man alone will have seen the real motive of doing good to others, because there is only one. It cannot be called egoistic, because that would be differentiation. It is the only selflessness. It is the perception of the universal, not of the individual. Every case of love and sympathy is an assertion of this universal. "Not I, but thou." Help another because you are in him and he is in you, is the philosophical way of putting it. The real Vedantist alone will give up his life for a fellow man without any compunction, because he knows he will not die. As long as there is one insect left in the world, he is living. As long as one mouth eats, he eats. So he goes on doing good to others and is never hindered by the modern ideas of caring for the body. When a man reaches this point of abnegation, he goes beyond the moral struggle, beyond everything. He sees in the most learned priest, in the cow, in the dog, in the most miserable places, neither the learned man, nor the cow, nor the dog, nor the miserable place, but the same divinity manifesting itself in them all. He alone is the happy man. And the man who has acquired that sameness has, even in this life, conquered all existence. God is pure; therefore such a man is said to be living in God. Jesus says, "Before Abraham was, I am." That means that Jesus and others like him are free spirits. And Jesus of Nazareth took human form, not by the compulsion of his past actions, but just to do good to mankind. It is not that when a man becomes free, he will stop and become a dead lump. But he will be more active than any other being, because every other being acts only under compulsion—he alone through freedom.

If we are inseparable from God, have we no individuality? Oh, yes. That is God. Our individuality is God. This is not the individuality you have now; you are coming toward that.

Individuality means what cannot be divided. How can you call this individuality? One hour you are thinking one way, and the next hour another way, and two hours after, another way. Individuality is that which changes not—[that which] is beyond all things, changeless. It would be tremendously dangerous for this state to remain in eternity, because then the thief would always remain a thief and the blackguard, a blackguard. If a baby died, he would have to remain a baby. The real individuality is that which never changes and will never change, and that is the God within us.

Vedantism is an expansive ocean on the surface of which a man-of-war could be near a catamaran. So in the Vedantic ocean a real yogi can be by the side of an idolater or even an atheist. What is more, in the Vedantic ocean, the Hindu, Mohammedan, Christian, and Parsee are all one, all children of the Almighty God. (V. 281-86)

THE THREE MAIN SCHOOLS OF VEDANTA

There are three principal variations among the Vedantists. But on one point they all agree, and that is that they all believe in God.

The first school I will tell you about is styled the dualistic school. The dualists believe that God, who is the creator of the universe and its ruler, is eternally separate from nature, eternally separate from the human soul. God is eternal, nature is eternal, and so are all souls. Nature and the souls become manifest and change, but God remains the same. According to the dualists, again, this God is personal in that He has qualities—not that He has a body. He has human attributes. He is merciful, He is just, He is powerful, He is almighty, He can be approached, He can be prayed to, He can be loved, He loves in return, and so forth. In one word, He is a human God, only infinitely greater than man. He has none of the evil qualities which men have. "He is the repository of an infinite number of blessed qualities"—that is their definition.

Another peculiar doctrine of the dualists is that every soul must eventually come to salvation. No one will be left out. Through various vicissitudes, through various sufferings and enjoyments, each one of them will come out in the end.

The real Vedanta philosophy begins with those known as the qualified nondualists. They make the statement that the effect is never different from the cause; the effect is but the cause reproduced in another form. If the universe is the effect and God the cause, it must be God Himself—it cannot be anything but that. They start with the assertion that God is both the efficient and the material cause of the universe—that He Himself is the creator, and He Himself is the material out of which the whole of nature is projected. Now, the whole universe, according to this sect, is God Himself. He is the material of the universe. We read in the Vedas, "As the *urnanabhi* [spider] spins the thread out of its own body,...even so the whole universe has come out of the Being."[3]

They say that these three existences—God, nature, and the soul—are one. God is, as it were, the Soul, and nature and souls are the body of God. Just as I have a body and I have a soul, so the whole universe and all souls are the body of God, and God is the Soul of all souls.

Now both the dualists and the qualified nondualists admit that the soul is by its nature pure, but through its own deeds it becomes impure. Every wicked deed contracts the nature of the soul, and every good deed expands it, and these souls are all parts of God. "As from a blazing fire, fly millions of sparks of the same nature, even so from this Infinite Being, God, these souls have come."[4] Each soul has the same goal.

Now we come to Advaita, the last of the Vedanta schools, and, as we think, the fairest flower of philosophy and religion that any country in any age has produced, where human thought attains its highest expression and even goes beyond the mystery which seems to be impenetrable. This is the nondualistic Vedanta. It is too abstruse, too elevated, to be the religion of the masses.

What does the Advaitist declare? He says: If there is a God, that God must be both the material and the efficient cause of the universe. Not only is He the creator, but He is also the created. He Himself is this universe.

How can that be? God, the pure, the Spirit, has become the universe? Yes—apparently so. That which all ignorant people see as the universe does not really exist. What are you and I and all these things we see? Mere self-hypnotism. There is but one Existence, the Infinite, the Ever-blessed One. In that

Existence we dream all these various dreams. It is the Atman, beyond all, the Infinite, beyond the known, beyond the knowable. In and through That we see the universe. It is the only reality. It is this table, It is the audience before me, It is the wall, It is everything, minus the name and form. Take away the form of the table, take away the name—what remains is the Atman.

The Vedantist does not call the Atman either He or She—these are fictions, delusions of the human brain. There is no sex in the soul. People who are under illusion, who have become like animals, see a woman or a man. Living gods do not see men or women. How can they who are beyond everything have any sex idea? Everyone and everything is the Atman, the Self—the sexless, the pure, the ever-blessed. It is the name, the form, the body, which are material, and they make all this difference. If you take away these two differences of name and form, the whole universe is one. There are not two, but one everywhere. You and I are one.

What does the Advaitist preach? He dethrones all the gods that ever existed or ever will exist in the universe, and places on that throne the Self of man, the Atman, higher than the sun and the moon, higher than the heavens, greater than this great universe itself. No books, no scriptures, no science, can ever imagine the glory of the Self, which appears as man—the most glorious God that ever was, the only God that ever existed, exists, or ever will exist. I am to worship, therefore, none but my Self. "I worship my Self," says the Advaitist. "To whom shall I bow down? I salute my Self. To whom shall I go for help? Who can help me, the Infinite Being of the universe?" These are foolish dreams, hallucinations. Who ever helped anyone? None. Wherever you see a weak man, a dualist, weeping and wailing for help from somewhere above the skies, it is because he does not know that the skies also are in him. He wants help from the skies, and the help comes. We see that it comes, but it comes from within himself, and he mistakes it as coming from without. Sometimes a sick man lying on his bed may hear a tap on the door. He gets up and opens it and finds no one there. He goes back to bed, and again he hears a tap. He gets up and opens the door. Nobody is there. At last he finds that it was his own heartbeat, which he fancied was a knock at the door.

Thus man, after this vain search for various gods outside himself, completes the circle and comes back to the point from which he started—the human soul. And he finds that the God whom he was searching for in hill and dale, whom he was seeking in every brook, in every temple, in churches and heavens, that God whom he was even imagining as sitting in heaven and ruling the world, is his own Self. I am He, and He is I. None but I was God, and this little *I* never existed.

"Know the truth and be free in a moment." All the darkness will then vanish. When man has seen himself as one with the Infinite Being of the universe, when all separateness has ceased, when all men and women, all gods and angels, all animals and plants, and the whole universe have melted into that Oneness, then all fear disappears. Can I hurt myself? Can I kill myself? Can I injure myself? Whom shall I fear? Can you fear yourself? Then will all sorrow disappear. What can cause me sorrow? I am the One Existence of the Universe. Then all jealousies will disappear. Of whom shall I be jealous? Of myself? Then will all bad feelings disappear. Against whom can I have any bad feeling? Against myself? There is none in the universe but me. And this is the one way, says the Vedantist, to Knowledge. Kill out this differentiation, kill out this superstition that there are many. "He who in this world of many sees that One, he who in this mass of insentiency sees that one sentient Being, he who in this world of shadows catches that Reality, unto him belongs eternal peace, unto none else, unto none else."[5]

The Advaitist or the qualified Advaitist does not say that dualism is wrong; it is a right view, but a lower one. It is on the way to truth; therefore let everybody work out his own vision of this universe according to his own ideas. Injure none, deny the position of none. Take a man where he stands and, if you can, lend him a helping hand and put him on a higher platform, but do not injure and do not destroy. All will come to truth in the long run. (II. 239-40, 242, 245-53)

MONISTIC VEDANTA

The solution of Vedanta is that we are not bound, we are free already. Not only so, but to say or to think that we are bound is dangerous—it is a mistake. It is self-hypnotism. As soon as you say, "I am bound," "I am weak," "I am helpless," woe unto you! You rivet one more chain upon yourself. Do not say it, do not think it. I have heard of a man who lived in a forest and used to repeat day and night, "Shivoham"—"I am the Blessed One"—and one day a tiger fell upon him and dragged him away to kill him. People on the other side of the river saw it and heard the voice, so long as voice remained in him, saying, "Shivoham"—even in the very jaws of the tiger. There have been many such men. There have been cases of men who, while being cut to pieces, have blessed their enemies. "I am He, I am He, and so art thou. I am pure and perfect, and so are all my enemies. You are He, and so am I." That is the position of strength. Nevertheless, there are great and wonderful things in the religions of the dualists. Wonderful is the idea of the Personal God apart from nature, whom we worship and love. Sometimes this idea is very soothing. But, says Vedanta, that feeling is something like the effect that comes from an opiate. It is not natural. It brings weakness in the long run, and what this world wants today more than it ever did before is strength. It is weakness, says Vedanta, that is the cause of all misery in this world. Weakness is the one cause of suffering. We become miserable because we are weak. We lie, steal, kill, and commit other crimes because we are weak. We suffer because we are weak. We die because we are weak. Where there is nothing to weaken us, there is no death or sorrow. We are miserable through delusion. Give up the delusion and the whole thing vanishes. It is plain and simple indeed. Through all these philosophical discussions and tremendous mental gymnastics we come to this one religious idea, the simplest in the whole world.

Monistic Vedanta is the simplest form in which you can put truth. To teach dualism was a tremendous mistake made in India and elsewhere, because people did not look at the ultimate principles, but only thought of the process, which is very intricate indeed. To many these tremendous philosophical and logical propositions were alarming. They thought that these things could not be made universal, could not be followed in everyday practical life, and that under the guise of such a philosophy much laxity of living would arise.

But I do not believe at all that monistic ideas preached to the world would produce immorality and weakness. On the contrary, I have reason to believe that they are the only remedy there is. If this be the truth, why let people drink ditchwater when the stream of life is flowing by? If this be the truth, that they are all pure, why not at this moment teach it to the whole world? Why not teach it, with the voice of thunder, to every man that is born, to saints and sinners, men, women, and children, to the man on the throne, and to the man sweeping the streets?

It appears now to be a very big and a very great undertaking—to many it appears very startling. But that is because of superstition, nothing else. By eating all sorts of bad and indigestible food, or by starving ourselves, we have become incompetent to eat a good meal. We have listened to words of weakness from our childhood. You hear people say that they do not believe in ghosts, but at the same time, there are very few who do not get a little creepy sensation in the dark. It is simply superstition. So with all religious superstitions. There are people in this country [England] who, if I told them there was no such being as the devil, would think all religion was gone. Many people have said to me: "How can there be religion without a devil? How can there be religion without someone to direct us? How can we live without being ruled by somebody? We like to be so treated, because we have become used to it. We are not happy until we feel we have been reprimanded by somebody every day." The same superstition! But however terrible it may seem now, the time will come when we shall look back, each one of us, and smile at every one of those superstitions which covered the pure and eternal soul, and repeat with gladness, with truth, and with strength, "I am free, and was free, and always will be free."

This monistic idea will come out of Vedanta, and it is the one idea that deserves to live. For this is the truth and truth is eternal. And truth itself teaches that it is not the special property of any individual or nation. Men, animals, and gods are all common recipients of this one truth. Let them all receive it. Why make life miserable? Why let people fall into all sorts of superstitions? I will give ten thousand lives, if twenty of them will give up their superstitions. Not only in this country, but in the land of its very birth, if you tell people this truth they are frightened. They say: "This idea is for *sannyasins* [monks], who give up the world and live in forests; for them it is all right. But for us poor householders, we must all have some sort of fear, we must have ceremonies," and so on.

Dualistic ideas have ruled the world long enough, and this is the result. Why not make a new experiment? It may take ages for all minds to receive monism, but why not begin now? If we have told it to twenty persons in our lives, we have done a great work. (II. 197-200)

THE ABSOLUTE AND ITS MANIFESTATION

The one question that is most difficult to grasp in understanding the Advaita philosophy, and the one question which will be asked again and again and which will always remain unanswered, is: How has the Infinite, the Absolute, become the finite? I will now take up this question, and in order to illustrate it I will use a figure.

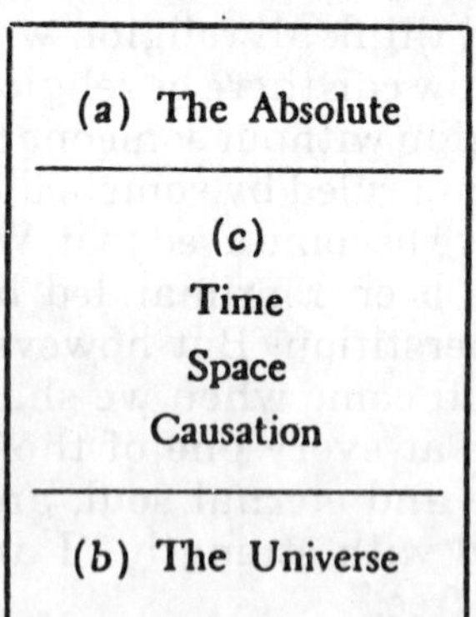

Here is the Absolute (a), and this is the universe (b). The Absolute has become the universe. By this is meant not only the material world, but the mental world, the spiritual world—heavens and earths, and in fact, everything that exists. Mind is the name of a change, and body the name of another change, and so on, and all these changes compose our universe. This Absolute (a) has become the universe (b) by coming through time, space, and causation (c). This is the central idea of Advaita. Time, space, and causation are like the glass through which the Absolute is seen, and when It is seen on the lower side, It appears as the universe.

Now, we at once gather from this that in the Absolute there is neither time, space, nor causation. The idea of time cannot be there, seeing that there is no mind, no thought. The idea of space cannot be there, seeing that there is no external change.

What you call motion and causation cannot exist where there is only one. We have to understand this and impress it on our minds—that what we call causation begins after, if we may be permitted to say so, the degeneration of the Absolute into the phenomenal, and not before; that our will, our desire, and all these things always come after that.

Now the question is: What are time, space, and causation? Advaita means nonduality—there are not two, but one. Yet we see that here is a proposition that the Absolute is manifesting Itself as many, through the veil of time, space, and causation. Therefore it seems that here are two: the Absolute and *maya*, the sum total of time, space, and causation. It seems apparently very convincing that there are two. To this the Advaitist replies that there cannot be two. To have two, we must have two absolute, independent existences which cannot be caused. But time, space, and causation cannot be said to be independent existences. In the first place, time is entirely a dependent existence; it changes with every change of our mind. Sometimes in a dream one imagines that one has lived several years; at other times several months have passed as one second. So time is entirely dependent on our state of mind. Secondly, the idea of time sometimes vanishes altogether. So with space. We cannot know what space is. Yet it is there, indefinable, and cannot exist separate from anything else. So with causation.

The whole of this universe, therefore, is, as it were, a peculiar form [of the Absolute]. The Absolute is that ocean, while you and I, and suns and stars, and everything else are various waves of that ocean. And what makes the waves different? Only the form—and that form is time, space, and causation, which are all entirely dependent on the wave. As soon as the wave goes they vanish. As soon as the individual gives up this maya it vanishes for him and he becomes free. (II. 130, 135-36)

AN ANALYSIS OF PERCEPTION

I am looking at you. How many things are necessary for this vision? First, the eyes. For if I am perfect in every other way, and yet have no eyes, I shall not be able to see you. Secondly, the real organ of vision. For the eyes are not the organs. They are but the instruments of vision, and behind them is the real organ, the nerve center in the brain. If that center be injured, a man may have the clearest pair of eyes, yet he will not be able to see anything. So it is necessary that this center, or the real organ, be there. Similarly, the external ear is but the instrument for carrying the vibration of sound inward to the center. Thus with all our senses. Yet that is not sufficient. Suppose in your library you are intently reading a book, and the clock strikes, yet you do not hear it. The sound is there, the pulsations in the air are there, the ear and the center are also there, and these vibrations have been carried through the ear to the center, and yet you do not hear it. What is wanting? The mind is not there. Thus we see that the third thing necessary is that the mind must be there. First there must be the external instrument, then the organ to which this external instrument will carry the sensation, and lastly the organ itself must be joined to the mind. When the mind is not joined to the organ, the organ and the ear may take the impression and yet we shall not be conscious of it. The mind, too, is only the carrier. It has to carry the sensation still forward and present it to the intellect. The intellect is the determinative faculty and decides upon what is brought to it. Still this is not sufficient. The intellect must carry it forward and present the whole thing before the ruler in the body, the human soul, the king on the throne. Before him this is presented, and then from him comes the order as to what to do or what not to do. And the order goes down, in the same sequence, to the intellect, to the mind, to the organs, and the organs convey it to the instruments, and perception is complete.

Now we see that the body, the external shape, has no light as its own essence, is not self-luminous, and cannot know itself; neither can the mind. Why not? Because the mind waxes and wanes; because it is vigorous at one time and weak at another; because it can be acted upon by anything and everything. Therefore the light which shines through the mind is not its own. Whose is it, then? It must belong to That which has it as Its own essence and, as such, can never decay or die, never become stronger or weaker—to the Soul. It is self-luminous. It is luminosity itself. (II. 213-16)

GOOD AND EVIL

In this world we find that all happiness is followed by misery as its shadow. Life has its shadow, death. They must go together, because they are not contradictory, not two separate existences, but different manifestations of the same unit—life and death, sorrow and happiness, good and evil. The dualistic conception that good and evil are two separate entities, and that they are both going on eternally, is absurd on the face of it. They are the diverse manifestations of one and the same fact, one time appearing as bad, and at another time as good. The difference does not exist in kind, but only in degree. They differ from each other in degree of intensity.

We find, as a matter of fact, that the same nerve systems carry good and bad sensations alike, and when the nerves are injured, neither sensation comes to us. The same phenomenon will produce pleasure in one and pain in another. The eating of meat produces pleasure in a man, but pain in the animal that is eaten. There has never been anything that gives pleasure to all alike. Some are pleased, others displeased. So on it will go.

The history of the world shows that evil, as well as good, is a continuously increasing quantity. Take the lowest man. He lives in the forest. His sense of enjoyment is very small, and so also is his power to suffer. His misery is entirely on the sense plane. If he does not get plenty of food he is miserable. But give him plenty of food and freedom to rove and to hunt, and he is perfectly happy. His happiness consists only in the senses, and so does his misery also. But if that man increases in knowledge, his happiness will increase, the intellect will open to him, and his sense enjoyment will evolve into intellectual enjoyment. He will feel pleasure in reading a beautiful poem, and a mathematical problem will be of absorbing interest to him. But, with these, the finer nerves will become more and more susceptible to the miseries of mental pain, of which the savage does not think.

Take your country [England], which is the richest in the world, and which is more luxurious than any other, and see how intense is the misery, how many more lunatics you have, compared with other races, only because the desires are so keen. Vedanta does not take the position that this world is only a miserable one. That would be untrue. At the same time it is a mistake to say that this world is full of happiness and blessings. So it is useless to tell children that this world is all good, all flowers, all milk and honey—which is what we have all dreamt. At the same time it is erroneous to think that because one man has suffered more than another, all is evil. It is this duality, this play of good and evil, that makes our world of experiences. At the same time Vedanta says, "Do not think that good and evil are two, are two separate essences, for they are one and the same thing appearing in different degrees and in different guises and producing differences of feeling in the same mind." So the first thought of Vedanta is the finding of unity in the external—the one Existence manifesting Itself, however different It may appear in manifestation.

Think of the old theory of the Persians: two gods creating this world, the good god doing everything that is good, and the bad one, everything bad. On the very face of it you see the absurdity, for if it is carried out, every law of nature must have two parts, one of which is manipulated by one god, and then he goes away and the other god manipulates the other part. There the difficulty comes: both are working in the same world, and these two gods keep themselves in harmony by injuring one portion and doing good to another. This is a crude case, of course, the crudest way of expressing the duality of existence. But take the more advanced, the more abstract theory, that this world is partly good and partly bad. This also is absurd, arguing from the same standpoint. It is the same force that gives us our food and that kills many through accidents or misadventure.

We find, then, that this world is neither good nor evil. It is a mixture of both. And as we go on we shall find that the whole blame is taken away from nature and put upon our own shoulders. At the same time Vedanta shows the way out—but not by denial of evil, because it boldly analyzes the fact as it is and does not seek to conceal anything. It is not a creed of hopelessness. It is not agnosticism. It finds out a remedy, but it wants to place that remedy on adamantine foundations—not by shutting the child's mouth and blinding its eyes with something which is untrue, and which the child will find out in a few days.

I remember when I was young, a young man's father died

and left him poorly off, with a large family to support, and he found that his father's friends were unwilling to help him. He had a conversation with a clergyman, who offered this consolation, "Oh, it is all good. All is sent for our good." That is the old method of trying to put a piece of gold leaf on an old sore. It is a confession of weakness, of absurdity. The young man went away, and six months afterward a son was born to the clergyman, and he gave a thanksgiving party to which the young man was invited. The clergyman prayed, "Thank God for His mercies." And the young man stood up and said, "Stop! This is all misery." The clergyman asked, "Why?" "Because when my father died you said it was good, though apparently evil, so now this is apparently good, but really evil." Is this the way to cure the misery of the world? Be good and have mercy on those who suffer. Do not try to patch it up. Nothing will cure this world. Go beyond it.

This is a world of good and evil. Wherever there is good, evil follows, but beyond and behind all these manifestations, all these contradictions, Vedanta finds that Unity. It says, "Give up what is evil and give up what is good." What remains then? Behind good and evil stands something that is yours, the real "you"—beyond every evil, and beyond every good too—and it is that which is manifesting itself as good and bad.

Know *that* first, and then, and then alone, will you be a true optimist, and not before; for then you will be able to control everything. Control these manifestations and you will be at liberty to manifest the real "you." First be master of yourself, stand up and be free, go beyond the pale of these laws. For these laws do not absolutely govern you; they are only part of your being. First, find out that you are not the slave of nature, never were and never will be—that this nature, infinite as you may think it, is only finite, a drop in the ocean, and your Soul is the ocean. You are beyond the stars, the sun, and the moon. They are like mere bubbles compared with your infinite being. Know that, and you will control both good and evil. Then alone will the whole vision change, and you will stand up and say, "How beautiful is good and how wonderful is evil!"

That is what Vedanta teaches. It does not propose any slipshod remedy by covering wounds with gold leaf and the more the wound festers, putting on more gold leaf. This life is a hard fact. Work your way through it boldly, though it may be adamantine. No matter! The soul is stronger. Vedanta lays no responsibility on little gods, for you are the makers of your own fortunes. You make yourselves suffer, you make good and evil, and it is you who put your hands before your eyes and say it is dark. Take your hands away and see the light. You are effulgent, you are perfect already, from the very beginning. We now understand the verse: "He goes from death to death who sees the many here." See the One and be free. (II. 178-82)

CHANGE IS ALWAYS SUBJECTIVE

What is the theory of evolution? There are two factors: First, a tremendous potential power trying to express itself, and secondly, circumstances holding it down, its environment not allowing it to express itself. So in order to fight with this environment, the power takes new bodies again and again. An amoeba, in the struggle, gets another body and conquers some obstacles, then gets another body, and so on until it becomes man. Now, if you carry this idea to its logical conclusion, there must come a time when that power that was in the amoeba, and which evolved as man, will have conquered all the obstructions that nature can bring before it and will thus escape from all its environments. This idea expressed in metaphysics will take this form: There are two components in every action—the one is the subject, the other the object—and the one aim of life is to make the subject master of the object. For instance, I feel unhappy because a man scolds me. My struggle will be to make myself strong enough to conquer the environment, so that he may scold and I shall not feel. That is how we are all trying to conquer nature. What is meant by morality? Making the subject strong by attuning it to the Absolute, so that finite nature ceases to have control over us. It is a logical conclusion of our philosophy that there must come a time when we shall have conquered all the environments, because nature is finite.

Here is another thing to learn. How do you know that nature is finite? You can only know this through metaphysics. Nature is that Infinite under limitations. Therefore it is finite. So there must come a time when we shall have conquered all environments. And how are we to conquer them? We cannot possibly conquer all the objective environments. We cannot. The little fish wants to fly from its enemies in the water. How does it do so? By evolving wings and becoming a bird. The fish does not change the water or the air; the change is in itself. Change is always subjective. All through evolution you find that the conquest of nature comes by change in the subject. Apply this to religion and morality, and you will find that the conquest of evil comes by the change in the subject alone. That is how the Advaita system gets its whole force, on the subjective side of man. To talk of evil and misery is nonsense, because they do not exist outside. If I am inured against all anger, I never feel angry. If I am proof against all hatred, I never feel hatred. This is, therefore, the process by which to achieve that conquest—through the subjective, by perfecting the subjective.

I may make bold to say that the only religion which agrees with and even goes a little further than modern researches, both on physical and moral lines, is Advaita, and that is why it appeals to modern scientists so much. (II. 136-38)

SOUL, GOD, AND RELIGION

In the first, or dualistic, stage man knows he is a little personal soul—John, James, or Tom—and he says, "I will be John, James, or Tom to all eternity and never anything else." As well might the murderer come along and say, "I will remain a murderer forever." But as time goes on, Tom vanishes and goes back to the original pure Adam.

"Blessed are the pure in heart, for they shall see God." Can we see God? Of course not. Can we know God? Of course not. If God can be known he will be God no longer. Knowledge is limitation. But I and my Father are one. I find the reality in my soul. These ideas are expressed in some religions, and only hinted at in others. In some they were expatriated. Christ's teachings are now very little understood in this country [America]. If you will excuse me, I will say that they have never been very well understood.

The different stages of growth are absolutely necessary for the attainment of purity and perfection. The varying systems of religion are, at bottom, founded on the same ideas. Jesus says, "The kingdom of heaven is within you." Again he says, "Our Father, who art in heaven." How do you reconcile the two sayings? In this way: He was talking to the uneducated masses when he said the latter, the masses who were uneducated in religion. It was necessary to speak to them in their own language. The masses want concrete ideas, something the senses can grasp. A man may be the greatest philosopher in the world, but a child in religion. When a man has developed a high state of spirituality he can understand that the kingdom of heaven is within him. That is the real kingdom of the mind. Thus we see that the apparent contradictions and perplexities in every religion mark but different stages of growth. And, as such, we have no right to blame anyone for his religion. There are stages of growth in which forms and symbols are necessary; they are the language that the souls in that stage can understand.

The next idea that I want to bring to you is that religion does not consist of doctrines or dogmas. It is not what you read nor what dogmas you believe that is of importance, but what you realize. "Blessed are the pure in heart, for they shall see God," yea, in this life. And that is salvation. There are those who teach that this can be gained by the mumbling of words. But no great master ever taught that external forms were necessary for salvation. The power of attaining it is within ourselves. We live and move in God. Creeds and sects have their parts to play, but they are for children; they last but temporarily. Books never make religions, but religions make books. We must not forget that. No book ever created God, but God inspired all the great books. And no book ever created a soul. We must never forget that. The end of all religions is the realization of God in the soul. That is the one universal religion. If there is one universal truth in all religions, I place it here—in realizing God. Ideals and methods may differ, but that is the central point. There may be a thousand different radii, but they all converge to the one center, and that is the realization of God—something behind this world of sense, this world of eternal eating and drinking and talking nonsense, this world of false shadows and selfishness. There is that, beyond all books, beyond all creeds, beyond the vanities of this world, and it is the realization of God within yourself. A man may believe in all the churches in the world, he may carry in his head all the sacred books ever written, he may baptize himself in all the rivers of the earth—still, if he has no perception of God, I would class him with the rankest atheist. And another man may have never entered a church or a mosque, nor performed any ceremony, but if he feels God within himself and is thereby lifted above the vanities of the world, that man is a holy man, a saint, call him what you will.

As soon as a man stands up and says he is right or his church is right and all others are wrong, he is himself all wrong. He does not know that upon the proof of all the others depends the proof of his own. Love and charity for the whole human race—that is the test of true religiousness. I do not mean the sentimental statement that all men are brothers, but that one must feel the oneness of human life. So far as they are not exclusive, I see that the sects and creeds are all mine; they are all grand. They are all helping men toward the real religion.

I will add, it is good to be born in a church, but it is bad to die there. It is good to be born a child, but bad to remain a child. Churches, ceremonies, and symbols are good for children, but when the child is grown he must burst the church or himself. We must not remain children forever. It is like trying to fit one coat to all sizes and growths. I do not deprecate the existence of sects in the world. Would to God there were twenty million more, for the more there are, the greater the field for selection there will be. What I do object to is trying to fit one religion to every case. Though all religions are essentially the same, they must have the varieties of form produced by dissimilar circumstances among different nations. We must each have our own individual religion—individual so far as the externals of it go.

Many years ago I visited a great sage of our country, a very holy man. We talked of our revealed book, the Vedas, of your Bible, of the Koran, and of revealed books in general. At the close of our talk this good man asked me to go to the table and take up a book. It was a book which, among other things, contained a forecast of the rainfall during the year. The sage said, "Read that." And I read out the quantity of rain that was to fall. He said, "Now take the book and squeeze it." I did so and he said, "Why, my boy, not a drop of water comes out.

Until the water comes out, it is all book, book." So until your religion makes you realize God, it is useless. He who only studies books for religion reminds one of the fable of the ass that carried a heavy load of sugar on its back, but did not know the sweetness of it. (I. 323-26)

Notes

1 "Shiva Mahimnah Stotram," 7.
2 Avadhuta Gita, adapted.
3 Mundaka Upanishad, 1.1.7.
4 Mundaka Upanishad, 2.1.1.
5 Katha Upanishad, 2.2.13.

III

THE RELIGION OF VEDANTA

Swami Vivekananda, Chicago, October 1893

MANY FACETS OF THE TRUTH

Man has wanted to look beyond, wanted to expand himself, and all that we call progress, evolution, has been always measured by that one search, the search for human destiny, the search for God. We find that, though there is nothing that has brought man more blessings than religion, yet at the same time, there is nothing that has brought him more horror than religion. Nothing has made more for peace and love than religion; nothing has engendered fiercer hatred than religion. Nothing has made the brotherhood of man more tangible than religion; nothing has bred more bitter enmity between man and man than religion. Nothing has built more charitable institutions, more hospitals for men, and even for animals, than religion; nothing has deluged the world with more blood than religion. We know, at the same time, that there has always been an undercurrent of thought; there have always been parties of men, philosophers, students of comparative religion, who have tried and are still trying to bring about harmony in the midst of all these jarring and discordant sects.

For certain countries these attempts have succeeded, but for the whole world, they have failed.

We must remember that all the great religions of the world are very ancient—not one has been formed at the present time—and that every religion of the world owes its origin to the country between the Ganga and the Euphrates. Not one great religion has arisen in Europe, not one in America—not one. Every religion is of Asiatic origin and belongs to that part of the world. Preaching has always been the business of the Asiatics. The Western people are grand in organization—social institutions, armies, governments, and so forth. But when it comes to preaching religion, they cannot come near the Asiatics, whose business it has been all the time—and they know it and do not use too much machinery.

This, then, is a fact in the present history of the human race: that all these great religions exist and are spreading and multiplying. Now, there is a meaning, certainly, to this. And had it been the will of an all-wise and all-merciful Creator that one of these religions should exist and the rest should die, it would have become a fact long, long ago. If it were a fact that only one of these religions was true and all the rest were false, by this time it would have covered the whole world. But this is not so; not one has gained all the ground. All religions sometimes advance, sometimes decline. In every country, probably, if the statistics were taken, you would find that religions are sometimes progressing and sometimes going back. Sects are multiplying all the time. If the claims of a religion that it has all the truth, and that God has given it all this truth in a certain book, were true, why are there so many sects? Fifty years do not pass before there are twenty sects founded upon the same book. If God has put all the truth in certain books, He does not give us those books in order that we may quarrel over texts. That seems to be the fact. Why is it? Even if a book were given by God that contained all the truth about religion, it would not serve the purpose, because nobody could understand the book. Take the Bible, for instance, and all the sects that exist among the Christians. Each one puts its own interpretation upon the same text, and each says that it alone understands that text and all the rest are wrong. So with every religion. There are many sects among the Mohammedans and among the Buddhists, and hundreds among the Hindus.

Now, I bring these facts before you in order to show you that any attempt to bring all humanity to one method of thinking in spiritual things has been a failure and always will be a failure. You cannot make all conform to the same ideas. That is a fact, and I thank God that it is so. I am not against any sect. I am glad that sects exist, and I only wish they may go on multiplying more and more. Why? Simply because of this: If you and I and all who are present here were to think exactly the same thoughts, there would be no thoughts for us to think. We know that two or more forces must come into collision in order to produce motion. It is the clash of thought, the differentiation of thought, that awakes thought. Now, if we all thought alike, we would be like Egyptian mummies in a museum, looking vacantly at one another's faces—no more than that! Whirls and eddies occur only in a rushing, living stream. There are no whirlpools in stagnant, dead water. When religions are dead, there will be no more sects. It will be the perfect peace and harmony of the grave. But so long as mankind thinks, there will be sects. Variation is the sign of life, and it must be there. I pray that sects may multiply so that at last there will be as many sects as human beings, and each one will have his own method, his individual method of thought in religion. (II. 359-64)

RELIGION IS REALIZATION

Religion is a question of fact, not of talk. We have to analyze our own souls and find what is there. We have to understand it and realize what is understood. That is religion. No amount of talk will make religion. So the question of whether there is a God or not can never be proved by argument, for the arguments are as much on one side as on the other. But if there is a God, He is in our own hearts. Have you ever seen Him?

The sages of the world alone have the right to tell us that they have analyzed their minds and have found these facts, and if we do the same we shall also believe, and not before. That is all that there is in religion. But you must always remember this: that as a matter of fact, ninety-nine percent of those who attack religion have never analyzed their minds, have never struggled to get at the facts. So their arguments do not have any weight against religion any more than the words of a blind man who cries out, "You are all fools who believe in the sun," would affect us.

This is one great idea to learn and to hold on to, this idea of realization. This turmoil and fight and difference in religions will cease only when we understand that religion is not in books and temples. It is in actual perception. Only the man who has actually perceived God and the soul has religion. There is no real difference between the highest ecclesiastical giant, who can talk by the volume, and the lowest, most ignorant materialist. We are all atheists—let us confess it. Mere intellectual assent does not make us religious.

Take a Christian or a Mohammedan or a follower of any other religion in the world. Any man who truly realized the truth of the Sermon on the Mount would be perfect and become a god immediately. Yet it is said that there are many millions of Christians in the world. What is meant is that mankind may at some time try to realize that Sermon. Not one in twenty million is a real Christian. So, in India there are said to be three hundred million Vedantists. But if there were one in a thousand who had actually realized religion, this world would soon be greatly changed. We are all atheists, and yet we try to fight the man who admits it. We are all in the dark. Religion is to us mere intellectual assent, mere talk, mere nothing.

We often consider a man religious who can talk well. But this is not religion. "Wonderful methods of joining words, rhetorical powers, and explaining the texts of the books in various ways—these are only for the enjoyment of the learned, and are not religion." Religion comes when that actual realization in our own souls begins. That will be the dawn of religion, and then alone we shall be moral. Now we are not much more moral than the animals. We are only held down by the whips of society. If society said today, "I will not punish you if you steal," we would just make a rush for each other's property. It is the policeman who makes us moral. It is social opinion that makes us moral, and really we are little better than animals. We understand how much this is so in the secret of our own hearts. So let us not be hypocrites. Let us confess that we are not religious and have no right to look down on others. We are all brothers, and we shall be truly moral when we have realized religion.

If you have seen a certain country and a man forces you to say that you have not seen it, still in your heart of hearts you know you have. So when you see religion and God in a more intense sense than you see this external world, nothing will be able to shake your belief. Then you will have real faith. That is what is meant by the words in your Gospel, "If ye have faith as a grain of mustard seed." Then you will know the Truth because you have become the Truth.

This is the watchword of Vedanta: Realize religion. No talking will do. (II. 163-65)

RELIGION OF TODAY

We find that in almost every religion these are the three primary things which we have in the worship of God: forms or symbols, names, and God-men. All religions have these, but you find that they want to fight with each other. One says: "My name is the only name, my form is the only form, and my God-men are the only God-men in the world. Yours are simply myths."

These are the external forms of devotion through which man has to pass. But if he is sincere, if he really wants to reach the truth, he goes higher than these, to a plane where forms are as nothing. Temples or churches, books or forms, are simply the kindergarten of religion, to make the spiritual child strong enough to take higher steps, and these first steps are necessary if he wants religion. With the thirst, the longing for God, comes real devotion, real *bhakti*. Who has the longing? That is the question. Religion is not in doctrines, in dogmas, nor in intellectual argumentation. It is being and becoming. It is realization. We hear so many talking about God and the soul and all the mysteries of the universe, but if you take them one by one and ask them: "Have you realized God? Have you seen your soul?"—how many can say they have? And yet they are all fighting with one another!

At one time in India, representatives of different sects met together and began to dispute. One said that the only God was

Shiva; another said the only God was Vishnu; and so on. And there was no end to their discussion. A sage was passing that way and was invited by the disputants to decide the matter. He first asked the man who was claiming Shiva to be the greatest God: "Have you seen Shiva? Are you acquainted with Him? If not, how do you know He is the greatest God?" Then turning to the worshipper of Vishnu, he asked, "Have you seen Vishnu?" And after asking this question to all of them, he found out that not one of them knew anything of God. That was why they were disputing so much, for had they really known, they would not have argued.

When a jar is being filled with water, it makes a noise, but when it is full, there is no noise. So the very fact of these disputations and fighting among sects shows that they do not know anything about religion. Religion to them is a mere mass of frothy words, to be written in books. Each one hurries to write a big book, to make it as massive as possible, stealing his materials from every book he can lay his hands upon and never acknowledging his indebtedness. Then he launches this book upon the world, adding to the disturbance that is already existing there.

The vast majority of men are atheists. I am glad that, in modern times, another class of atheists has come into existence in the Western world—I mean the materialists. They are sincere atheists. They are better than the religious atheists, who are insincere, who fight and talk about religion and yet do not want it, never try to realize it, never try to understand it. Remember the words of Christ: "Ask, and it shall be given you; seek, and ye shall find; knock, and it shall be opened unto you." These words are literally true—not figures or fiction. Who wants God? That is the question. Do you think that all this mass of people in the world want God and cannot get Him? That cannot be. What want is there without its object outside? Man wants to breathe, and there is air for him to breathe. Man wants to eat, and there is food to eat. What creates these desires? The existence of external things. It was the light that made the eyes; it was the sound that made the ears. So every desire in human beings has been created by something which already existed outside. This desire for perfection, for reaching the goal and getting beyond nature—how can it be there until something has created it and drilled it into the soul of man and made it live there? He, therefore, in whom this desire is awakened will reach the goal.

We want everything but God. This is not religion that you see all around you. My lady has furniture in her parlor from all over the world, and now it is the fashion to have something Japanese, so she buys a vase and puts it in her room. Such is religion with the vast majority. They have all sorts of things for enjoyment, and unless they add a little flavor of religion, life is not all right, because society would criticize them. Society expects it, so they must have some religion. This is the present state of religion in the world. (II. 42-45)

ON DOING GOOD TO THE WORLD

We are asked: "What good is your religion to society?" Society is made a test of truth. Now this is very illogical. Society is only a stage of growth through which we are passing. We might just as well judge the good or the utility of a scientific discovery by its use to the baby. It is simply monstrous. If the social state were permanent, it would be the same as if the baby remained a baby. There can be no perfect man-baby—the words are a contradiction in terms. So there can be no perfect society. Man must, and will, grow out of such early stages. Society is good at a certain stage, but it cannot be our ideal. It is a constant flux. The present mercantile civilization must die, with all its pretensions and humbug—all a kind of "Lord Mayor's Show." What the world wants is thought-power through individuals. My Master used to say: "Why don't you help your own lotus flower to bloom? The bees will then come of themselves." The world needs people who are mad with the love of God. You must believe in yourself, and then you will believe in God. The history of the world is that of six men of faith, six men of deep, pure character.

We need to have three things: the heart to feel, the brain to conceive, and the hand to work. First, we must go out of the world and make ourselves fit instruments. Make yourself a dynamo. *Feel* first for the world. At a time when all men are ready to work, where is the man of *feeling*? Where is the feeling that produced an Ignatius Loyola? Test your love and humility. That man is not humble or loving who is jealous. Jealousy is a terrible, horrible sin. It enters a man so mysteriously. Ask yourself, does your mind react in hatred or jealousy? Good works are continually being undone by the tons of hatred and anger that are being poured out on the world. If you are pure, if you are strong, *you, one* man, are equal to the whole world.

The brain to conceive, the next condition of doing good works, is only a dry Sahara after all. It cannot do anything alone unless it has the *feeling* behind it. Take love, which has never failed, and then the brain will conceive and the hand will work righteousness. Sages have dreamed of and have *seen* the vision of God. "The pure in heart shall see God." All the great ones claim to have *seen* God. Thousands of years ago has the vision been seen, and the unity that lies beyond has been recognized, and now the only thing we can do is to fill in these glorious outlines. (VI. 144-45)

THE GOAL OF RELIGION

Life will be a desert, human life will be vain, if we cannot know the beyond. It is very well to say, "Be content with the things of the present." The cows and the dogs are, and so are all animals, and that is what makes them animals. So if man rests content with the present and gives up all search into the beyond, mankind will have to go back to the animal plane again. It is religion, the inquiry into the beyond, that makes the difference between a man and an animal.

Religion does not live on bread, does not dwell in a house. Again and again you hear this objection advanced: "What good can religion do? Can it take away the poverty of the poor?" Supposing it cannot, would that prove the untruth of religion? Suppose a baby stands up among you when you are trying to demonstrate an astronomical theorem, and says, "Does it bring gingerbread?" "No, it does not," you answer. "Then," says the baby, "it is useless." Babies judge the whole universe from their own standpoint, that of producing gingerbread, and so do the babies of the world. We must not judge higher things from a low standpoint. Everything must be judged by its own standard, and the infinite must be judged by the standard of infinity. Religion permeates the whole of man's life—not only the present, but the past, present, and future. It is, therefore, the eternal relationship between the eternal soul and the eternal God. Is it logical to measure its value by its action upon five minutes of human life? Certainly not. These are all negative arguments.

Now comes the question: Can religion really accomplish anything? It can. It brings to man eternal life. It has made man what he is, and will make of this human animal a god. That is what religion can do. Take religion from human society and what will remain? Nothing but a forest of brutes. Sense happiness is not the goal of humanity. Wisdom (jnana) is the goal of all life. We find that man enjoys his intellect more than an animal enjoys its senses. And we see that man enjoys his spiritual nature even more than his rational nature. So the highest wisdom must be this spiritual knowledge. With this knowledge will come bliss. All the things of this world are but shadows, the manifestations in the third or fourth degree, of the real Knowledge and Bliss.

One question more: What is the goal? Nowadays it is asserted that man is infinitely progressing, forward and forward, and there is no goal of perfection to attain to. Ever approaching, never attaining—whatever that may mean and however wonderful it may be—it is absurd on the face of it. Is there any motion in a straight line? A straight line infinitely projected becomes a circle. It returns to the starting point. You must end where you began, and as you began in God, you must go back to God. What remains? Detail work. Through eternity you have to do the detail work.

Yet another question: Are we to discover new truths of religion as we go on? Yes and no. In the first place, we cannot know anything more of religion. It has all been known. In all religions of the world you will find it claimed that there is a unity within us. Being one with divinity, there cannot be any further progress in that sense. Knowledge means finding this unity.

The next question is: Can such a unity be found? In India the attempt has been made from the earliest times to reach a science of religion and philosophy—for the Hindus do not separate these as is customary in Western countries. We regard religion and philosophy as but two aspects of one thing, which must equally be grounded in reason and scientific truth.

Vedanta is not satisfied to end in dualism, but continues its search for the final unity, which is alike the goal of science and religion. (III. 3-5)

FUNDAMENTALS OF RELIGION

My mind can best grasp the religions of the world, ancient or modern, dead or living, through this fourfold division:

1. Symbology—The employment of various external aids to preserve and develop the religious faculty of man.
2. History—The philosophy of each religion as illustrated in the lives of divine or human teachers acknowledged by each religion. This includes mythology, for what is mythology to one race or period, is, or was, history to other races or periods. Even in cases of human teachers, much of their history is taken as mythology by successive generations.
3. Philosophy—The rationale of the whole scope of each religion.
4. Mysticism—The assertion of something superior to sense knowledge and reason, which particular persons, or all persons under certain circumstances, possess. [This] runs through the other divisions also.

All the religions of the world, past or present, embrace one or more of these principles, the highly developed ones having all the four. (IV. 374)

VEDANTA: AN UNORGANIZED RELIGION

Religion is the realization of spirit as spirit. What are we doing now? Just the opposite—realizing spirit as matter. Out of the immortal God we manufacture death and matter, and out of dead, dull matter we manufacture spirit.

Religion is a [matter of] growth, not a mass of foolish words. Two thousand years ago a man saw God. Moses saw God in a burning bush. Does what Moses did when he saw God save you? No man's seeing God can help you the least bit, except that it may excite you and urge you to do the same thing. That is the whole value of the ancients' examples. Nothing more. [Just] signposts on the way. No man's eating can satisfy another man. No man's seeing God can save another man. You have to see God yourself. All these people fighting about what God's nature is—whether He has three heads in one body or five heads in six bodies. Have you seen God? No.... And they do not believe they can ever see Him. What fools we mortals are! Sure, lunatics!

[In India] it has come down as a tradition that if there is a God, He must be your God and my God. To whom does the sun belong? You say Uncle Sam is everybody's uncle. If there is a God, you ought to be able to see Him. If not, let Him go.

Each one thinks his method is best. Very good! But remember, it may be good for *you*. One food which is very indigestible to one is very digestible to another. Because it is good for you, do not jump to the conclusion that your method is everybody's method, that Jack's coat fits John and Mary. All the uneducated, uncultured, unthinking men and women have been put into that sort of strait jacket! Think for yourselves. Become atheists! Become materialists! That would be better. Exercise the mind!... What right have you to say that this man's method is wrong? It may be wrong for you. That is to say, if you undertake the method, you will be degraded. But that does not mean that he will be degraded. Therefore, says Krishna, if you have knowledge and see a man weak, do not condemn him. Go to his level and help him if you can. He must grow.

We start a religion and make a set of dogmas and betray the goal of mankind and treat everyone [as having] the same nature. No two persons have the same mind or the same body.... No two persons have the same religion....

If you want to be religious, enter not the gate of any organized religions. They do a hundred times more evil than good, because they stop the growth of each one's individual development. Study everything, but keep your own seat firm. If you take my advice, do not put your neck into the trap. The moment they try to put their noose on you, get your neck out and go somewhere else. [As] the bee culling honey from many flowers remains free, not bound by any flower, be not bound.... Enter not the door of any organized religion. [Religion] is only between you and your God, and no third person must come between you. Think what these organized religions have done! What Napoleon was more terrible than these religious persecutions?. . . If you and I organize, we begin to hate every person. It is better not to love, if loving only means hating others. That is not love. That is hell! If loving your own people means hating everybody else, it is the quintessence of selfishness and brutality, and the effect is that it will make you brutes.

Let us be no more the worshippers of creeds or sects with small, limited notions of God, but see Him in everything in the universe. If you are knowers of God, you will everywhere find the same worship as in your own heart.

Get rid, in the first place, of all these limited ideas and see God in every person—working through all hands, walking through all feet, and eating through every mouth. In every being He lives, through all minds He thinks. He is self-evident, nearer unto us than ourselves. To know this is religion, is faith, and may it please the Lord to give us this faith! When we shall feel that oneness, we shall be immortal. (I. 469-70, 473-74, 341)

REASON AND RELIGION

The question is: Is religion to justify itself by the discoveries of reason, through which every other science justifies itself? Are the same methods of investigation that we apply to sciences and knowledge outside, to be applied to the science of religion? In my opinion this must be so, and I am also of the opinion that the sooner it is done the better. If a religion is destroyed by such investigations, it was then all the time useless, unworthy superstition, and the sooner it goes the better. I am thoroughly convinced that its destruction would be the best thing that could happen. All that is dross will be taken off, no doubt, but the essential parts of religion will emerge triumphant out of this investigation. Not only will it be made scientific—as scientific, at least, as any of the conclusions of physics or chemistry—but it will have greater strength, because physics or chemistry has no internal mandate to vouch for its truth, which religion has.

The religion of Vedanta can satisfy the demands of the scientific world in regard to the highest generalization and to the law of evolution. That the explanation of a thing comes from within itself is still more completely satisfied by Vedanta. Brahman, the God of Vedanta, has nothing outside of Himself—nothing at all. All this indeed is He. He is in the universe; He Himself is the universe. "Thou art the man, Thou art the woman, Thou art the young man walking in the pride of youth, Thou art the old man tottering in his step."[1] He is here. Him we see and feel. In Him we live and move and have our being. You have that conception in the New Testament. It is that idea—God immanent in the universe, the very essence, the heart, the soul of things. He manifests Himself, as it were, in this universe. You and I are little bits, little points, little channels, little expressions, all living inside of that infinite ocean of Existence, Knowledge, and Bliss.

The difference between man and man, between angels and man, between man and animals, between animals and plants, between plants and stones, is not in kind—because everyone, from the highest angel to the lowest particle of matter, is but an expression of that one infinite ocean—but the difference is only in degree. I am a low manifestation; you may be a higher; but in both the materials are the same. You and I are both outlets of the same channel, and that is God; as such, your nature is God, and so is mine. You are of the nature of God by your birthright; so am I. You may be an angel of purity, and I may be the blackest of demons. Nevertheless, my birthright is that infinite ocean of Existence, Knowledge, and Bliss, and so is yours. You have manifested yourself more today. Wait, I will manifest myself more yet, for I have it all within me.

No extraneous explanation is sought—none is asked for. The sum total of this whole universe is God Himself. Is God then matter? No, certainly not, for matter is that God perceived by the five senses. That God, as perceived through the intellect, is *mind*; and when the Spirit sees, He is seen as *Spirit*. He is not matter, but whatever is real in matter is He. (I. 367, 374-75)

THE BASIS OF ETHICS

The Vedanta philosophers discovered the basis of ethics. Though all religions have taught ethical precepts, such as,

"Do not kill, do not injure, love your neighbor as yourself," etc., yet none of these has given the reason. Why should I not injure my neighbor? To this question there was no satisfactory or conclusive answer forthcoming until it was evolved by the metaphysical speculations of the Hindus, who could not rest satisfied with mere dogmas. So the Hindus say that this Atman is absolute and all-pervading, and therefore infinite. There cannot be two infinites, for they would limit each other and would become finite. Also, each individual soul is a part and parcel of that universal Soul, which is infinite. Therefore in injuring his neighbor, the individual actually injures himself. This is the basic metaphysical truth underlying all ethical codes.

It is too often believed that a person in his progress toward perfection passes from error to truth—that when he passes on from one thought to another, he must necessarily reject the first. But no error can lead to truth. The soul passing through its different stages goes from truth to truth, and each stage is true. It goes from lower truth to higher truth. This point may be illustrated in the following way: A man is journeying toward the sun and takes a photograph at each step. How different would be the first photograph from the second, and still more from the third or the last, when he reaches the real sun! But all these, though differing so widely from each other, are true, only they are made to appear different by the changing conditions of time and space. It is the recognition of this truth which has enabled the Hindus to perceive the universal truth of all religions, from the lowest to the highest. It has made of them the only people who never had religious persecutions. (I. 384-85)

MORALITY IN VEDANTA

Once a gigantic attempt was made [in India] to preach Vedantic ethics, which succeeded to a certain extent for several hundred years—and we know historically that those years were the best times of that nation. I mean the Buddhistic attempt to break down privilege. Some of the most beautiful epithets addressed to Buddha that I remember are, "Thou the breaker of castes, destroyer of privileges, preacher of equality to all beings." He preached this one idea of equality. Its power has been misunderstood to a certain extent in the brotherhood of *shramanas* [Buddhist monks], where we find that hundreds of attempts have been made to make them into a church, with superiors and inferiors. You cannot make much of a church when you tell people they are all gods. One of the good effects of Vedanta has been freedom of religious thought, which India has enjoyed throughout its history. It is something to glory in, that it is the land where there was never a religious persecution, where people are allowed perfect freedom in religion.

This practical side of Vedantic morality is necessary as much today as it ever was—more necessary, perhaps, than it ever was—for all this privilege-claiming has become tremendously intensified with the extension of knowledge. The idea of God and the devil, or *Ahura Mazda* and *Ahriman*, has a good deal of poetry in it. The difference between God and the devil is in nothing except in unselfishness and selfishness. The devil knows as much as God, is as powerful as God, only he has no holiness—that makes him a devil. Apply the same idea to the modern world: excess of knowledge and power, without holiness, makes human beings devils.

Those of you who have studied the Gita will remember the memorable passages: "He who looks upon the learned brahmin, upon the cow, the elephant, the dog, or the outcast with the same eye, he indeed is the sage and the wise man. Even in this life he has conquered relative existence whose mind is firmly fixed on this sameness; for the Lord is one and the same to all, and the Lord is pure. Therefore, those who have this sameness for all and are pure are said to be living in God."[2] This is the gist of Vedantic morality—this sameness for all. We have seen that it is the subjective world that rules the objective. Change the subject, and the object is bound to change. Purify yourself, and the world is bound to be purified. This one thing needs to be taught now more than ever before. We are becoming more and more busy about our neighbors, and less and less about ourselves. The world will change if we change. If we are pure, the world will become pure. The question is why I should see evil in others. I cannot see evil unless I am evil. I cannot be miserable unless I am weak. Things that used to make me miserable when I was a child do not do so now. The subject changed, so the object was bound to change—so says Vedanta. All these things that we call causes of misery and evil, we shall laugh at when we arrive at that wonderful state of equality, that sameness. This is what is called, in Vedanta, attaining freedom. The sign of approaching that freedom is more and more of this sameness and equality. In misery and happiness the same, in success and defeat the same—such a mind is nearing that state of freedom. (I. 424-26)

PRACTICAL RELIGION

We read many books, many scriptures. We get various ideas from our childhood and change them every now and then. We understand what is meant by theoretical religion. We think we understand what is meant by practical religion. Now I am going to present to you my idea of practical religion.

What is the goal of life? Is this world the goal of life? Nothing more? Are we to be just what we are—nothing more? Is man to be a machine that runs smoothly without a hitch anywhere? Are all the sufferings he experiences today all he can have, and doesn't he want anything more?

The highest dream of many religions is the world. The vast majority of people are dreaming of the time when there will be no more disease, sickness, poverty, or misery of any kind. They will have a good time all around. Practical religion, therefore, simply means: "Clean the streets! Make it nice!" We see how all enjoy it.

Is enjoyment the goal of life? Were it so, it would be a tremendous mistake to become a man at all. What man can enjoy a meal with more gusto than the dog or the cat? Go to a menagerie and see the [wild animals] tearing the flesh from the bone. Go back and become a bird!... What a mistake then to become a man! Vain have been my years—hundreds of years—of struggle only to become the man of sense enjoyments.

Mark, therefore, the ordinary theory of practical religion, what it leads to. Charity is great, but the moment you say it is all, you run the risk of running into materialism. It is not religion. It is no better than atheism—a little less.

What is the ideal of religion, then, if this cannot be practical [religion]? And it certainly cannot be. What are we here for? We are here for freedom, for knowledge. We want to know in order to make ourselves free. That is our life—one universal cry for freedom. What is the reason the plant grows from the seed, overturning the ground and raising itself up to the skies? What is the offering for the earth from the sun? What is your life? The same struggle for freedom. Nature is trying all around to suppress us, and the soul wants to express itself. The struggle with nature is going on. Nature says, "I will conquer." The soul says, "I must be the conqueror." Nature says, "Wait! I will give you a little enjoyment to keep you quiet." The soul enjoys a little, becomes deluded a moment, but the next moment it [cries for freedom again]. Have you marked the eternal cry going on through the ages in every breast?

The infinite human soul can never be satisfied but by the Infinite itself.... Infinite desire can only be satisfied by infinite knowledge—nothing short of that.

What is practical religion, then? To get to that state—freedom—the attainment of freedom. And this world, if it helps us on to that goal, [is] all right. If not—if it begins to bind one more layer on the thousands already there—it becomes an evil. Possessions, learning, beauty, everything else—as long as they help us to that goal, they are of practical value. When they have ceased helping us on to that goal of freedom, they are a positive danger. What is practical religion, then? Utilize the things of this world and the next just for one goal—the attainment of freedom.

Renounce the lower so that you may get the higher. What is the foundation of society? Morality, ethics, laws. Renounce! Renounce all temptation to take your neighbor's property, to put hands upon your neighbor, all the pleasure of tyrannizing over the weak, all the pleasure of cheating others by telling lies. Is not morality the foundation of society? What is marriage but the renunciation of unchastity? The savage does not marry. Man marries because he renounces. So on and on. Renounce! Renounce! Sacrifice! Give up! Not for zero. Not for nothing. But to get the higher. But who can do this? You cannot until you have got the higher. You may talk, you may struggle, you may try to do many things, but renunciation comes by itself when you have got the higher. Then the lesser falls away by itself.

This is practical religion. What else? Cleaning streets and building hospitals? Their value consists only in this renunciation. And there is no end to renunciation. The difficulty is they try to put a limit to it—thus far and no farther. But there is no limit to this renunciation.

Where God is, there is no other. Where the world is, there is no God. These two will never unite—[like] light and darkness. That is what I have understood from Christianity and the life of the Teacher. Is not that Buddhism? Is not that Hinduism? Is not that Mohammedanism? Is not that the teaching of all the great sages and teachers?

You are all materialists, because you believe that you are the body. If a man gives me a hard punch I would say I am punched. If he strikes me I would say I am struck. If I am not the body, why should I say so? It makes no difference if I *say* I am the Spirit. I am the body just now. I have converted myself into matter. That is why I am to renounce the body, to go back to what I really am. I am the Spirit—the soul no instrument can pierce, no sword can cut asunder, no fire can burn, no air can dry. Unborn and uncreated, without beginning and without end, deathless, birthless, and omnipresent—that is what I am. And all misery comes just because I think this little lump of clay is myself. I am identifying myself with matter and taking all the consequences.

Practical religion is identifying myself with my Self. Stop this wrong identification! How far are you advanced in that? You may have built two thousand hospitals, built fifty thousand roads, and yet what of that if you have not realized that you are the Spirit? You die a dog's death, with the same feelings that the dog does. The dog howls and weeps because he knows that he is only matter and he is going to be dissolved.

You must see God. The Spirit must be realized, and that is practical religion. It is not what Christ preached that *you* call practical religion: "Blessed are the poor in spirit for theirs is the kingdom of heaven." Was it a joke? What is the practical religion you are thinking of? Lord help us! "Blessed are the pure in heart, for they shall see God." That means street cleaning, hospital building, and all that? Good works, when you do them with a pure mind. Don't give the man twenty dollars and buy all the papers in San Francisco to see your name!

The kingdom of heaven is within us. He is there. He is the Soul of all souls. See Him in your own soul. That is practical religion. That is freedom. Let us ask each other how much we are advanced in that—how much we are worshippers of the body, or real believers in God, the Spirit; how much we believe ourselves to be Spirit. That is selflessness. That is freedom. That is real worship. Realize yourself. That is all there is to do. Know yourself as you are—infinite Spirit. That is practical religion. (IV. 238-41, 243-46)

THE VEDANTIC VIEW OF FAMILY LIFE

The life of every individual, according to the Hindu scriptures, has its peculiar duties apart from those which are common to humanity. The Hindu begins life as a student; then he marries and becomes a householder; in old age he retires; and lastly he gives up the world and becomes a sannyasin. To each of these stages of life certain duties are attached. No one of these stages is intrinsically superior to another. The life of the married man is quite as great as that of the celibate who has devoted himself to religious work. The scavenger in the street is quite as great and glorious as the king on his throne. It is useless to say that the man who lives outside the world is a greater man than he who lives in the world. It is much more difficult to live in the world and worship God than to give it up and live a free and easy life. The four stages of life in India have, in later times, been reduced to two—that of the householder and that of the monk. The householder marries and carries on his duties as a citizen, and the duty of the other is to devote his energies wholly to religion, to preach, and to worship God. I shall read to you a few passages from the Mahanirvana Tantra, which treats of this subject, and you will see that it is a very difficult task for a man to be a householder and perform all his duties perfectly:

The householder should be devoted to God—knowledge of God should be the goal of his life. Yet he must work constantly, perform all his duties. He must give up the fruits of his actions to God.

The great duty of the householder is to earn a living, but he must take care that he does not do it by telling lies or by cheating or by robbing others. And he must remember that his life is for the service of God and the poor.

Knowing that his mother and father are the visible representatives of God, the householder, always and by all means, must please them. If the mother is pleased, and the father, God is pleased with that man. That child is really a good child who never speaks harsh words to his parents.

Before one's parents one must not utter jokes, must not show restlessness, must not show anger or temper. Before his mother or father a child must bow down low, and he must stand up in their presence, and must not take a seat until they order him to sit.

If the householder has food and drink and clothes without first seeing that his mother and his father, his children, his wife, and the poor are supplied, he is committing a sin. The mother and the father are the causes of this body. So a man must undergo a thousand troubles in order to do good to them.

Even so is his duty to his wife. No man should scold his wife, and he must always maintain her as if she were his own mother. And even when he is in the greatest difficulties and troubles, he must not show anger to his wife.

He who thinks of another woman besides his wife, if he touches her even with his mind—that man goes to dark hell.

Before women, a man must not use improper language, and must never brag of his powers. He must not say, "I have done this, and I have done that."

The householder must always please his wife with money, clothes, love, faith, and words like nectar, and must never do anything to disturb her. That man who has succeeded in getting the love of a chaste wife has succeeded in his religion and has all the virtues.

The following are a man's duties toward his children:

A son should be lovingly reared up to his fourth year. He should be educated till he is sixteen. When he is twenty years of age he should be employed in some work. He should then be treated affectionately by his father as his equal. Exactly in the same manner the daughter should be brought up and should be educated with the greatest care. And when she marries, the father ought to give her jewels and wealth.

Excessive attachment to food, clothes, and the tending of the body and dressing of the hair should be avoided. The householder must be pure in heart and clean in body, always active, and always ready for work.

To his enemies the householder must be a hero. He must resist them. That is the duty of the householder. He must not sit down in a corner and weep, and talk nonsense about non-resistance. If he does not show himself a hero to his enemies he has not done his duty. And to his friends and relatives he must be as gentle as a lamb.

It is the duty of the householder not to pay reverence to the wicked, because if he reverences the wicked people of the world, he patronizes wickedness. And it will be a great mistake if he disregards those who are worthy of respect, the good people.

The householder is the center of life and society. It is a worship for him to acquire and spend wealth nobly; for the householder who struggles to become rich by good means and for good purposes is doing practically the same thing for the attainment of salvation as the anchorite does in his cell when he is praying. For in them we see only the different aspects of the same virtue of self-surrender and self-sacrifice prompted by the feeling of devotion to God and to all that is His.

The householder must struggle to acquire a good name by all means. He must not gamble, he must not move in the company of the wicked, he must not tell lies, and must not be the cause of trouble to others.

The householder must speak the truth and speak gently, using words which people like, which will do good to others; nor should he talk of the business of other men.

The householder, by digging tanks, by planting trees on the roadsides, by establishing resthouses for men and animals, by making roads and building bridges, goes toward the same goal as the greatest yogi. (I. 42-46)

UNITY IN VARIETY

At the very outset, I may tell you that there is no polytheism in India. In every temple, if one stands by and listens, one will find the worshippers applying all the attributes of God, including omnipresence, to the images. It is not polytheism, nor would the name *henotheism* explain the situation. "The rose called by any other name would smell as sweet." Names are not explanations.

I remember, as a boy, hearing a Christian missionary preach to a crowd in India. Among other sweet things he was telling them was that if he gave a blow to their idol with his stick, what could it do? One of his hearers sharply answered, "If I abuse your God, what can He do?" "You would be punished," said the preacher, "when you die." "So my idol will punish you when you die," retorted the Hindu.

The tree is known by its fruits. When I have seen, amongst them that are called idolaters, men the like of whom in morality and spirituality and love I have never seen anywhere, I stop and ask myself, "Can sin beget holiness?"

Superstition is a great enemy of man, but bigotry is worse. Why does a Christian go to church? Why is the Cross holy? Why is the face turned toward the sky in prayer? Why are there so many images in the Catholic Church? Why are there so many images in the minds of Protestants when they pray? My brethren, we can no more think about anything without a mental image than we can live without breathing. By the law of association, the material image calls up the mental idea and vice versa. This is why the Hindu uses an external symbol when he worships. He will tell you that it helps to keep his mind fixed on the Being to whom he prays. He knows as well as you do that the image is not God, is not omnipresent. After all, how much does omnipresence mean to most of the world? It stands merely as a word, a symbol. Has God superficial area? If not, when we repeat that word *omnipresent*, we think of the extended sky or of space—that is all.

As we find that, somehow or other, by the laws of our mental constitution, we have to associate our ideas of infinity with the image of the blue sky or of the sea, so we naturally connect our idea of holiness with the image of a church, a mosque, or a cross. The Hindus have associated the ideas of holiness, purity, truth, omnipresence, and such other ideas with different images and forms, but with this difference—that while some people devote their whole lives to their idol of a church and never rise higher, because with them religion means an intellectual assent to certain doctrines and doing good to their fellows, the whole religion of the Hindu is centered in realization. Man is to become divine by realizing the divine. Idols or temples or churches or books are only the supports, the helps, of his spiritual childhood; but on and on he must progress. He must not stop anywhere. "External worship, material worship," say the Hindu scriptures, "is the lowest stage; struggling to rise high, mental prayer, is the next stage; but the highest stage is when the Lord has been realized."[3]

Mark, the same earnest man who is kneeling before the idol tells you, "Him the sun cannot express, nor the moon, nor the stars; the lightning cannot express Him, not to speak of fire. Through Him they shine." But he does not abuse anyone's idol or call its worship sin. He recognizes in it a necessary stage of life. "The child is father of the man." Would it be right for an old man to say that childhood is a sin or youth a sin?

If a man can realize his divine nature with the help of an image, would it be right to call that a sin? Or, even when he has passed that stage, should he call it an error? To the Hindu, man is not traveling from error to truth, but from truth to truth—from lower to higher truth. To him all religions, from the lowest fetishism to the highest absolutism, mean so many attempts of the human soul to grasp and realize the Infinite, each determined by the conditions of its birth and association, and each of these marks a stage of progress. And every soul is a young eagle soaring higher and higher, gathering more and more strength, till it reaches the glorious Sun.

Unity in variety is the plan of nature, and the Hindu has recognized it. Every other religion lays down certain fixed dogmas and tries to force society to adopt them. It places before society only one coat, which must fit Jack and John and Henry all alike. If it does not fit John or Henry, he must go without a coat to cover his body. The Hindus have discovered that the Absolute can only be realized, or thought of, or stated, through the relative, and the images, crosses, and crescents are simply so many symbols—so many pegs to hang the spiritual ideas on. It is not that this help is necessary for everyone, but those who do not need it have no right to say that it is wrong. Nor is it compulsory in Hinduism.

One thing I must tell you. Idolatry in India does not mean anything horrible. It is not the mother of harlots. On the other hand, it is the attempt of undeveloped minds to grasp high spiritual truths. The Hindus have their faults—they sometimes have their exceptions. But mark this: They are always for punishing their own bodies, and never for cutting the throats of their neighbors. If the Hindu fanatic burns himself on the pyre, he never lights the fire of Inquisition. And even this [self-immolation] cannot be laid at the door of his religion any more than the burning of witches can be laid at the door of Christianity.

To the Hindu, then, the whole world of religions is only a traveling, a coming up, of different men and women, through various conditions and circumstances, to the same goal. Every religion is only evolving a God out of the material man, and the same God is the inspirer of all of them. Why, then, are there so many contradictions? They are only apparent, says the Hindu. The contradictions come from the same truth adapting itself to the varying circumstances of different natures.

It is the same light coming through glasses of different colors. And these little variations are necessary for purposes of adaptation. But in the heart of everything the same truth reigns. The Lord has declared to the Hindu in His incarnation as Krishna: "I am in every religion, as the thread through a string of pearls."[4] "Wherever thou seest extraordinary holiness and extraordinary power raising and purifying humanity, know thou that I am there."[5] (I. 15-18)

Notes

1 Shvetashvatara Upanishad, 4.3.
2 Bhagavad Gita, 5.18-19.
3 Atmajnana Nirnaya, 14.
4 Bhagavad Gita, 7.7.
5 Bhagavad Gita, 10.41.

IV

GOD AND MAN IN VEDANTA

Swami Vivekananda, Chicago, October 1893

GOD: PERSONAL AND IMPERSONAL

The Advaita system is nondestructive. This is its glory, that it has the boldness to preach, "Do not disturb the faith of any, even of those who through ignorance have attached themselves to lower forms of worship." That is what it says—do not disturb, but help everyone to get higher and higher; include all humanity. This philosophy preaches a God who is a sum total. If you seek a universal religion which can apply to everyone, that religion must not be composed of only the parts, but it must always be their sum total and include all degrees of religious development. This idea is not clearly found in any other religious system. They are all parts, equally struggling to attain to the whole. The existence of the part is only for this.

So, from the very first, Advaita had no antagonism with the various sects existing in India. There are dualists existing today, and their number is by far the largest in India because dualism naturally appeals to less educated minds. It is a very convenient, natural, commonsense explanation of the universe. But with these dualists, Advaita has no quarrel. The dualist thinks that God is outside the universe, somewhere in heaven, and the Advaitist, that He is his own Soul, and that it would be blasphemy to call Him anything more distant. Any idea of separation would be terrible. He is the nearest of the near. There is no word in any language to express this nearness except the word *Oneness*. With any other idea, the Advaitist is not satisfied, just as the dualist is shocked with the concept of Advaita and thinks it blasphemous. At the same time the Advaitist knows that these other ideas must be, and so he has no quarrel with the dualist, who is on the right road. From his standpoint the dualist will have to see the many. It is a constitutional necessity of his standpoint. Let him have it. The Advaitist knows that whatever may be the dualist's theories, he is going to the same goal as he himself. There he differs entirely from the dualist, who is forced by his point of view to believe that all differing views are wrong.

The dualists all the world over naturally believe in a Personal God who is purely anthropomorphic, who, like a great potentate in this world, is pleased with some and displeased with others. He is arbitrarily pleased with some people or races and showers blessings upon them. Naturally the dualist comes to the conclusion that God has favorites, and he hopes to be one of them. You will find that in almost every religion is the idea: "We are the favorites of our God, and only by believing as we do, can you be taken into favor with Him." Some dualists are so narrow as to insist that only the few who have been predestined to the favor of God can be saved; the rest may try ever so hard, but they cannot be accepted. I challenge you to show me one dualistic religion that has not more or less of this exclusiveness. And therefore, in the nature of things, dualistic religions are bound to fight and quarrel with each other, and this they have ever been doing. Again, these dualists win popular favor by appealing to the vanity of the uneducated, who like to feel that they enjoy exclusive privileges.

The dualist thinks you cannot be moral until you have a God with a rod in His hand, ready to punish you. The unthinking masses are generally dualists, and they, poor fellows, have been persecuted for thousands of years in every country, and their idea of salvation is, therefore, freedom from the fear of punishment. I was asked by a clergyman in America: "What! You have no devil in your religion? How can that be?" But we find that the best and the greatest men that have been born in the world have worked with that high impersonal idea. It is the man who said, "I and my Father are one," whose power has descended unto millions. For two thousand years he has worked for good. And we know that the same man, because he was a nondualist, was merciful to others. To the masses, who could not conceive of anything higher than a Personal God, he said, "Pray to your Father in heaven." To others, who could grasp a higher idea, he said, "I am the vine, ye are the branches." But to his disciples, to whom he revealed himself more fully, he proclaimed the highest truth, "I and my Father are one."

The Vedantist gives no other attributes to God except these three—that He is Infinite Existence, Infinite Knowledge, and Infinite Bliss, and he regards these three as one. Existence without Knowledge and Love cannot be. Knowledge without Love and Love without Knowledge cannot be. What we want is the harmony of Existence, Knowledge, and Bliss Infinite. For that is our goal. (II. 141-43)

GOD IN EVERYTHING

From my childhood I have heard of seeing God everywhere and in everything, and then I can really enjoy the world. But as soon as I mix with the world and get a few blows from it, the idea vanishes. I am walking in the street thinking that God is in every man, and a strong man comes along and gives me a push and I fall flat on the footpath. Then I rise up quickly with clenched fist, the blood has rushed to my head, and the reflection goes. Immediately I have become mad. Everything is forgotten. Instead of encountering God I see the devil. Ever since we were born we have been told to see God in all. Every religion teaches that—see God in everything and everywhere. Do you not remember that in the New Testament Christ says so? We have all been taught that, but it is when we come to the practical side that the difficulty begins.

You all remember how in *Aesop's Fables* a fine stag is looking at his form reflected in a lake and is saying to his young one: "How powerful I am! Look at my splendid head. Look at my limbs, how strong and muscular they are. And how swiftly I can run." Then he hears the barking of dogs in the distance and immediately takes to his heels, and after he has run several miles he comes back panting. The young one says: "You just told me how strong you were. How is it that when the dog barked you ran away?" "Yes, my son, but when the dogs bark all my confidence vanishes." Such is the case with us. We think highly of humanity, we feel ourselves strong and valiant, we make grand resolves, but when the dogs of trial and temptation bark, we are like the stag in the fable.

Then, if such is the case, what is the use of teaching all these things? There is the greatest use. The use is this, that perseverance will finally conquer. Nothing can be done in a day.

"This Self is first to be heard about, then to be thought upon, and then meditated upon."[2] Everyone can see the sky. Even the very worm crawling upon the earth sees the blue sky—but how very far away it is! So it is with our ideal. It is far away, no doubt, but at the same time we know that we must have it. We must even have the highest ideal. Unfortunately, in this life the vast majority of persons are groping through the dark without any ideal at all. If a man with an ideal makes a thousand mistakes, I am sure that the man without an ideal makes fifty thousand. Therefore it is better to have an ideal.

The ideal of man is to see God in everything. But if you cannot see Him in everything, see Him in one thing, in that thing you like best, and then see Him in another. So on you can go. There is infinite life before the soul. Take your time and you will achieve your end. (II. 151-53)

WORSHIP OF THE IMPERSONAL GOD

When Vedanta says that you and I are God, it does not mean the Personal God. To take an example: Out of a mass of clay a huge elephant of clay is manufactured, and out of the same clay a little clay mouse is made. Would the clay mouse ever be able to become the clay elephant? But put them both in water and they are both clay. As clay they are both one, but as mouse and elephant there will be an eternal difference between them. The Infinite, the Impersonal, is like the clay in the example.

We and the Ruler of the universe are one, but as manifested beings, men, we are His eternal slaves, His worshippers. Thus we see that the Personal God remains. Everything else in this relative world remains, and religion is made to stand on a better foundation. Therefore it is necessary that we first know the Impersonal in order to know the Personal.

Prayers will remain, only they will get a better meaning. All those senseless ideas of prayer, the low stages of prayer, which are simply giving words to all sorts of silly desires in our minds, will perhaps have to go. To ask God to give you a breath of air, to send down a shower of rain, to make fruits grow in your garden, and so on, is quite unnatural. To pray to the Ruler of the universe, prating about every little need of ours, and from our childhood saying, "O Lord, I have a headache—let it go," is ridiculous. To Him we must go for higher things. A fool indeed is he who, resting on the banks of the Ganga, digs a little well for water. A fool indeed is he who, living near a mine of diamonds, digs for bits of crystal.

And indeed we shall be fools if we go to the Father of all mercy, the Father of all love, for trivial earthly things. To Him, therefore, we shall go for light, for strength, for love. But so long as there is weakness and a craving for servile dependence in us, there will be these little prayers and ideas of the worship of the Personal God. But those who are highly advanced do not care for such little helps. They have well-nigh forgotten all about this seeking things for themselves, wanting things for themselves. The predominant idea in them is "Not I, but thou, my brother." Those are the fit persons to worship the Impersonal God. And what is the worship of the Impersonal God? No slavery there—"O Lord, I am nothing. Have mercy on me." You know the old Persian poem, translated into English:

> I came to see my beloved. The doors were closed. I knocked and a voice came from inside, "Who art thou?" "I am so-and-so." The door was not opened. A second time I came and knocked. I was asked the same question and gave the same answer. The door opened not. I came a third time, and the same question came. I answered, "I am thou, my love," and the door opened.

Worship of the Impersonal God is through truth. And what is truth? That I am He. When I say that I am not Thou, it is untrue. When I say I am separate from you, it is a lie, a terrible lie. I am one with this universe—born one. It is self-evident to my senses that I am one with the universe. I am one with the air that surrounds me, one with heat, one with light, eternally one with the whole Universal Being, who is called this universe, who is mistaken for the universe. For it is He and nothing else, the Eternal Subject in the heart, who says, "I am," in every heart—the Deathless One, the Sleepless One, ever awake, the Immortal, whose glory never dies, whose powers never fail. I am one with That.

This is all the worship of the Impersonal. And what is the result? The whole life of man will be changed. Strength, strength it is that we want so much in this life. For what we call sin and sorrow have all one cause, and that is our weakness. With weakness comes ignorance, and with ignorance comes misery. The Impersonal will make us strong. Then miseries will be laughed at; then the vileness of the vile will be smiled at, and the ferocious tiger will reveal, behind its tiger's nature, my own Self. That will be the result. That soul is strong that has become one with the Lord; none else is strong. In your own Bible, what do you think was the cause of that strength of Jesus of Nazareth—that immense, infinite strength which laughed at traitors and blessed those who were willing to murder him? It was that "I and my Father are one." It was that prayer, "Father, just as I am one with you, so make them all one with me." That is the worship of the Impersonal God. (I. 379-81)

WORSHIP THE LIVING GOD

We want to worship a living God. I have not seen anything but God all my life, nor have you. To see this chair you first see God, and then the chair in and through Him. He is everywhere, saying, "I am." The moment you feel "I am," you are conscious of Existence. Where shall we go to find God if we cannot see Him in our own hearts and in every living being? "Thou art the man, Thou art the woman, Thou art the girl, and Thou art the boy. Thou art the old man tottering with a stick. Thou art the young man walking in the pride of his strength. Thou art all that exists"—a wonderful living God, who is the only fact in the universe.

This seems to many to be a terrible contradiction of the traditional God, who lives behind a veil somewhere and whom nobody ever sees. The priests only give us an assurance that if we follow them, listen to their admonitions, and walk in the way they mark out for us, then, when we die, they will give us a passport to enable us to see the face of God! What are all these heaven ideas but simply modifications of this nonsensical priestcraft?

Of course, the impersonal idea is very destructive; it takes away all trade from the priests, churches, and temples. In India there is a famine now, but there are temples in each one of which there are jewels worth a king's ransom! If the priests taught this Impersonal idea to the people, their occupation would be gone. Yet we have to teach it unselfishly, without priestcraft. You are God and so am I. Who obeys whom? Who worships whom? You are the highest temple of God. I would rather worship you than any temple, image, or Bible. Why are some people so contradictory in their thought? They are like fish slipping through our fingers. They say they are hard-headed, practical men. Very good. But what is more practical than worshipping here, worshipping you? I see you, feel you, and I know you are God. The Mohammedan says there is no God but Allah. Vedanta says there is nothing that is not God. It may frighten many of you, but you will understand it by degrees. The living God is within you, and yet you are building churches and temples and believing all sorts of imaginary nonsense. The only God to worship is the human soul in the human body. Of course all animals are temples too, but man is the highest, the Taj Mahal of temples. If I cannot worship in that, no other temple will be of any advantage. The moment I have realized God sitting in the temple of every human body, the moment I stand in reverence before every human being and see God in him, that moment I am free from bondage. Everything that binds vanishes, and I am free.

This is the most practical of all worship. It has nothing to do with theorizing and speculation. Yet it frightens many. They say it is not right. They go on theorizing about old ideals told them by their grandfathers—that a God somewhere in heaven had told someone that he was God. Since that time we have only theories. This is practicality according to them, and our ideas are impractical! No doubt, Vedanta says, each one must have his own path, but the path is not the goal. The worship of a God in heaven and all these things are not bad, but they are only steps toward the Truth and not the Truth itself. They are good and beautiful, and some wonderful ideas are there, but Vedanta says at every point:

> My friend, Him whom you are worshipping as unknown, I worship Him as you. He whom you are worshipping as unknown and are seeking for, throughout the universe, has been with you all the time. You are living through Him, and He is the Eternal Witness of the universe.

> He whom all the Vedas worship, nay, more, He who is always present in the eternal "I"—He existing, the whole universe exists. He is the light and life of the universe. If the "I" were not in you, you would not see the sun; everything would be a dark mass. He shining, you see the world.

One question is generally asked, and it is this: Won't this lead to a tremendous amount of difficulty? Every one of us will think, "I am God, and whatever I do or think must be good, for God can do no evil." In the first place, even taking this danger of misinterpretation for granted, can it be proved that on the other side the same danger does not exist? They have been worshipping a God in heaven separate from them and of whom they are much afraid. They have been born shaking with fear, and all their life they will go on shaking. Has the world been made much better by this?

It is not right to say that the Impersonal idea will lead to a tremendous amount of evil in the world, as if the other doctrine never lent itself to works of evil, as if it did not lead to sectarianism, deluging the world with blood and causing men to tear each other to pieces. "My God is the greatest God. Let us decide it by a free fight." That is the outcome of dualism all over the world. Come out into the broad, open light of day. Come out from the little narrow paths. For how can the infinite soul rest content to live and die in small ruts? Come out into the universe of light. Everything in the universe is yours. Stretch out your arms and embrace it with love. If you ever felt you wanted to do that, you have felt God. (II. 320-23)

THE REAL NATURE OF MAN

The body is not the Real Man; neither is the mind, for the mind waxes and wanes. It is the Spirit beyond, which alone can live forever. The body and mind are continually changing and are, in fact, only names of series of changeful phenomena, like rivers whose waters are in a constant state of flux, yet present the appearance of unbroken streams. Every particle in this body is continually changing; no one has the same body for many minutes together, and yet we think of it as the same body. So with the mind: One moment it is happy, another moment unhappy; one moment strong, another weak—an ever-changing whirlpool. That cannot be the Spirit, which is infinite. Change can only be in the limited. To say that the infinite changes in any way is absurd; it cannot be. You can move and I can move, as limited bodies; every particle in this universe is in a constant state of flux. But taking the universe as a unit, as one whole, it cannot move, it cannot change. Motion is always a relative thing. I move in relation to something else. Any particle in this universe can change in relation to any other particle. But take the whole universe as one, and in relation to what can it move? There is nothing besides it. So this infinite Unit is unchangeable, immovable, absolute, and this is the Real Man. Our reality, therefore, consists in the Universal and not in the limited. These are old delusions, however comfortable they are, to think that we are little limited beings, constantly changing.

People are frightened when they are told that they are Universal Being, everywhere present. Through everything you work, through every foot you move, through every lip you talk, through every heart you feel. People are frightened when they are told this. They will again and again ask you if they are not going to keep their individuality. What is individuality? I should like to see it. A baby has no moustache. When he grows to be a man perhaps he has a moustache and beard. His individuality would be lost if it were in the body. If I lose one eye, or if I lose one of my hands, my individuality would be lost if it were in the body. Then a drunkard should not give up drinking because he would lose his individuality. A thief should not be a good man because he would thereby lose his individuality. No man ought to change his habits for fear of this. There is no individuality except in the Infinite. That is the only condition which does not change. Everything else is in a constant state of flux. Neither can individuality be in memory. Suppose, on account of a blow on the head, I forget all about my past; then I have lost all individuality; I am gone. I do not remember two or three years of my childhood, and if memory and existence are one, then whatever I forget is gone. That part of my life which I do not remember, I did not live. That is a very narrow idea of individuality.

We are not individuals yet. We are struggling toward individuality, and that is the Infinite; that is the real nature of man. He alone lives whose life is in the whole universe, and the more we concentrate our lives on limited things, the faster we go toward death. Those moments alone we live when our lives are in the universe, in others; and living this little life is death—simply death—and that is why the fear of death comes. The fear of death can only be conquered when man realizes that as long as there is one life in this universe, he is living. When he can say, "I am in everything, in everybody; I am in all lives; I am the universe," then alone comes the state of fearlessness. To talk of immortality in constantly changing things is absurd. Says an old Sanskrit philosopher, "It is only the Spirit that is the individual, because it is infinite." Infinity cannot be divided. Infinity cannot be broken into pieces. It is the same one, undivided unit forever, and this is the individual man, the Real Man. The apparent man is merely a struggle to express, to manifest, this individuality which is beyond. Evolution is not in the Spirit.

These changes which are going on—the wicked becoming good, the animal becoming man; take them in whatever way you like—are not in the Spirit. They are the evolution of nature and the manifestation of the Spirit. Suppose there is a screen hiding you from me, in which there is a small hole through which I can see some of the faces before me, just a few faces. Now suppose the hole begins to grow larger and larger, and as it does so, more and more of the scene before me reveals itself. When at last the whole screen has disappeared, I stand face to face with you all. You did not change at all in this case. It was the hole that was evolving, and you were gradually manifesting yourselves. So it is with the Spirit. No perfection is going to be attained. You are already free and perfect.

What are these ideas of religion and God and searching for the hereafter? Why does man look for a God? Why does man, in every nation, in every state of society, want a perfect ideal somewhere, either in man, in God, or elsewhere? Because that idea is within you. It was your own heart beating and you did not know; you were mistaking it for something external. It is the God within your own self that is impelling you to seek for Him, to realize Him. After long searches here and there, in temples and in churches, in earths and in heavens, at last you come back, completing the circle from where you started, to your own soul, and find that He for whom you have been seeking all over the world, for whom you have been weeping and praying in churches and temples, on whom you were looking as the mystery of all mysteries, shrouded in the clouds, is the nearest of the near, is your own Self, the reality of your life, body, and soul. That is your own nature. Assert it, manifest it. You are not to become pure; you are pure already. You are not to become perfect; you are that already. Nature is like that screen, which is hiding the reality beyond. Every good thought that you think or act upon is simply tearing the veil, as it were, and the purity, the Infinity, the God behind, manifests Itself more and more. This is the whole history of man. Finer and finer becomes the veil, more and more of the light behind shines forth; for it is its nature to shine.

It [the Self] cannot be known; in vain we try to know It. Were It knowable, It would not be what It is, for It is the eternal Subject. Knowledge is a limitation; knowledge is objectifying. He is the eternal Subject of everything, the eternal witness of this universe, your own Self. Knowledge is, as it were, a lower step, a degeneration. We are that eternal Subject already; how can we know It? It is the real nature of every man, and he is struggling to express it in various ways. Otherwise, why are there so many ethical codes? Where is the explanation of all ethics? One idea stands out as the center of all ethical systems, expressed in various forms—namely, doing good to others. The guiding motive of mankind should be charity toward men, charity toward all animals. But these are all various expressions of that eternal truth that "I am the universe; this universe is one." Or else, where is the reason? Why should I do good to my fellowmen? Why should I do good to others? What compels me? It is sympathy, the feeling of sameness everywhere. The hardest hearts feel sympathy for other beings sometimes. Even the man who gets frightened if he is told that this assumed individuality is really a delusion—that it is ignoble to try to cling to this apparent individuality—that very man will tell you that extreme self-abnegation is the center of all morality. And what is perfect self-abnegation? It means the abnegation of this apparent self, the abnegation of all selfishness.

This idea of "me and mine"—*ahamkara* and *mamata*—is the result of past superstition, and the more this present self passes away, the more the Real Self becomes manifest. This is true self-abnegation, the center, the basis, the gist of all moral teaching; and whether man knows it or not, the whole world is slowly going toward it, practicing it more or less. Only the vast majority of mankind are doing it unconsciously. Let them do it consciously. Let them make the sacrifice, knowing that this "me and mine" is not the Real Self, but only a limitation. Only one glimpse of that infinite reality which is behind—only one spark of that infinite fire which is the All—represents the present man. The Infinite is his true nature. (II. 79-83)

THE LIVING FREE

In worshipping God we have been always worshipping our own hidden Self. The worst lie that you can ever tell yourself is that you were born a sinner or a wicked man. He alone is a sinner who sees a sinner in another man. Suppose there is a baby here, and you place a bag of gold on the table. Suppose a robber comes and takes the gold away. To the baby it is all the same; because there is no robber inside, so he sees no robber outside. To sinners and vile men there is vileness outside, but not to good men. So the wicked see this universe as a hell, and the partially good see it as heaven, while the perfect beings realize it as God Himself. Only when a man sees this universe as God does the veil fall from his eyes; then that man, purified and cleansed, finds his whole vision changed. The bad dreams that have been torturing him for millions of years all vanish, and he who was thinking of himself as either a man or a god or a demon, he who was thinking of himself as living in low places, in high places, on earth, in heaven, and so on, finds that he is really omnipresent; that all time is in him, and that he is not in time; that all the heavens are in him, that he is not in any heaven; and that all the gods that man ever worshipped are in him, and that he is not in any one of those gods. He was the manufacturer of gods and demons, of men and plants and animals and stones. And the real nature of man now stands unfolded to him as being higher than heaven, more perfect than this universe of ours, more infinite than infinite time, more omnipresent than the omnipresent ether.

Thus alone does a man become fearless and free. Then all delusions cease, all miseries vanish, all fears come to an end forever. Birth goes away and with it death; pains fly, and with them fly away pleasures; earths vanish, and with them vanish heavens; bodies vanish, and with them vanishes the mind also. For that man, disappears the whole universe, as it were. This searching, moving, continuous struggle of forces stops forever, and that which was manifesting itself as force and matter, as the struggles of nature, as nature itself, as heavens and earths and plants and animals and men and angels—all that becomes transfigured into one infinite, unbreakable, unchangeable Existence, and the knowing man finds that he is one with that Existence. "Even as clouds of various colors come before the sky, remain there for a second, and then vanish away," even so, before this soul are all these visions coming—of earths and heavens, of the moon and the gods, of pleasures and pains. But they all pass away, leaving the one infinite, blue, unchangeable Spirit. The sky never changes; it is the clouds that change. It is a mistake to think that the Spirit changes. It is a mistake to think that we are impure, that we are limited, that we are separate. The Real Man is the one Unit Existence.

Two questions now arise. The first is: "Is it possible to realize this? So far, it is doctrine, philosophy. But is it possible to realize it?" It is. There are men still living in this world for whom delusion has vanished forever. The second question is: "Do they immediately die after such realization?" Not so soon as we might think. Two wheels joined by one pole are running together. If I get hold of one of the wheels and, with an axe, cut the pole asunder, the wheel I have got hold of stops. But upon the other wheel is its past momentum, so it runs on a little and then falls down. This pure and perfect being, the soul, is one wheel, and this external hallucination of body and mind is the other wheel, and they are joined together by the pole of work, of *karma*. Knowledge is the axe that will sever the bond between the two, and the wheel of the soul will stop—stop thinking that it is coming and going, living and dying, stop thinking that it is nature and has wants and desires—and will find that it is perfect, desireless. But upon the other wheel, that of the body and mind, will be the momentum of past acts. So it will live for some time, until that momentum of past work is exhausted, until that momentum is worked away, and then the body and mind will fall, and the soul will be free. No more is there any going to heaven and coming back—not even any going to *Brahmaloka* or to any of the highest of the spheres. For where is he to come from or to go to? The man who has in this life attained to this state, for whom, for a minute at least, the ordinary vision of the world has changed and the reality has been apparent—he is called the "living free." This is the goal of the Vedantist, to attain freedom while living.

Once in western India I was traveling in the desert country. For days and days I traveled on foot through the desert, but it was to my surprise that I saw, every day, beautiful lakes, with trees all round them, and the reflections of the trees upside down and vibrating there. "How wonderful it looks—and they call this a desert country!" I said to myself. Nearly a month I traveled, seeing these wonderful lakes and trees and plants. One day I was very thirsty and wanted to have a drink of water, so I started to go to one of these clear, beautiful lakes. But as I approached, it vanished. With a flash it came to my brain, "This is the mirage about which I have read all my life." And with that came also the idea that throughout the whole of that month, every day, I had been seeing the mirage and did not know it. The next morning I began my march. There was again the lake, but with it came also the idea that it was the mirage and not a true lake.

So is it with this universe. We are all traveling in this mirage of the world, day after day, month after month, year after year, not knowing that it is a mirage. One day it will break up, but it will come back again. The body has to remain under the power of past karma, and so the mirage will come back. This world will come back upon us so long as we are bound by karma. Men, women, animals, plants, our attachments and duties—all will come back to us, but not with the same power. Under the influence of the new knowledge the strength of karma will be broken; its poison will be lost. It will become transformed, for along with it there will come the idea that we know it now, that the sharp distinction between the reality and the mirage has been known. This world will not then be the same world as before.

He who reaches the Self—what remains attached to him? A little karma, a little bit of the momentum of his past life; but it is all good momentum. Until the bad momentum is entirely worked out and past impurities are entirely burnt, it is impossible for any man to see and realize truth. So what is left attached to the man who has reached the Self and seen Truth is the remnant of the good impressions of his past life, the good momentum. Even if he lives in the body and works incessantly, he works only to do good. His lips speak only benediction to all. His hands do only good works. His mind can only think good thoughts. His presence is a blessing wherever he goes. He is himself a living blessing. Such a man will, by his very presence, change even the most wicked persons into saints. Even if he does not speak, his very presence will be a blessing to mankind. (II. 279-82, 284)

WHAT MAKES US MISERABLE?

What makes us miserable? The cause of all miseries from which we suffer is desire. You desire something, and the desire is not fulfilled; the result is distress. If there is no desire, there is no suffering. But here, too, there is the danger of my being misunderstood. So it is necessary to explain what I mean by giving up desire and becoming free from all misery. The walls have no desire, and they never suffer. True, but they never evolve. This chair has no desires; it never suffers; but it is always a chair. There is a glory in happiness; there is a glory in suffering. If I may dare to say so, there is a utility in evil too. The great lesson in misery we all know. There are hundreds of things we have done in our lives which we wish we had never done, but which, at the same time, have been great teachers. As for me, I am glad I have done something good and many things bad; glad I have done something right, and glad I have committed many errors, because every one of them has been a great lesson. I, as I am now, am the resultant of all I have done, all I have thought. Every action and thought have had their effect, and these effects are the sum total of my progress.

We all understand that desires are wrong, but what is meant by giving up desires? How could life go on? It would be the same suicidal advice, killing the desire and the man too. The solution is this: not that you should not have property, not that you should not have things which are necessary and things which are even luxuries—have all that you want, and more, only know the truth and realize it. Wealth does not belong to anybody. Have no idea of proprietorship, possession. You are nobody, I am not anybody, nor is anyone else. All belong to the Lord. God is in the wealth that you enjoy. He is in the desire that rises in your mind. He is in the things you buy to satisfy your desire. He is in your beautiful attire, in your beautiful ornaments. This is the line of thought. All will be metamorphosed as soon as you begin to see things in that light. If you put God in your every movement, in your conversation, in your form, in everything, the whole scene will change, and the world, instead of appearing as one of woe and misery, will become a heaven.

"The kingdom of heaven is within you," says Jesus. So says Vedanta and every great teacher. "He that hath eyes to see, let him see, and he that hath ears to hear, let him hear." Vedanta proves that the truth for which we have been searching all this time is present now and was all the time with us. In our ignorance we thought we had lost it, and went about the world crying and weeping, struggling to find the truth, while all along it was dwelling in our own hearts. There alone can we find it.

If we understand the giving up of the world in its old, crude sense, then it would come to this: that we must not work—that we must be idle, sitting like lumps of earth, neither thinking nor doing anything—but must become fatalists, driven about by every circumstance, ordered about by the laws of nature, drifting from place to place. That would be the result. But that is not what is meant. We must work. Ordinary men, driven everywhere by false desires—what do they know of work? The man impelled by his own feelings and his own senses—what does he know about work? He works who is not impelled by his own desires, by any selfishness whatsoever. He works who has no ulterior motive in view. He works who has nothing to gain from work.

If a man plunges headlong into foolish luxuries of the world without knowing the truth, he has missed his footing. He cannot reach the goal. And if a man curses the world, goes into a forest, mortifies his flesh, and kills himself little by little by starvation, makes his heart a barren waste, kills out all feelings, and becomes harsh, stern, and dried up, that man also has missed the way. These are the two extremes, the two mistakes at either end. Both have lost the way. Both have missed the goal.

So work, says Vedanta, putting God in everything and knowing Him to be in everything. Work incessantly, holding life as something deified, as God Himself, and knowing that this is all we have to do, this is all we should ask for. God is in everything. Where else shall we go to find Him? He is already in every work, in every thought, in every feeling. Thus knowing, we must work. This is the only way. There is no other. Thus the effects of work will not bind us. We have seen how false desires are the cause of all the misery and evil we suffer from, but when they are thus deified, purified, through God, they bring no evil, they bring no misery. Those who have not learned this secret will have to live in a demoniacal world until they discover it. Many do not know what an infinite mine of bliss is in them, around them, everywhere. They have not yet discovered it. What is a demoniacal world? Vedanta says it is ignorance. (II. 147-50)

MISERY: ITS CAUSE AND CURE

If we examine our own lives, we find that the greatest cause of sorrow is this: We take up something and put our whole energy on it—perhaps it is a failure, and yet we cannot give it up. We know that it is hurting us, that any further clinging to it will simply bring misery on us; still we cannot tear ourselves away from it. A bee came to sip honey, but its feet stuck to the honeypot and it could not get away. Again and again we find ourselves in that state. That is the whole secret of existence. Why are we here? We came here to sip the honey, and we find our hands and feet sticking to it. We are caught, though we came to catch. We came to enjoy; we are being enjoyed. We came to rule; we are being ruled. We came to work; we are being worked. All the time we find that. And this comes into every detail of our life. We are being worked upon by other minds, and we are always struggling to work on other minds. We want to enjoy the pleasures of life, and they eat into our vitals. We want to get everything from nature, but we find in the long run that nature takes everything from us—depletes us and casts us aside.

Had it not been for this, life would have been all sunshine. Never mind! With all its failures and successes, with all its joys and sorrows, it can be one succession of sunshine if only we are not caught.

That is the one cause of misery: We are attached; we are being caught. Therefore says the Gita: Work constantly; work, but be not attached, be not caught. Reserve to yourself the power of detaching yourself from everything, however beloved, however much the soul might yearn for it, however great the pangs of misery you would feel if you were going to leave it. Still, reserve the power of leaving it whenever you want. The weak have no place here, in this life or in any other life. Weakness leads to slavery. Weakness leads to all kinds of misery, physical and mental. Weakness is death. There are hundreds of thousands of microbes surrounding us, but they cannot harm us unless we become weak, until the body is ready and predisposed to receive them. There may be a million microbes of misery floating about us. Never mind! They dare not approach us; they have no power to get a hold on us until the mind is weakened. This is the great fact: Strength is life; weakness is death. Strength is felicity, life eternal, immortal; weakness is constant strain and misery. Weakness is death.

Attachment is the source of all our pleasures now. We are attached to our friends, to our relatives. We are attached to our intellectual and spiritual works. We are attached to external objects so we get pleasure from them. What, again, brings misery but this very attachment? We have to detach ourselves to earn joy. If only we had the power to detach ourselves at will, there would not be any misery. That man alone will be able to get the best of nature who, having the power of attaching himself to a thing with all his energy, has also the power to detach himself when he should do so. The difficulty is that there must be as much power of attachment as that of detachment. There are men who are never attracted by anything. They can never love. They are hardhearted and apathetic. They escape most of the miseries of life. But a wall never feels misery; a wall never loves, is never hurt. But it is a wall, after all. Surely it is better to be attached and caught than to be a wall. Therefore the man who never loves, who is hard and stony, escaping most of the miseries of life, escapes also its joys. We do not want that. That is weakness; that is death. That soul has not been awakened that never feels weakness, never feels misery. That is a callous state. We do not want that.

At the same time, we not only want this mighty power of love, this mighty power of attachment, the power of throwing our whole soul upon a single object, losing ourselves and letting ourselves be annihilated, as it were, for other souls—which is the power of the gods—but we want to be higher even than the gods. The perfect man can put his whole soul upon that one point of love, yet he is unattached. How does this come about? There is another secret to learn.

The beggar is never happy. The beggar only gets a dole, with pity and scorn behind it—at least with the thought behind it that the beggar is a low object. He never really enjoys what he gets.

We are all beggars. Whatever we do, we want a return. We are all traders. We are traders in life, we are traders in virtue, we are traders in religion. And alas! we are also traders in love.

If you come to trade, if it is a question of give-and-take, if it is a question of buy-and-sell, abide by the laws of buying and selling. There is a bad time and there is a good time; there is a rise and there is a fall in prices. You always expect the blow to come. It is like looking at the mirror. Your face is reflected: you make a grimace—there is one in the mirror; if you laugh, the mirror laughs. This is buying and selling, giving and taking.

We get caught. How? Not by what we give, but by what we expect. We get misery in return for our love—not from the fact that we love, but from the fact that we want love in return.

There is no misery where there is no want. Desire, want, is the father of all misery. Desires are bound by the laws of success and failure. Desires must bring misery.

The great secret of true success, of true happiness, then, is this: The man who asks for no return, the perfectly unselfish man, is the most successful. It seems to be a paradox. Do we not know that every man who is unselfish in life gets cheated, gets hurt? Apparently, yes. Christ was unselfish, and yet he was crucified. True, but we know that his unselfishness is the reason, the cause, of a great victory—the crowning of millions upon millions of lives with the blessing of true success.

Ask nothing; want nothing in return. Give what you have to give. It will come back to you—but do not think of that now. It will come back multiplied a thousandfold, but the attention must not be on that. Yet have the power to give. Give, and let it end there. Learn that the whole of life is giving, that nature will force you to give. So give willingly. Sooner or later you will have to give up. You come into life to accumulate. With clenched hands you want to take. But nature puts a hand on your throat and makes your hands open. Whether you will it or not, you have to give. The moment you say, "I will not," the blow comes; you are hurt. None is there who will not be compelled in the long run to give up everything. And the more one struggles against this law, the more miserable one feels. It is because we dare not give, because we are not resigned enough to accede to this grand demand of nature, that we are miserable. The forest is gone, but we get heat in return. The sun is taking up water from the ocean to return it in showers. You are a machine for taking and giving. You take in order to give. Ask, therefore, nothing in return; but the more you give, the more will come to you. The quicker you can empty the air out of this room, the quicker it will be filled up by the external air. And if you close all the doors and every aperture, that which is within will remain, but that which is outside will never come in, and that which is within will stagnate, degenerate, and become poisoned. A river is continually emptying itself into the ocean and is continually filling up again. Bar not the exit into the ocean. The moment you do that, death seizes you.

Be, therefore, not a beggar; be unattached. This is the most difficult task in life. (II. 2-6)

MAN, THE MAKER OF HIS DESTINY

I have seen some astrologers who predicted wonderful things, but I have no reason to believe they predicted them only from the stars or anything of the sort. In many cases it is simply mind reading. Sometimes wonderful predictions are made, but in many cases it is arrant trash.

It is people who are getting old who talk of fate. Young men generally do not come to astrology. We *may* be under planetary influence, but it should not matter much to us. Buddha said, "Those who make a living by calculation of the stars, by such art and other lying tricks, are to be avoided." And he ought to know, because he was the greatest Hindu ever born. Let stars come. What harm is there? If a star disturbs my life, it would not be worth a cent. You will find that astrology and all these mystical things are generally signs of a weak mind. Therefore, as soon as they become prominent in our minds, we should see a physician, take good food, and rest.

The more I live, the more I become convinced every day that every human being is divine. In no man or woman, however vile, does that divinity die. Only he or she does not know how to reach it and is waiting for the Truth. And wicked people are trying to deceive him or her with all sorts of fooleries. If one man cheats another for money, you say he is a fool and a blackguard. How much greater is the iniquity of one who wants to fool others spiritually! This is too bad. It is the one test, that truth must make you strong and put you above superstition. The duty of the philosopher is to raise you above superstition. Even this world, this body and mind, are superstitions. What infinite souls you are! And to be tricked by twinkling stars! It is a shameful condition. You are divinities. The twinkling stars owe their existence to you.

I was once traveling in the Himalayas, and the long road stretched before us. We poor monks cannot get anyone to carry us, so we had to make all the way on foot. There was an old man with us. The way goes up and down for hundreds of miles, and when that old monk saw what was before him, he said: "Oh, sir, how to cross it. I cannot walk anymore. My chest will break." I said to him, "Look down at your feet." He did so, and I said: "The road that is under your feet is the road that you have passed over and is the same road that you see before you. It will soon be under your feet." The highest things are under your feet, because you are Divine Stars. All these things are under your feet. You can swallow the stars by the handful if you want—such is your real nature. Be strong, get beyond all superstitions, and be free. (VIII. 183, 184, 186-87)

Notes

1 Bhagavad Gita, 3.26.
2 Brihadaranyaka Upanishad, 2.4.5.

V

THE CONCEPT OF MAYA

Swami Vivekananda in London, 1895

WHAT IS MAYA?

Almost all of you have heard of the word *maya*. Generally it is used, though incorrectly, to denote illusion or delusion or some such thing. But the theory of maya forms one of the pillars upon which Vedanta rests. It is therefore necessary that it should be properly understood. I ask a little patience of you, for there is a great danger of its being misunderstood.

The oldest use of [the word] *maya* that we find in Vedic literature is in the sense of delusion. But then, the real theory had not been reached. We find such passages as, "Indra through his maya assumed various forms." Here, it is true, the word *maya* means something like magic, and we find various other passages always taking the same meaning. The word *maya* then dropped out of sight altogether. But in the meantime the idea was developing. Later the question was raised, "Why can't we know the secret of the universe?" And the answer given was very significant: "Because we talk in vain, and because we are satisfied with the things of the senses, and because we are running after desires. Therefore, we cover the

Reality, as it were, with a mist." Here the word *maya* is not used at all, but we get the idea that the cause of our ignorance is a kind of mist that has come between us and the truth. Much later on, in one of the latest Upanishads, we find the word *maya* reappearing, but by this time a transformation had taken place in it, and a mass of new meaning had attached itself to the word. Theories had been propounded and repeated, others had been taken up, until at last the idea of maya became fixed. We read in the Shvetashvatara Upanishad, "Know nature to be maya, and the Ruler of this maya is the Lord Himself."

Coming to later philosophers, we find that this word *maya* has been manipulated in various fashions, until we come to the great Shankaracharya. The theory of maya was manipulated a little by the Buddhists, too, but in the hands of the Buddhists it became very much like what is called idealism, and that is the meaning which is now generally given to the word *maya*. When the Hindu says the world is maya, at once people get the idea that the world is an illusion. This interpretation has some basis, as coming through the Buddhist philosophers, because there was one group of philosophers who did not believe in the external world at all. But the maya of Vedanta, in its last developed form, is neither idealism nor realism, nor is it a theory. It is a simple statement of fact—what we are and what we see around us.

As no man can jump out of his own self, so no man can go beyond the limits that have been put upon him by the laws of time and space. Every attempt to solve the laws of causation, time, and space would be futile, because the very attempt would have to be made by taking for granted the existence of these three.

"This world has no existence." What is meant by that? It means that it has no absolute existence. It exists only in relation to my mind, to your mind, and to the mind of everyone else. We see this world with the five senses, but if we had another sense we would see in it something more. If we had yet another sense it would appear as something still different. It has, therefore, no real existence. It has no unchangeable, immovable, infinite existence. Nor can it be called nonexistence, seeing that it exists and we have to work in and through it. It is a mixture of existence and nonexistence. (II. 88-89, 91)

THIS IS MAYA

Every child is a born optimist. He dreams golden dreams. In youth he becomes still more optimistic. It is hard for a young man to believe that there is such a thing as death, such a thing as defeat or degradation. Old age comes, and life is a mass of ruins. Dreams have vanished into the air, and the man becomes a pessimist. Thus we go from one extreme to another, buffeted by nature, without knowing where we are going.

Then there is the tremendous fact of death. The whole world is going toward death. Everything dies. All our progress, our vanities, our reforms, our luxuries, our wealth, our knowledge, have that one end—death. That is all that is certain. Cities come and go, empires rise and fall, planets break into pieces and crumble into dust, to be blown about by the atmospheres of other planets. Thus it has been going on from time without beginning. Death is the end of everything. Death is the end of life, of beauty, of wealth, of power, of virtue too. Saints die and sinners die, kings die and beggars die. They are all going to death. And yet this tremendous clinging to life exists. Somehow, we do not know why, we cling to life. We cannot give it up. And this is maya.

A mother is nursing a child with great care. All her soul, her life, is in that child. The child grows, becomes a man, and perchance becomes a blackguard and a brute, kicks her and beats her every day, and yet the mother clings to the child. And when her reason awakes, she covers it up with the idea of love. She little thinks that it is not love, but something else, which has got hold of her nerves and which she cannot shake off. However she may try, she cannot shake off the bondage she is in. And this is maya.

We are all after the golden fleece. Every one of us thinks that it will be his. Every reasonable man sees that his chance is, perhaps, one in twenty million, yet everyone struggles for it. And this is maya.

Death is stalking day and night over this earth of ours, but at the same time we think we shall live eternally. A question was once asked of King Yudhishthira, "What is the most wonderful thing on this earth?" And the king replied, "Every day people are dying around us, and yet men think they will never die."[1] And this is maya.

These tremendous contradictions in our intellect, in our knowledge, indeed, in all the facts of our life, face us on all sides. A reformer arises and wants to remedy the evils that are existing in a certain nation, and before they have been remedied a thousand other evils arise in another place. It is like an old house that is falling. You patch it up in one place and the ruin extends to another. In India our reformers cry and preach against the evils of enforced widowhood. In the West nonmarriage is the great evil. Help the unmarried on one side; they are suffering. Help the widows on the other; they are suffering. It is like chronic rheumatism: you drive it from the head and it goes to the body; you drive it from there and it goes to the feet. Reformers arise and preach that learning, wealth, and culture should not be in the hands of a select few, and they do their best to make them accessible to all. These may bring more happiness to some, but perhaps, as culture comes, physical happiness lessens. The knowledge of happiness brings the knowledge of unhappiness. Which way then shall we go? The least amount of material prosperity that we enjoy is causing the same amount of misery elsewhere. This is the law. The young, perhaps, do not see it clearly, but those who have lived long enough and those who have struggled enough will understand it. And this is maya.

These things are going on day and night, and to find a solution to this problem is impossible. Why should it be so? It is impossible to answer this, because the question cannot be logically formulated. There is neither *how* nor *why* in fact. We only know that it *is* and that we cannot help it. Even to grasp it, to draw an exact image of it in our own mind, is beyond our power. How can we solve it, then?

Maya is a statement of the fact of this universe, of how it is going on. People generally get frightened when these things are told to them. But bold we must be. Hiding facts is not the way to find a remedy. As you all know, a hare hunted by dogs puts its head down and thinks itself safe. So when we take refuge in optimism we act just like the hare. But that is no remedy. There are objections to this idea, but you may remark that they are generally from people who possess many of the good things of life. In this country [England] it is very difficult to become a pessimist . Everyone tells me how wonderfully the world is going on, how progressive. But what he himself is, is his own world. Old questions arise: Christianity must be the only true religion of the world because Christian nations are prosperous! But that assertion contradicts itself, because the prosperity of the Christian nation depends on the misfortune of non-Christian nations. There must be some to prey on. Suppose the whole world were to become Christian. Then the Christian nations would become poor, because there would be no non-Christian nations for them to prey upon. Thus the argument kills itself. Animals are living upon plants, men upon animals and, worst of all, upon one another—the strong upon the weak. This is going on everywhere. And this is maya.

What solution do you find for this? We hear every day many explanations and are told that in the long run all will be good. Taking it for granted that this is possible, why should there be this diabolical way of doing good? Why cannot good be done through good instead of through these diabolical methods? The descendants of the human beings of today will be happy. But why must there be all this suffering now? There is no solution. This is maya.

As we increase our power to be happy we also increase our power to suffer, and sometimes I am inclined to think that if we increase our power to become happy in arithmetical progression, we shall increase, on the other hand, our power to become miserable in geometrical progression. We who are progressing know that the more we progress, the more avenues are opened to pain as well as to pleasure. And this is maya.

Thus we find that maya is not a theory for the explanation of the world. It is simply a statement of facts as they exist—that the very basis of our being is contradiction, that everywhere we have to move through this tremendous contradiction, that wherever there is good, there must also be evil, and wherever there is evil, there must be some good. Wherever there is life, death must follow as its shadow. And everyone who smiles will have to weep, and vice versa. Nor can this state of things be remedied. We may vainly imagine that there will be a place where there will be only good and no evil, where we shall only smile and never weep. This is impossible in the very nature of things, for the conditions will remain the same. Wherever there is the power of producing a smile in us, there lurks the power of producing tears. Wherever there is the power of producing happiness, there lurks somewhere the power of making us miserable.

The very same phenomenon that appears to be good now may appear to be bad tomorrow. The same thing that produces misery in one may produce happiness in another. The fire that burns the child may cook a good meal for a starving man. The same nerves that carry the sensations of misery carry also the sensations of happiness. The only way to stop evil, therefore, is to stop good also. There is no other way. To stop death we shall have to stop life also. Life without death and happiness without misery are contradictions, and neither can be found alone, because each of them is but a different manifestation of the same thing.

Let me repeat once more that the Vedantic position is neither pessimism nor optimism. It does not say that this world is all evil or all good. It says that our evil is of no less value than our good, and our good of no more value than our evil. They are bound together. This is the world, and knowing this you work with patience.

This maya is everywhere. It is terrible. Yet we have to work through it. The man who says that he will work when the world has become all good and then he will enjoy bliss is as likely to succeed as the man who sits beside the Ganga and says, "I will ford the river when all the water has run into the ocean." The way is not *with* maya, but *against* it. This is another fact to learn. We are not born as helpers of nature, but as competitors with nature. We are its masters, but we bind ourselves down. Why is this house here? Nature did not build it. Nature says, "Go and live in the forest." Man says, "I will build a house and fight with nature," and he does so. The whole history of humanity is a continuous fight against the so-called laws of nature, and man gains in the end. Coming to the internal world, there too the same fight is going on—this fight between the animal man and the spiritual man, between light and darkness. And here too man becomes victorious. He cuts his way, as it were, out of nature to freedom. (II. 91-95, 97-98, 102, 104)

THE SNARE OF MAYA

Once Narada [a great sage] said to Krishna, "Lord, show me maya." A few days passed, and Krishna asked Narada to make a trip with him toward a desert. After walking several miles Krishna said: "Narada, I am thirsty. Can you fetch some water for me?" "I will go at once, sir, and get you water." So Narada went.

At a little distance there was a village. He entered the village in search of water and knocked at a door, which was opened by a most beautiful young girl. At the sight of her he immediately forgot that his Master was waiting for water, perhaps dying for want of it. He forgot everything and began to talk with the girl. All that day he did not return to his Master. The next day he was again at the house, talking to the girl. The talk ripened into love. He asked the father for the daughter, and they were married and lived there and had children. Thus twelve years passed. His father-in-law died, and he inherited his property. He lived, as he seemed to think, a very happy life with his wife and children, his fields and his cattle, and so forth.

Then came a flood. One night the river rose until it overflowed its banks and flooded the whole village. Houses fell, men and animals were swept away and drowned, and everything was floating in the rush of the stream. Narada had to escape. With one hand he held his wife, and with the other, two of his children. Another child was on his shoulders, and he was trying to ford this tremendous flood. After a few steps he found the current was too strong, and the child on his shoulders fell and was borne away. A cry of despair came from Narada. In trying to save that child, he lost his grasp upon the others, and they also were lost. At last his wife, whom he clasped with all his might, was torn away by the current, and he was thrown on the bank, weeping and wailing in bitter lamentation.

Behind him there came a gentle voice: "My child, where is the water? You went to fetch a pitcher of water, and I am waiting for you. You have been gone for quite half an hour." "Half an hour!" Narada exclaimed. Twelve whole years had passed through his mind, and all these scenes had happened in half an hour! And this is maya. (II. 120-21)

TEARING THE VEIL OF MAYA

I am complete and perfect, and I was never bound—boldly preaches Vedanta. If you think you are bound, bound you will remain. If you know that you are free, free you are. Thus the end and aim of this philosophy is to let us know that we have been free always and shall remain free forever. We never change, we never die, and we are never born. What are all these changes, then? What becomes of this phenomenal world? This world is admitted as an apparent world, bound by time, space, and causation. And this is called the *vivartavada* in Vedanta: illusory superimposition of names and forms upon the Absolute. The Absolute does not change. In the little amoeba, that infinite perfection is latent. It is called amoeba from its amoeba covering. And from the amoeba to the perfect man, the change is not in what is inside—that remains the same, unchangeable—but the change occurs in the covering.

There is a screen here, and some beautiful scenery outside. There is a small hole in the screen through which we can catch only a glimpse of it. Suppose this hole begins to increase. As it grows larger and larger, more and more of the scenery comes into view, and when the screen has vanished we come face to face with the whole of the scenery. This scene outside is the soul, and the screen between us and the scenery is maya—time, space, and causation. There is a little hole somewhere, through which I can catch only a glimpse of the soul. As the hole grows bigger I see more and more, and when the screen has vanished, I know that I am the soul.

So changes in the universe are not in the Absolute. They are in nature. Nature evolves more and more until the Absolute manifests Itself. In everyone It exists. In some It is manifested more than in others. The whole universe is really one. In speaking of the soul, to say that one person is superior to another has no meaning. In speaking of the soul, to say that man is superior to the animal or the plant has no meaning. The whole universe is one. In plants the obstacle to soul-manifestation is very great; in animals, a little less; and in man, still less; in cultured, spiritual men, still less; and in perfect men it has vanished altogether. All our struggles, exercises, pains, pleasures, tears, and smiles, all that we do and think, tend toward that goal—the tearing up of the screen, making the hole bigger, thinning the layers that remain between the manifestation and the reality behind. Our work, therefore, is not to make the soul free, but to get rid of the bondages. The sun is covered by layers of clouds but remains unaffected by them. The work of the wind is to drive the clouds away, and the more the clouds disappear, the more the light of the sun appears. There is no change whatsoever in the Soul—infinite, absolute, eternal Existence, Knowledge, and Bliss. (I. 419-21)

GOD'S PLAY

Blame none. If evil comes, know the Lord is playing with you and be exceedingly glad. After every happiness comes misery; they may be far apart or near. The more advanced the soul, the more quickly does one follow the other. What we want is neither happiness nor misery. Both make us forget our true nature. Both are chains—one iron, one gold. Behind both is the Atman, who knows neither happiness nor misery. These are states, and states must ever change; but the nature of the soul is bliss, peace—unchanging. We have not to get it; we have it. Only wash away the dross and see it.

Stand upon the Self. Then only can we truly love the world. Take a very, very high stand. Knowing our universal nature, we must look with perfect calmness upon all the panorama of the world. It is but baby's play, and we know that, so cannot be disturbed by it. If the mind is pleased with praise it will be displeased with blame. All pleasures of the senses or even of the mind are evanescent, but within ourselves is the one true unrelated pleasure, dependent upon nothing. It is perfectly free. It is bliss. The more our bliss is within, the more spiritual we are. The pleasure of the Self is what the world calls religion.

The internal universe, the real, is infinitely greater than the external, which is only a shadowy projection of the true one. This world is neither true nor untrue; it is the shadow of truth. "Imagination is the gilded shadow of truth," says the poet.

We enter into creation, and then for us it becomes living.

Things are dead in themselves; only we give them life, and then, like fools, we turn around and are afraid of them or enjoy them. But be not like certain fisherwomen who, caught in a storm on their way home from market, took refuge in the house of a florist. They were lodged for the night in a room next to the garden, where the air was full of the fragrance of flowers. In vain did they try to rest, until one of their number suggested that they wet their fish baskets and place them near their heads. Then they all fell into a sound sleep.

The world is our fish basket. We must not depend upon it for enjoyment. Those who do are the *tamasikas*, the bound. Then there are the *rajasikas*, the egotistical, who talk always about "I," "I." They do good work sometimes and may become spiritual. But the highest are the *sattvikas*, the introspective, those who live only in the Self. These three qualities—*tamas*, *rajas*, and *sattva* [idleness, activity, and illumination]—are in everyone, and different ones predominate at different times.

There is no possibility of ever having pleasure without pain, good without evil; for life itself is just lost equilibrium. What we want is freedom—not life, nor pleasure, nor good. Creation is infinite, without beginning and without end—the ever-moving ripple in an infinite lake. There are yet unreached depths in this lake where equilibrium has been regained; but the ripple on the surface is always there. The struggle to regain the balance is eternal.

To regain the balance we must counteract tamas by rajas, then conquer rajas by sattva, the calm, beautiful state that will grow and grow until all else is gone. Give up bondage. Become a son of God, be free, and then you can "see the Father," as did Jesus. Infinite strength is religion and God. Avoid weakness and slavery. You are the Soul only if you are free; there is immortality for you only if you are free; there is God only if He is free.

The world is for me, not I for the world. Good and evil are our slaves, not we theirs. It is the nature of the brute to remain where he is. It is the nature of man to seek good and avoid evil. It is the nature of God to seek neither, but just to be eternally blissful. Let us be God! Make the heart like an ocean; go beyond all the trifles of the world. Be mad with joy even at evil. See the world as a picture and then enjoy its beauty, knowing that nothing affects you. Do you know what good is? It is like glass beads that children find in a mud puddle. Look at the world with calm complacency. See good and evil as the same—both are merely "God's play." Enjoy all. (VII. 11-13)

Note

Mahabharata, Vanaparvan, 313.116.

VI

KARMA YOGA
(The Path of Action)

Swami Vivekananda in London, May 1896

KARMA AND ITS EFFECT ON CHARACTER

The word *karma* is derived from the Sanskrit *kri*, "to do." All action is karma. Technically this word also means the effects of actions. In connection with metaphysics it sometimes means the effects of which our past actions were the causes. But in karma yoga we have simply to do with the word *karma* as meaning work.

The goal of mankind is knowledge. That is the one ideal placed before us by Eastern philosophy. Pleasure is not the goal of man, but knowledge. Pleasure and happiness come to an end. It is a mistake to suppose that pleasure is the goal. The cause of all the miseries we have in the world is that men foolishly think pleasure to be the ideal to strive for. After a time man finds that it is not happiness, but knowledge, toward which he is going, and that both pleasure and pain are great teachers, and that he learns as much from evil as from good. As pleasure and pain pass before his soul, they leave upon it different pictures, and the result of these combined impressions is what is called man's "character." If you take the character of any man, it really is but the aggregate of tendencies, the sum total of the bent of his mind. You will find that misery and happiness are equal factors in the formation of that character. Good and evil have an equal share in molding character, and in some instances misery is a greater teacher than happiness. In studying the great characters the world has produced, I dare say, in the vast majority of cases, it would be found that it was misery that taught more than happiness. It was poverty that taught more than wealth. It was blows that brought out their inner fire more than praise.

Now this knowledge, again, is inherent in man. No knowledge comes from outside; it is all inside. What we say a man *knows* should, in strict psychological language, be what he *discovers* or *unveils*. What a man *learns* is really what he *discovers* by taking the cover off his own soul, which is a mine of infinite knowledge. We say that Newton discovered gravitation. Was it sitting anywhere in a corner waiting for him? It was in his own mind. The time came and he found it out. All the knowledge that the world has ever received comes from the mind. The infinite library of the universe is in your own mind. The external world is simply the suggestion, the occasion, which sets you to study your own mind, but the object of your study is always your own mind. The falling of an apple gave the suggestion to Newton, and he studied his own mind. He rearranged all the previous links of thought in his mind and discovered a new link among them, which we call the law of gravitation. It was not in the apple nor in anything in the center of the earth.

Like fire in a piece of flint, knowledge exists in the mind. Suggestion is the friction that brings it out. So with all our feelings and actions. Our tears and our smiles, our joys and our griefs, our weeping and our laughter, our curses and our blessings, our praises and our blames—every one of these we shall find, if we calmly study our own selves, to have been brought out from within ourselves by so many blows. The result is what we are. All these blows taken together are called *karma*—work, action. Every mental and physical blow that is given to the soul, by which, as it were, fire is struck from it, and by which its own power and knowledge are discovered, is *karma*—this word being used in its widest sense. Thus we are all doing karma all the time. I am talking to you: that is karma. You are listening:

that is karma. We breathe: that is karma. We walk: that is karma. Everything we do, physical or mental, is karma, and it leaves its marks on us. (I. 27-29)

THE MYSTERY OF KARMA

Whatever work we do, the mind is thrown into a wave, and after the work is finished we think the wave is gone. No. It has only become fine [subtle], but it is still there. When we try to remember the work, it comes up again and becomes a wave. So it was there—if not, there would not have been memory. Thus every action, every thought, good or bad, just goes down and becomes fine, and is stored up there. Both happy and unhappy thoughts are called pain-bearing obstructions, because, according to the yogis, in the long run they bring pain. All happiness which comes from the senses will eventually bring pain. All enjoyment will make us thirst for more, and that brings pain as its result. There is no limit to man's desires. He goes on desiring, and when he comes to a point where desire cannot be fulfilled, the result is pain. Therefore, the yogis regard the sum total of impressions, good or evil, as pain-bearing obstructions. They obstruct the way to the freedom of the soul. (I. 243)

THE PHILOSOPHY OF KARMA

Disciple: Sir, what is the necessity for doing good to others?

Swami Vivekananda: Well, it is necessary for one's own good. We become forgetful of the ego when we think of the body as dedicated to the service of others—the body, which most complacently we identify with the ego. And in the long run comes the loss of body-consciousness. The more intently you think of the well-being of others, the more oblivious of yourself you become. In this way, as your heart gradually gets purified by work, you will come to feel the truth that your own Self is pervading all beings and all things. Thus it is that doing good to others constitutes a way, a means, of revealing one's own Self, or Atman. Know this also to be one of the spiritual practices, a discipline for God-realization. Its aim also is Self-realization. Exactly as that aim is attained by jnana (knowledge), bhakti (devotion), and so on, so also by work for the sake of others.

Disciple: But, sir, if I am to keep thinking of others day and night, when shall I contemplate on the Atmân? If I remain wholly occupied with something particular and relative, how can I realize the Atman, which is Absolute?

Swamiji[1]: The highest aim of all disciplines, all spiritual paths, is the attainment of the knowledge of the Atman. If you, by being devoted to the service of others and by getting your heart purified by such work, attain to the vision of all beings as the Self, what else remains to be attained in the way of Self-realization? Would you say that Self-realization is the state of existing as inert matter, such as this wall or this piece of wood?

Disciple: Though that is not the meaning, yet what the scriptures speak of as the withdrawal of the Self into Its real nature consists in the cessation of all mind-functions and all work.

Swamiji: Yes, this samadhi of which the scriptures speak is a state not at all easy to attain. When, very rarely, it appears in somebody, it does not last for long. So what will that person keep himself occupied with? Thus it is that after realizing that state described in the scriptures, the saint sees the Self in all beings and, in that consciousness, devotes himself to service so that any karma that was yet left to be worked out through the body may exhaust itself. It is this state which has been described by the authors of the *shastras* [scriptures] as *jivanmukti*, "free while living."

Disciple: So after all it comes about, sir, that unless this state of jivanmukti is attained, work for the sake of others can never be pursued in the truest sense of the term.

Swamiji: Yes, that is what the shastras say. But they also say that work, or service, for the good of others leads to this state of jivanmukti. Otherwise there would be no need on the part of the shastras to teach us a separate path of religious practice called karma yoga. (VII. 111-13)

WORK AND ITS SECRET

One of the greatest lessons I have learned in my life is to pay as much attention to the means of work as to its end. He was a great man from whom I learned it, and his own life was a practical demonstration of this great principle. I have always been learning great lessons from that one principle. And it appears to me that all the secret of success is there: to pay as much attention to the means as to the end.

Our great defect in life is that we are so much drawn to the ideal; the goal is so much more enchanting, so much more alluring, so much bigger in our mental horizon, that we lose sight of the details altogether. But whenever failure comes, if we analyze it critically, in ninety-nine percent of cases we shall find that it was because we did not pay attention to the means. Proper attention to the finishing, strengthening, of the means is what we need. With the means all right, the end must come. We forget that it is the cause that produces the effect. The effect cannot come by itself. And unless the causes are exact, proper, and powerful, the effect will not be produced. (II. 1)

THE TEACHINGS OF KARMA YOGA

Karma yoga teaches: "Do not give up the world. Live in the world, imbibe its influences as much as you can, but if it be for your own enjoyment's sake, work not at all." Enjoyment should not be the goal. First kill your self and then take the whole world as yourself. As the old Christians used to say, "The old man must die." This "old man" is the selfish idea that the whole world is made for our enjoyment. Foolish parents teach their children to pray, "O Lord, Thou hast created this sun for me and this moon for me"—as if the Lord has had nothing else to do but create everything for these babies. Do not teach your children such nonsense. Then again, there are people who are foolish in another way. They teach us that all these animals were created for us to kill and eat, and that this universe is for the enjoyment of men. That is all foolishness. A tiger may say, "Man was created for me," and pray: "O Lord, how wicked are these men who do not come and place themselves before me to be eaten! They are breaking Your law." If the world is created for us, we are also created for the world. That this world is created for our enjoyment is the most wicked idea that holds us down. This world is not for our sake. Millions pass out of it every year; the world does not feel it. Millions of others are supplied in their place. Just as much as the world is created for us, so also we are created for the world.

To work properly, therefore, you have first to give up the idea of attachment. Secondly, do not mix in the fray. Hold yourself as a witness and go on working. My Master used to say, "Look upon your children as a nurse does." The nurse will take your baby and fondle it and play with it and behave toward it as gently as if it were her own child. But as soon as you give her notice to quit, she is ready to start off, bag and baggage, from the house. Everything in the shape of attachment is forgotten. It will not give the ordinary nurse the least pang to leave your children and take up other children. Even so are you to be with all that you consider your own. You are like the nurse. If you believe in God, believe that all these things which you consider yours are really His. (I. 88-89)

KARMA YOGA ACCORDING TO THE GITA

What is the meaning of the idea "to work without motive"? Nowadays many understand it in the sense that one is to work in such a way that neither pleasure nor pain can affect one's mind. If this is its real meaning, then the animals might be said to work without motive. Some animals devour their own offspring, and they do not feel any pangs at all in doing so. Robbers ruin other people by robbing them of their possessions, but if they feel quite callous to pleasure or pain, then they also would be working without motive. If the meaning of it is such, then one who has a stony heart, the worst of criminals, might be considered to be working without motive. The walls have no feelings of pleasure or pain; neither has a stone; and it cannot be said that they are working without motive. In the above sense, the doctrine is a potent instrument in the hands of the wicked. They would go on doing wicked deeds and would claim that they are working without motive. If such be the significance of working without motive, then a fearful doctrine has been put forth by the teachings of the Gita. Certainly this is not the meaning.

The Gita teaches karma yoga. We should work through yoga

[concentration]. In such concentration in action [karma yoga] there is no consciousness of the lower ego present. The consciousness that I am doing this and that is never present when one works through *yoga*. The Western people do not understand this. They say that if there is no consciousness of the ego, if this ego is gone, how then can a man work? But when one works with concentration, losing all consciousness of oneself, the work that is done will be infinitely better, and this everyone may have experienced in his own life. We perform many works subconsciously, such as digestion of food, many others consciously, and others, again, by becoming immersed in samadhi, as it were, when there is no consciousness of the lower ego. If a painter, losing the consciousness of his ego, becomes completely immersed in his painting, he will be able to produce masterpieces. A good cook concentrates his whole self on the food he handles. Then he loses consciousness of everything else for the time being. But these people are only able to do a single work perfectly in this way, [work] to which they are habituated. The Gita teaches that all work should be done thus. He who is one with the Lord through yoga performs all his work by becoming immersed in concentration, and does not seek any personal benefit. Such performance of work brings only good to the world—no evil can come out of it. Those who work thus never do anything for themselves.

The result of every work is mixed with good and evil. There is no good work that has not a touch of evil in it. Like smoke surrounding fire, some evil always clings to work. We should engage in such work as brings the largest amount of good and the smallest measure of evil. Arjuna killed Bhishma and Drona. If this had not been done, Duryodhana could not have been conquered, the force of evil would have triumphed over the force of good, and thus a great calamity would have fallen on the country.

We are reading the Gita by candlelight, but numerous insects are being burned to death. Thus it is seen that some evil always clings to work. Those who work without any consciousness of their lower ego are not affected by evil, for they work for the good of the world. To work without motive, to work unattached, brings the highest bliss and freedom. This secret of karma yoga is taught by the Lord Sri Krishna in the Gita. (V. 247-49)

WORK FOR WORK'S SAKE

Man works with various motives. There cannot be work without motive. Some people want to get fame and they work for fame. Others want money and they work for money. Others want to have power and they work for power. Others want to get to heaven and they work for that. Others want to leave a name when they die, as they do in China, where no man gets a title until he is dead; and that is a better way, after all, than with us. When a man does something very good there, they give a title of nobility to his dead father or grandfather. Some people work for that. Some of the followers of certain Mohammedan sects work all their lives to have a big tomb built for them when they die. Other [people] work as a penance. They do all sorts of wicked things, then erect a temple or give something to the priests to buy them off and obtain from them a passport to heaven. They think this kind of beneficence will clear them and they will go scot-free in spite of their sinfulness. Such are some of the various motives for work.

Work for work's sake. There are some in every country who are really the salt of the earth, who work for work's sake, who do not care for name or fame or even to go to heaven. They work just because good will come of it. There are others who do good to the poor and help mankind from still higher motives, because they believe in doing good and they love good. As a rule, the desire for name and fame seldom brings immediate results; they come to us when we are old and have almost done with life. If a man works without any selfish motive in view, does he not gain anything? Yes, he gains the highest. Unselfishness is more paying, only people have not the patience to practice it. It is more paying from the point of view of health also. Love, truth, and unselfishness are not merely moral figures of speech. They form our highest ideal, because in them lies such a manifestation of power.

All outgoing energy following from a selfish motive is frittered away. It will not cause power to return to you. But if selfishness is restrained, it will result in development of power. This self-control will tend to produce a mighty will, a character which makes a Christ or a Buddha. Foolish men do not know this secret. (I. 31-33)

BE UNATTACHED

Be unattached. Let things work; let brain centers work; work incessantly, but let not a ripple conquer the mind. Work as if you were a stranger in this land, a sojourner. Work incessantly, but do not bind yourselves. Bondage is terrible. This world is not our habitation. It is only one of the many stages through which we are passing. Remember that great saying of the Sankhya philosophy, "The whole of nature is for the soul, not the soul for nature." The very reason for nature's existence is the education of the soul. It has no other meaning. It is there because the soul must have knowledge, and through knowledge free itself. If we remember this always, we shall never be attached to nature. We shall know that nature is a book we are to read, and that when we have gained the required knowledge, the book is of no more value to us.

Work like a master and not as a slave. Work incessantly, but do not do slave's work. Do you not see how everybody works? Nobody can be altogether at rest. Ninety-nine percent of mankind work like slaves, and the result is misery. It is all selfish work. Work through freedom! Work through love! The word *love* is very difficult to understand. Love never comes until there is freedom. There is no true love possible in the slave. If you buy a slave and tie him down in chains and make him work for you, he will work like a drudge, but there will be no love in him. So when we ourselves work for the things of the world as slaves, there can be no love in us, and our work is not true work. This is true of work done for relatives and friends, and it is true of work done for our own selves. Selfish work is slave's work. And here is a test: Every act of love brings happiness. There is no act of love which does not bring peace and blessedness as its reaction. Therefore true love can never react so as to cause pain either to the lover or to the beloved. Suppose a man loves a woman. He wishes to have her all to himself and feels extremely jealous about her every movement. He wants her to sit near him, to stand near him, and to eat and move at his bidding. He is a slave to her and wishes to have her as his slave. That is not love. It is a kind of morbid affection of the slave, insinuating itself as love. It cannot be love because it is painful. If she does not do what he wants, it brings him pain. With love there is no painful reaction; love only brings a reaction of bliss. If it does not, it is not love; it is mistaking something else for love. When you have succeeded in loving your husband, your wife, your children, the whole world, the universe, in such a manner that there is no reaction of pain or jealousy, no selfish feeling, then you are in a fit state to be unattached.

Krishna says: "Look at Me, Arjuna! If I stop working for one moment the whole universe will die. I have nothing to gain from work. I am the one Lord. But why do I work? Because I love the world."[2] God is unattached because He loves. That real love makes us unattached. Wherever there is attachment, the clinging to the things of the world, you must know that it is all physical attraction between sets of particles of matter—something that attracts two bodies nearer and nearer all the time, and, if they cannot get near enough, produces pain. But where there is real love, it does not rest on physical attachment at all. Such lovers may be a thousand miles away from one another, but their love will be all the same. It does not die and will never produce any painful reaction. To attain this nonattachment is almost a lifework, but as soon as we have reached this point, we have attained the goal of love and become free.

Do you ask anything from your children in return for what you have given them? It is your duty to work for them, and there the matter ends. In whatever you do for a particular person, city, or state, assume the same attitude toward it as you have toward your children—expect nothing in return. If you can invariably take the position of a giver, in which everything given by you is a free offering to the world, without any thought of return, then your work will bring you no attachment. Attachment comes only where we expect a return. (I. 56-59)

EACH IS GREAT IN HIS OWN PLACE

A certain king used to inquire of all the sannyasins that came to his country, "Which is the greater man—he who gives up the world and becomes a sannyasin, or he who lives in the world and performs his duties as a householder?" Many wise men sought to solve the problem. Some asserted that the sannyasin was the greater, upon which the king demanded that they should prove their assertion. When they could not, he ordered them to marry and become householders. Then others came and said, "The householder who performs his duties is the greater man." Of them, too, the king demanded proofs. When they could not give them, he made them also settle down as householders.

At last there came a young sannyasin, and the king similarly inquired of him also. He answered, "Each, O King, is equally great in his own place." "Prove this to me," demanded the king. "I will prove it to you," said the sannyasin, "but you must first come and live as I do for a few days, that I may be able to prove to you what I say." The king consented and followed the sannyasin out of his own territory. They passed through many other countries until they came to a great kingdom. In the capital of that kingdom a great ceremony was going on. The king and the sannyasin heard the noise of drums and music, and heard also the criers. The people were assembled in the streets in gala dress, and a great proclamation was being made. The king and the sannyasin stood there to see what was going on. The crier was proclaiming loudly that the princess, daughter of the king of that country, was about to choose a husband from among those assembled before her.

It was an old custom in India for princesses to choose husbands in this way. Each princess had certain ideas of the sort of man she wanted for a husband. Some would have the handsomest man, others would have only the most learned, others again the richest, and so on. All the princes of the neighborhood would put on their best attire and present themselves before her. Sometimes they too had their own criers to enumerate their virtues and the reasons why they hoped the princess would choose them. The princess would be taken round on a throne, in the most splendid array, and would look at them and hear about them. If she was not pleased with what she saw and heard, she would say to her bearers, "Move on," and would take no more notice of the rejected suitor. If, however, the princess was pleased with any one of them, she would throw a garland of flowers over him and he would become her husband.

The princess of the country to which our king and the sannyasin had come was having one of these interesting ceremonies. She was the most beautiful princess in the world, and her husband would be ruler of the kingdom after her father's death. The idea of this princess was to marry the handsomest man, but she could not find the right one to please her. Several times these meetings had taken place, but the princess could not select a husband. This meeting was the most splendid of all. More people than ever before had attended it. The princess came in on a throne, and the bearers carried her from place to place. She did not seem to care for anyone, and everyone became disappointed that this meeting also was going to be a failure.

Just then a young man, a sannyasin, handsome as if the sun had come down to the earth, came and stood in one corner of the assembly, watching what was going on. The throne with the princess came near him, and as soon as she saw the beautiful sannyasin, she stopped and threw the garland over him. The young sannyasin seized the garland and threw it off, exclaiming: "What nonsense is this? I am a sannyasin. What is marriage to me?" The king of that country thought that perhaps this man was poor and so dared not marry the princess, and said to him, "With my daughter goes half my kingdom now, and the whole kingdom after my death!" and put the garland on the sannyasin again. The young man threw it off once more, saying, "Nonsense! I do not want to marry," and walked quickly away from the assembly.

Now the princess had fallen so much in love with this young man that she said, "I must marry this man or I shall die," and she went after him to bring him back. Then our other sannyasin, who had brought the king there, said to him, "King, let us follow this pair." So they walked after them, but at a good distance behind. The young sannyasin who had refused to marry the princess walked out into the country for several miles. When he came to a forest and entered into it, the princess followed him, and the other two followed them. Now this young sannyasin was well acquainted with that forest and knew all the intricate paths in it. He suddenly passed into one of these and disappeared, and the princess could not discover him. After trying for a long time to find him she sat down under a tree and began to weep, for she did not know the way out. Then our king and the other sannyasin came up to her and said: "Do not weep. We will show you the way out of this forest, but it is too dark for us to find it now. Here is a big tree. Let us rest under it, and in the morning we will go early and show you the road."

Now a little bird and his wife and their three young ones lived on that tree in a nest. This little bird looked down and saw the three people under the tree and said to his wife: "My dear, what shall we do? Here are some guests in the house, and it is winter, and we have no fire." So he flew away and got a bit of burning firewood in his beak and dropped it before the guests, to which they added fuel and made a blazing fire. But the little bird was not satisfied. He said again to his wife: "My dear, what shall we do? There is nothing to give these people to eat, and they are hungry. We are householders; it is our duty to feed anyone who comes to the house. I must do what I can. I will give them my body." So he plunged into the midst of the fire and perished. The guests saw him falling and tried to save him, but he was too quick for them.

The little bird's wife saw what her husband did, and she said: "Here are three persons and only one little bird for them to eat. It is not enough. It is my duty as a wife not to let my husband's effort go in vain. Let them have my body also." Then she fell into the fire and was burned to death.

Then the three baby birds, when they saw what was done and that there was still not enough food for the three guests, said: "Our parents have done what they could and still it is not enough. It is our duty to carry on the work of our parents. Let our bodies go too." And they all dashed down into the fire also.

Amazed at what they saw, the three people could not of course eat these birds. They passed the night without food, and in the morning the king and the sannyasin showed the princess the way, and she went back to her father.

Then the sannyasin said to the king: "King, you have seen that each is great in his own place. If you want to live in the world, live like those birds, ready at any moment to sacrifice yourself for others. If you want to renounce the world, be like that young man to whom the most beautiful woman and a kingdom were as nothing. If you want to be a householder, hold your life a sacrifice for the welfare of others, and if you choose the life of renunciation, do not even look at beauty and money and power. Each is great in his own place, but the duty of the one is not the duty of the other." (I. 47-51)

THE QUALIFICATIONS OF A KARMA YOGI

Three things are necessary for great achievements. First, *feel from the heart*. What is in the intellect, or reason? It goes a few steps and there it stops. But through the heart comes inspiration. Love opens the most impossible gates. Love is the gate to all the secrets of the universe. Feel, therefore, my would-be reformers, my would-be patriots! Do you feel? Do you feel that millions and millions of the descendants of gods and of sages have become next-door neighbors to brutes? Do you feel that millions are starving today, and millions have been starving for ages? Do you feel that ignorance has come over the land as a dark cloud? Does it make you restless? Does it make you sleepless? Has it gone into your blood, coursing through your veins, becoming consonant with your heart-beats? Has it made you almost mad? Are you seized with that one idea of the misery of ruin, and have you forgotten all about your name, your fame, your wives, your children, your property, even your own bodies? Have you done that? That is the first step to become a patriot, the very first step.

You may feel, then, but instead of spending your energies in frothy talk, have you found any way out, any *practical solution*—some help instead of condemnation, some sweet words to soothe their miseries, to bring them out of this living death?

Yet that is not all. Have you got the *will to surmount mountain-high obstructions*? If the whole world stands against you, sword in hand, would you still dare to do what you think is right? If your wives and children are against you, if all your money goes, your name dies, your wealth vanishes, would you still stick to it? Would you still pursue it and go on steadily toward your own goal? As the great king Bhartrihari says: "Let the sages blame or let them praise; let the goddess of fortune come or let her go wherever she likes; let death come today or let it come in hundreds of years; he indeed is the steady man who does not move one inch from the way of truth."[3] Have you got that steadfastness? If you have these three things, each one of you will work miracles. You need not write in the newspapers; you need not go about lecturing; your very face will shine. If you live in a cave your thoughts will permeate even through the rock walls, will go vibrating all over the world for hundreds of years, maybe, until they will fasten on to some brain and work out there. Such is the power of thought, of sincerity, and of purity of purpose. (III. 225-27)

A STORY OF SELF-SACRIFICE

After the battle of Kurukshetra the five Pandava brothers performed a great sacrifice and made very large gifts to the poor. All the people expressed amazement at the greatness and richness of the sacrifice and said that such a sacrifice the world had never seen before. But after the ceremony there came a little mongoose, half of whose body was golden and the other half brown; and he began to roll on the floor of the sacrificial hall. He said to those around: "You are all liars! This was no sacrifice." "What!" they exclaimed. "You say this was no sacrifice! Do you not know how money and jewels were poured out to the poor and everyone became rich and happy? This was the most wonderful sacrifice any man ever performed."

But the mongoose said: "There was once a little village, and in it there dwelt a poor brahmin with his wife, his son, and his son's wife. They were very poor and lived on small gifts made to them for preaching and teaching. There came in that land a three years' famine, and the poor brahmin suffered more than ever. At last, when the family had starved for days, the father brought home one morning a little barley flour, which he had been fortunate enough to obtain, and he divided it into four parts, one for each member of the family. They prepared it for their meal, and just as they were about to eat there was a knock at the door. The father opened it, and there stood a guest." (Now in India a guest is a sacred person. He is like a god for the time being and must be treated as such.) "So the poor brahmin said, 'Come in, sir. You are welcome.' He set before the guest his own portion of the food, which the guest quickly ate and said, 'Oh, sir, you have almost killed me. I have been starving for ten days, and this little bit has but increased my hunger.' Then the wife said to her husband, 'Give him my share.' But the husband said, 'Not so.' The wife, however, insisted, saying, 'Here is a poor man, and it is our duty as householders to see that he is fed, and it is my duty as a wife to give him my portion, seeing that you have no more to offer him.' Then she gave her share to the guest, who, after eating it, said he was still burning with hunger. So the son said: 'Take my portion also. It is the duty of a son to help his father to fulfill his obligations.' The guest ate that but remained still unsatisfied, so the son's wife gave him her portion also. That was sufficient, and the guest departed, blessing them.

"That night those four people died of starvation. A few grains of that flour had fallen on the floor, and when I rolled my body on them, half of it became golden, as you see. Since then I have been traveling all over the world, hoping to find another sacrifice like that. But nowhere have I found one; not even here has the other half of my body been turned into gold. That is why I say this was no sacrifice." (I. 60-61)

WE HELP OURSELVES, NOT THE WORLD

Our duty to others means helping others, doing good to the world. Why should we do good to the world? Apparently to help the world, but really to help ourselves. We should always try to help the world. That should be the highest motive in us. But if we consider well, we find that the world does not require our help at all. This world was not made that you or I should come and help it. I once read a sermon in which it was said, "All this beautiful world is very good, because it gives us time and opportunity to help others." Apparently this is a very beautiful sentiment, but is it not blasphemy to say that the world needs our help? We cannot deny that there is much misery in it. To go out and help others is, therefore, the best thing we can do, although, in the long run, we shall find that helping others is only helping ourselves. As a boy I had some white mice. They were kept in a little box in which there were little wheels, and when the mice tried to cross the wheels, the wheels turned and turned, and the mice never got anywhere. So it is with the world and our helping it. The only help is that we get moral exercise.

This world is neither good nor evil. Each man manufactures a world for himself. If a blind man thinks of the world, it is either as soft or hard, or as cold or hot. We are a mass of happiness or misery; we have seen that hundreds of times in our lives. As a rule, the young are optimistic and the old pessimistic. The young have life before them. The old complain that their day is gone; hundreds of desires, which they cannot fulfill, struggle in their hearts. Both are foolish nevertheless. Life is good or evil according to the state of mind in which we look at it. In itself, it is neither. Fire, in itself, is neither good nor evil. When it keeps us warm we say, "How beautiful fire is!" When it burns our fingers we blame it. Still, in itself, it is neither good nor bad. According as we use it, it produces in us the feeling of good or bad. So also is this world. It is perfect. By perfection is meant that it is perfectly fitted to meet its ends. We may all be perfectly sure that it will go on beautifully without us, and we need not bother our heads wishing to help it.

Yet we must do good. The desire to do good is the highest motive power we have, if we know all the time that it is a privilege to help others. Do not stand on a high pedestal and take five cents in your hand and say, "Here, my poor man!" But be grateful that the poor man is there, so that by making a gift to him you are able to help yourself. It is not the receiver that is blessed, but it is the giver. Be thankful that you are allowed to exercise your power of benevolence and mercy in the world, and thus become pure and perfect. All good acts tend to make us pure and perfect. (I. 75-76)

THE WORLD: A DOG'S CURLY TAIL

There was a poor man who wanted some money. Somehow he had heard that if he could get hold of a ghost, he might command him to bring money or anything else he liked; so he was very anxious to get hold of a ghost. He went about searching for a man who would give him a ghost, and at last he found a sage with great powers, and besought his help. The sage asked him what he would do with a ghost. "I want a ghost to work for me. Teach me how to get hold of one, sir. I desire it very much," replied the man. But the sage said: "Don't disturb yourself. Go home." The next day the man went again to the sage and began to weep and pray: "Give me a ghost. I must have a ghost, sir, to help me." At last the sage was disgusted and said: "Take this charm, repeat this magic word, and a ghost will come. And whatever you say to him he will do. But beware! They are terrible beings and must be kept continually busy. If you fail to give him work, he will take your life." The man replied: "That is easy. I can give him work for his whole life."

Then he went to a forest and after long repetition of the magic word, a huge ghost appeared before him and said: "I am a ghost. I have been conquered by your magic; but you must keep me constantly employed. The moment you fail to give me work I will kill you." The man said, "Build me a palace," and the ghost said: "It is done. The palace is built." "Bring me money," said the man. "Here is your money," said the ghost. "Cut this forest down and build a city in its place." "That is done," said the ghost. "Anything more?" Now the man began to be frightened and thought he could give him nothing more to do. He did everything in a trice. The ghost said, "Give me something to do or I will eat you up." The poor man could find no further occupation for him and was frightened. So he ran and ran and at last reached the sage and said, "Oh, sir, save my life!" The sage asked him what the matter was, and the man replied: "I have nothing to give the ghost to do. Everything I tell him to do he does in a moment, and he threatens to eat me up if I do not give him work." Just then the ghost arrived, saying, "I'll eat you up," and he was about to swallow the man. The man began to shake, and begged the sage to save his life. The sage said: "I will find you a way out. Look at that dog with a curly tail. Draw your sword quickly and cut the tail off and give it to the ghost to straighten out." The man cut off the dog's tail and gave it to the ghost, saying, "Straighten that out for me." The ghost took it and slowly and carefully straightened it out, but as soon as he let it go, it instantly curled up again. Once more he laboriously straightened it out, only to find it again curled up as soon as he attempted to let go of it. Again he patiently straightened it out, but as soon as he let it go it curled up again. So he went on for days and days, until he was exhausted and said: "I was never in such trouble before in my life. I am an old, veteran ghost, but never before was I in such trouble. I will make a compromise with you. You let me off and I will let you keep all I have given you and will promise not to harm you." The man was much pleased and accepted the offer gladly.

This world is like a dog's curly tail, and people have been striving to straighten it out for hundreds of years. But when they let it go, it curls up again. How could it be otherwise? One must first know how to work without attachment; then one will not be a fanatic. When we know that this world is like a dog's curly tail and will never get straightened, we shall not become fanatics. If there were no fanaticism in the world, it would make much more progress than it does now. It is a mistake to think that fanaticism can make for the progress of mankind. On the contrary, it is a retarding element, creating hatred and anger, causing people to fight each other, and making them unsympathetic. We think that whatever we do or possess is the best in the world, and what we do not do or possess is of no value. So always remember the instance of the curly tail of the dog whenever you have a tendency to become a fanatic. You need not worry or make yourself sleepless about the world. It will go on without you. When you have avoided fanaticism, then alone will you work well. It is the level-headed man, the calm man of good judgment and cool nerves, of great sympathy and love, who does good work and so does good to himself. The fanatic is foolish and has no sympathy. He can never straighten out the world, nor can he himself become pure and perfect. (I. 77-79)

AN IDEAL KARMA YOGI

Let me tell you a few words about one man who actually carried this teaching of karma yoga into practice. That man is Buddha. He is the one man who ever carried it into perfect practice. All the prophets of the world, except Buddha, had external motives to move them to unselfish action. The prophets of the world, with this single exception, may be divided into two sets: one set holding that they are Incarnations of God come down on earth, and the other holding that they are only Messengers from God. And both draw their impetus for work from outside and expect reward from outside, however highly spiritual may be the language they use. But

Buddha is the only prophet who said: "I do not care to know your various theories about God. What is the use of discussing all the subtle doctrines about the soul? Do good and be good, and this will take you to freedom and to whatever truth there is."

He was, in the conduct of his life, absolutely without personal motives. And what man worked more than he? Show me in history one character who has soared so high above all. The whole human race has produced but one such character, such high philosophy, such wide sympathy. This great philosopher preached the highest philosophy, yet had the deepest sympathy for the lowest of animals and never put forth any claims for himself. He is the ideal karma yogi, acting entirely without motive, and the history of humanity shows him to have been the greatest man ever born—beyond compare the greatest combination of heart and brain that ever existed, the greatest soul-power that has ever been manifested. He is the greatest reformer the world has seen. He was the first who dared to say: "Believe not because some old manuscripts are produced. Believe not because it is your national belief, because you have been made to believe it from your childhood. But reason it all out, and after you have analyzed it, then, if you find that it will do good to one and all, believe it, live up to it, and help others to live up to it."

He works best who works without any motive—neither for money, nor for fame, nor for anything else. And when a man can do that, he will be a Buddha, and out of him will come the power to work in such a manner as will transform the world. This man represents the very highest ideal of karma yoga. (I. 116-18)

Notes

1 Swami Vivekananda is also called Swamiji.

2 Bhagavad Gita, 3.22, 24

3 Bhartrihari, *Nitishatakam*, 74.

VII

JNANA YOGA
(The Path of Knowledge)

Swami Vivekananda in London, December 1896

THE ETERNAL QUESTION

Great is the tenacity with which man clings to the senses. Yet, however substantial he may think the external world in which he lives and moves, there comes a time in the lives of individuals and of races when involuntarily they ask, "Is this real?" To the person who never finds a moment to question the credentials of his senses, whose every moment is occupied with some sort of sense enjoyment—even to him death comes, and he also is compelled to ask, "Is this real?" Religion begins with this question and ends with its answer. Even in the remote past, where recorded history cannot help us, in the mysterious light of mythology, back in the dim twilight of civilization, we find the same question was asked: "What becomes of this? What is real?"

One of the most poetical of the Upanishads, the Katha Upanishad, begins with the inquiry: "When a man dies, there is a dispute. One party declares that he has gone forever; the other insists that he is still living. Which is true?" Various answers have been given. The whole sphere of metaphysics, philosophy, and religion is really filled with various answers to this question. At the same time, attempts have been made to suppress it, to put a stop to the unrest of the mind, which asks: "What is beyond? What is real?" But as long as death remains, all these attempts at suppression will prove to be unsuccessful. We may talk about seeing nothing beyond and keeping all our hopes and aspirations confined to the present moment, and struggle hard not to think of anything beyond the world of the senses. And perhaps everything outside helps to keep us limited within its narrow bounds. The whole world may combine to prevent us from broadening out beyond the present. Yet, as long as there is death, the question must come again and again: "Is death the end of all these things to which we are clinging, as if they were the most real of all realities, the most substantial of all substances?" The world vanishes in a moment and is gone. Standing on the brink of a precipice beyond which is the infinite, yawning chasm, every mind, however hardened, is bound to recoil and ask, "Is this real?" The hopes of a lifetime, built up little by little with all the energies of a great mind, vanish in a second. Are they real? This question must be answered. Time never lessens its power; on the other hand, it adds strength to it.

Then there is the desire to be happy. We run after everything to make ourselves happy. We pursue our mad careers in the external world of the senses. If you ask the young man for whom life is successful, he will declare that it is real; and he really thinks so. Perhaps, when the same man grows old and finds fortune ever eluding him, he will then declare that it is fate. He finds at last that his desires cannot be fulfilled. Wherever he goes there is an adamantine wall beyond which he cannot pass. Every sense activity results in a reaction. Everything is evanescent. Enjoyment, misery, luxury, wealth, power, and poverty—even life itself—are all evanescent.

Two positions remain to mankind. One is to believe with the nihilists that all is nothing, that we know nothing, that we can never know anything about either the future, the past, or even the present. For we must remember that he who denies the past and the future and wants to stick to the present is simply a madman. One may as well deny the father and mother and assert the child. It would be equally logical. To deny the past and future, the present must inevitably be denied also. This is one position, that of the nihilists. I have never seen a man who could really become a nihilist for one minute. It is very easy to talk.

Then there is the other position—to seek for an explanation, to seek for the real, to discover in the midst of this eternally changing and evanescent world whatever is real. In this body, which is an aggregate of molecules of matter, is there anything that is real? This has been the search throughout the history of the human mind. In the very oldest times we often find glimpses of light coming into men's minds. We find men, even then, going a step beyond this body, finding something that is not this external body, although very much like it, something much more complete, much more perfect, something that remains even when this body is dissolved. We read in a hymn of the *Rig Veda* addressed to the god of fire, who is burning a dead body: "Carry him, O Fire, in your arms gently. Give him a perfect body, a bright body. Carry him where the fathers live, where there is no more sorrow, where there is no more death."

The same idea you will find present in every religion. And we get another idea with it. It is a significant fact that all religions, without one exception, hold that man is a degeneration of what he was, whether they clothe this in mythological words, or in the clear language of philosophy, or in the beautiful expressions of poetry. This is the one fact that comes out of every scripture and of every mythology: that the man that is, is a degeneration of what he was. This is the kernel of truth within the story of Adam's fall in the Jewish scripture. (II. 70-72)

WHAT IS THE ATMAN?

There is a great discussion going on as to whether the aggregate of materials we call the body is the cause of the manifestation of the force we call the soul, thought, etc., or whether it is thought that manifests this body. The religions of the world, of course, hold that the force called *thought* manifests the body, and not the reverse. There are schools of modern thought which hold that what we call thought is simply the outcome of the adjustment of the parts of the machine that we call the body. The second position—that the soul, or the mass of thought, or whatever you may call it, is the outcome of this machine, the outcome of the chemical and physical combinations of matter making up the body and brain—leaves the question unanswered. What makes the body? What force combines the molecules into the body form? What force is there that takes up material from the mass of matter around and forms my body one way, another body another way, and so on? What makes these infinite distinctions? To say that the force called the soul is the outcome of the combinations of the molecules of the body is putting the cart before the horse. How did the combinations come? Where was the force to make them? If you say that some other force was the cause of these combinations, and the soul was the outcome of that matter, and that soul, which combined a certain mass of matter, was itself the result of the combinations—it is no answer. That theory ought to be accepted which explains most of the facts, if not all, and that without contradicting other existing theories. It is more logical to say that the force that takes up the matter and forms the body is the same [as that] which manifests through that body.

To say, therefore, that the thought-forces manifested by the body are the outcome of the arrangement of molecules and have no independent existence has no meaning. Neither can force evolve out of matter. Rather it is possible to demonstrate that what we call matter does not exist at all. It is only a certain state of force. Solidity, hardness, or any other state of matter can be proved to be the result of motion. Increase of vortex motion imparted to fluids gives them the force of solids. A mass of air in vortex motion, as in a tornado, becomes solid-like and by its impact breaks or cuts through solids. A thread of a spider's web, if it could be moved at almost infinite velocity, would be as strong as an iron chain and would cut through an oak tree. Looking at it in this way, it would be easier to prove that what we call matter does not exist. But the other way cannot be proved.

What is the force that manifests itself through the body? It is obvious to all of us, whatever that force be, that it is taking particles up, as it were, and manipulating forms out of them—human bodies. None else comes here to manipulate bodies for you and me. I never saw anybody eat food for me. I have to assimilate it, manufacture blood and bones and everything out of that food. What is this mysterious force?

We know how in olden times, in all the ancient scriptures, this power, this manifestation of power, was thought to be a bright substance having the form of this body, and which remained even after this body fell. Later on, however, we find a higher idea coming—that this bright body did not represent the force. Whatsoever has form must be the result of combinations of particles and requires something else behind it to move it. If this body requires something which is not the body to manipulate it, the bright body by the same necessity will also require something other than itself to manipulate it. So that something was called the soul—the Atman, in Sanskrit. It was the Atman which through the bright body, as it were, worked on the gross body outside. The bright body is considered as the receptacle of the mind, and the Atman is beyond that. It is not the mind even. It works the mind, and through the mind, the body. You have an Atman. I have another. Each one of us has a separate Atman and a separate fine body, and through that we work on the gross external body. Questions were then asked about this Atman, about its nature. What is this Atman, this soul of man, which is neither the body nor the mind? Great discussions followed. Speculations were made, and various shades of philosophic inquiry came into existence. I shall try to place before you some of the conclusions that have been reached about this Atman.

The different philosophies seem to agree that this Atman, whatever it be, has neither form nor shape, and that which has neither form nor shape must be omnipresent. Time begins with mind; space also is in the mind. Causation cannot stand without time. Without the idea of succession there cannot be any idea of causation. Time, space, and causation, therefore, are in the mind. And as this Atman is beyond the mind and formless, it must be beyond time, beyond space, and beyond causation. Now, if it is beyond time, space, and causation, it must be infinite. Then comes the highest speculation in our philosophy. The infinite cannot be two. If the soul be infinite, there can be only one Soul, and all ideas of various souls—you having one soul, and I having another, and so forth—are not real. The Real Man therefore is one and infinite, the omnipresent Spirit. And the apparent man is only a limitation of that

Real Man. In that sense the mythologies are true in saying that the apparent man, however great he may be, is only a dim reflection of the Real Man, who is beyond. The Real Man, the Spirit, being beyond cause and effect, not bound by time and space, must therefore be free. He was never bound and could not be bound. The apparent man, the reflection, is limited by time, space, and causation, and is therefore bound. Or in the language of some of our philosophers, he appears to be bound but really is not. This is the reality in our souls, this omnipresence, this spiritual nature, this infinity. Every soul is infinite. Therefore there is no question of birth and death. (II. 75-78)

THE JOURNEY TOWARD FREEDOM

True it is that we are all slaves of maya, born in maya, and live in maya. Is there then no way out, no hope? That we are all miserable, that this world is really a prison, that even our so-called trailing beauty is but a prison house, and that even our intellects and minds are prison houses, has been known for ages upon ages. There has never been a man, there has never been a human soul, who has not felt this some time or other, however he may talk. And the old people feel it most, because in them is the accumulated experience of a whole life, because they cannot be easily cheated by the lies of nature. Is there no way out?

We find that, with all this, with this terrible fact before us, in the midst of sorrow and suffering, even in this world where life and death are synonymous, even here, there is a still small voice that is ringing through all ages, through every country, and in every heart: "This, My maya, is divine, made up of qualities, and very difficult to cross. Yet those who come unto Me cross the river of life." "Come unto Me all ye that labor and are heavy laden, and I will give you rest." This is the voice that is leading us forward. Man has heard it, and is hearing it, all through the ages. This voice comes to men when everything seems to be lost and hope has fled, when man's dependence on his own strength has been crushed down, and everything seems to melt away between his fingers, and life is a hopeless ruin. Then he hears it. This is called religion.

On the one side, therefore, is the bold assertion that this is all nonsense, that this is maya. But, along with it, there is the most hopeful assertion that beyond maya there is a way out. On the other hand, practical men tell us: "Don't bother your heads about such nonsense as religion and metaphysics. Live here. This is a very bad world indeed, but make the best of it." Which, put in plain language, means: Live a hypocritical, lying life, a life of continuous fraud, covering all sores in the best way you can. Go on applying patch after patch, until everything is lost and you are a mass of patchwork. This is what is called practical life. Those who are satisfied with this patchwork will never come to religion.

Religion begins with a tremendous dissatisfaction with the present state of things, with our lives, and a hatred—an intense hatred—for this patching up of life, an unbounded disgust for fraud and lies. He alone can be religious who dares say, as the mighty Buddha once said under the Bo-tree: "Death is better than a vegetating, ignorant life. It is better to die on the battlefield than to live a life of defeat." This is the basis of religion. When a man takes this stand he is on the way to find the truth. He is on the way to God. That determination must be the first impulse toward becoming religious. I will hew out a way for myself. I will know the truth or give up my life in the attempt. For on this side it is nothing, it is gone, it is vanishing every day. The beautiful, hopeful young person of today is the veteran of tomorrow. Hopes and joys and pleasures will die like blossoms with tomorrow's frost. That is one side. On the other, there are the great charms of conquest, victories over all the ills of life, victory over life itself, the conquest of the universe. On that side men can stand. Those who dare, therefore, to struggle for victory, for truth, for religion, are on the right path, and that is what the Vedas preach: "Be not in despair. The way is very difficult, like walking on the edge of a razor. Yet despair not. Arise, awake, and find the ideal, the goal."

One curious fact, present in the midst of all our joys and sorrows, difficulties and struggles, is that we are surely journeying toward freedom. The question was practically this: "What is this universe? From what does it arise? Into what does it go?" And the answer was: "In freedom it rises, in freedom it rests, and into freedom it melts away." This idea of freedom you cannot relinquish. Your actions, your very lives, will be lost without it. Every moment nature is proving us to be slaves and not free. Yet simultaneously rises the other idea, that still we are free. At every step we are knocked down, as it were, by maya, and shown that we are bound. And yet at the same moment, together with this blow, together with this feeling that we are bound, comes the other feeling that we are free. Some inner voice tells us that we are free. But if we attempt to realize that freedom, to make it manifest, we find the difficulties almost insuperable. Yet, in spite of that, it insists on asserting itself inwardly: "I am free, I am free." And if you study all the various religions of the world you will find this idea expressed.

Not only religion—you must not take this word in its narrow sense—but the whole life of society is the assertion of that one principle of freedom. All movements are the assertion of that one freedom. That voice has been heard by everyone, whether he knows it or not, that voice which declares, "Come unto Me all ye that labor and are heavy laden." It may not be in the same language or the same form of speech, but, in some form or other, that voice calling for freedom has been with us. Yes, we are born here on account of that voice. Every one of our movements is for that. We are all rushing toward freedom. We are all following that voice, whether we know it or not. As the children of the village were attracted by the music of the flute player, so we are all following the music of the voice without knowing it.

What happens then? The scene begins to shift. As soon as you know the voice and understand what it is, the whole scene changes. The same world that was the ghastly battlefield of maya is now changed into something good and beautiful. We no longer curse nature or say that the world is horrible and that it is all vain. We need no longer weep and wail. As soon as we understand the voice, we see the reason why this struggle should be here—this fight, this competition, this difficulty, this cruelty, these little pleasures and joys. We see that they are in the nature of things, because without them there would be no going toward the voice, which we are destined to attain, whether we know it or not.

All human life, all nature, therefore, is struggling to attain freedom. The sun is moving toward the goal; so is the earth in circling round the sun; so is the moon in circling round the earth. To that goal, the planet is moving and the air is blowing. Everything is struggling toward that. The saint is going toward that voice—he cannot help it. It is no glory to him. So is the sinner. The charitable man is going straight toward that voice and cannot be hindered. The miser is also going toward the same destination. The greatest worker of good hears the same voice within, and he cannot resist it. He must go toward the voice. So is the most arrant idler. One stumbles more than another, and he who stumbles more, we call bad; he who stumbles less, we call good. Good and bad are never two different things; they are one and the same. The difference is not one of kind, but of degree. (II. 122-27)

REGAIN YOUR OWN EMPIRE

When a man does anything evil, his soul begins to contract and his power is diminished and goes on decreasing until he does good works, when it expands again. One idea seems to be common to all the Indian systems, and I think to all the systems in the world, whether they know it or not, and that is what I should call the divinity of man. There is not one system in the world, not one real religion, that does not hold the idea that the human soul—whatever it be, or whatever its relation to God—is essentially pure and perfect, whether [this idea is] expressed in the language of mythology, allegory, or philosophy. Its real nature is blessedness and power, not weakness and misery. Somehow or other this misery has come. The one great idea that to me seems clear and comes out through masses of superstition in every country and in every religion is that man is divine, that divinity is our nature.

Whatever else comes is a mere superimposition, as Vedanta calls it. Something has been superimposed, but that divine nature never dies. In the most degraded, as well as in the most saintly, it is ever present. It has to be called out, and it will work itself out. We have to ask, and it will manifest itself. The people of old knew that fire existed in flint and in dry wood, but friction was necessary to call it out. So this fire of freedom and purity is the nature of every soul, and not a quality, because qualities can be acquired and therefore can be lost. The soul is one with Freedom, and the soul is one with Existence, and the soul is one with Knowledge. Sat-Chit-Ananda—Existence-Knowledge-Bliss Absolute—is the nature, the birthright, of the soul, and all the manifestations that we see are Its expressions, dimly or brightly manifesting Itself. The Vedantist boldly says that the enjoyments in this life, even the most degraded joys, are but manifestations of the One Divine Bliss, the Essence of the soul.

This idea seems to be the most prominent in Vedanta, and, as I have said, it appears to me that every religion holds it. I have yet to know the religion that does not. It is the one universal idea working through all religions. Take the Bible, for instance. You find there the allegorical statement that the first man, Adam, was pure, and that his purity was obliterated by his evil deeds afterward. It is clear from this allegory that the Hebrews thought that the original nature of man was perfect. The impurities that we see, the weaknesses that we feel, are but superimpositions on that nature. And the subsequent history of the Christian religion shows that they also believe in the possibility, nay, the certainty, of regaining that old state. This is the whole history of the Bible, Old and New Testaments together.

So it is with the Mohammedans. They also believe in Adam and the purity of Adam, and through Mohammed, the way was opened to regain that lost state. So with the Buddhists. They believe in the state called *nirvana*, which is beyond this relative world. It is exactly the same as the Brahman of the Vedantists. And the whole system of the Buddhists is founded upon the idea of regaining that lost state of nirvana.

In every system we find this doctrine present—that you cannot get anything which is not yours already. You are indebted to nobody in this universe. You claim your own birthright, as it has been most poetically expressed by a great Vedanta philosopher in the title of one of his books, *Swarajya-siddhi* (The attainment of our own empire). That empire is ours; we have lost it and we have to regain it. The *mayavadin*, however, says that this losing of the empire is a hallucination—you never lost it. This is the only difference.

Although all the systems agree so far that we had the empire and that we have lost it, they give us varied advice as to how to regain it. One says that you must perform certain ceremonies, pay certain sums of money to certain idols, eat certain sorts of food, live in a peculiar fashion, to regain that empire. Another says that if you weep and prostrate yourselves and ask pardon of some Being beyond nature, you will regain that empire. Again, another says if you love such a Being with all your heart, you will regain that empire. All this varied advice is in the Upanishads. As I go on, you will find it so.

But the last and the greatest counsel is that you need not weep at all. You need not go through all these ceremonies and need not take any notice of how to regain your empire, because you never lost it. Why should you go about seeking for what you never lost? You are pure already. You are free already. If you think you are free, free you are this moment, and if you think you are bound, bound you will be. This is a very bold statement, and as I told you at the beginning of this course, I shall have to speak to you very boldly. It may frighten you now, but when you think over it and realize it in your own life, then you will come to know that what I say is true. For if that freedom is not your nature, by no manner of means can you become free. Or, supposing you were free and in some way you lost that freedom—that shows that you were not free to begin with. Had you been free, what could have made you lose it? The independent can never be made dependent. If it is really dependent, its independence was a hallucination. (II. 192-96)

STEPS TO REALIZATION

First among the qualifications required of the aspirant for jnana, or wisdom, come *shama* and *dama*, which may be taken together. They mean the keeping of the organs in their own centers without allowing them to stray out. I shall explain to you first what the word *organ* means. Here are the eyes. The eyes are not the organs of vision, but only the instruments. Unless the organs also are present, I cannot see, even if I have eyes. But given both the organs and the instruments, unless the mind attaches itself to these two, no vision takes place. So in each act of perception, three things are necessary: first the external instruments, then the internal organs, and lastly the mind. If any one of them be absent, then there will be no perception. Thus the mind acts through two agencies—one external and the other internal. When I see things, my mind goes out, becomes externalized. But suppose I close my eyes and begin to think. The mind does not go out; it is internally active. But in either case there is activity of the organs. So in order to control the mind, we must first be able to control these organs. To restrain the mind from wandering outward or inward, and [to] keep the organs in their respective centers, is what is meant by the words *shama* and *dama*. Shama consists in not allowing the mind to externalize, and dama, in checking the external instruments.

Now comes *uparati*, which consists in not thinking of the things of the senses. Most of our time is spent in thinking about sense objects, things which we have seen or we have heard, which we shall see or shall hear, things which we have eaten or are eating or shall eat, places where we have lived, and so on. We think of them or talk of them most of our time. One who wishes to be a Vedantist must give up this habit.

Then comes the next preparation—(It is a hard task to be a philosopher!)—*titiksha*, the most difficult of all. It is nothing less than the ideal forbearance—"Resist not evil." This requires a little explanation. We may not resist an evil but, at the same time, we may feel very miserable. A man may say very harsh things to me, and I may not outwardly hate him for it, may not answer him back, and may restrain myself from apparently getting angry, but anger and hatred may be in my mind, and I may feel very badly toward that man. That is not nonresistance. I should be without any feeling of hatred or anger, without any thought of resistance. My mind must then be as calm as if nothing had happened. And only when I have got to that state have I attained nonresistance, and not before. Forbearance of all misery, without even a thought of resisting or driving it out, without even any painful feeling in the mind or any remorse—this is titiksha.

The next qualification required is *shraddha*, faith. One must have tremendous faith in religion and God. Until one has it, one cannot aspire to be a jnani. A great sage once told me that not one in twenty million in this world believed in God. I asked him why, and he told me: "Suppose there is a thief in this room, and he comes to know that there is a mass of gold in the next room, and only a very thin partition between the two rooms. What will be the condition of that thief?" I answered: "He will not be able to sleep at all. His brain will be actively thinking of some means of getting at the gold, and he will think of nothing else." Then he replied: "Do you believe that a man could believe in God and not go mad to get Him? If a man sincerely believes that there is that immense, infinite mine of Bliss, and that it can be reached, would not that man go mad in his struggle to reach it?" Strong faith in God and the consequent eagerness to reach Him constitute shraddha.

Then comes *samadhana*, or constant practice to hold the mind in God. Nothing is done in a day. Religion cannot be swallowed in the form of a pill. It requires hard and constant practice. The mind can be conquered only by slow and steady practice.

Next is *mumukshutva*, the intense desire to be free. All the misery we have is of our own choosing—such is our nature. The old Chinaman who, having been kept in prison for sixty years, was released on the coronation of a new emperor, exclaimed when he came out that he could not live. He must go back to his horrible dungeon among the rats and mice. He could not bear the light. So he asked them to kill him or send him back to the prison, and he was sent back. Exactly similar is the condition of all men. We run headlong after all sorts of misery and are unwilling to be freed from them. Every day we run after pleasure, and before we reach it, we find it is gone. It has slipped through our fingers. Still we do not cease from our mad pursuit, but on and on we go, blinded fools that we are.

Few men know that with pleasure there is pain, and with pain, pleasure; and as pain is disgusting, so is pleasure, since it is the twin brother of pain. It is derogatory to the glory of man that he should be going after pain, and equally derogatory that he should be going after pleasure. Both should be turned aside by men whose reason is balanced. Why will not men seek freedom from being played upon? This moment we are whipped, and when we begin to weep, nature gives us a dollar. Again we are whipped, and when we weep, nature gives us a piece of gingerbread and we begin to laugh again. The sage wants liberty. He finds that sense objects are all vain and that there is no end to pleasures and pains.

How the rich people in the world want to find fresh pleasures! All pleasures are old, and they want new ones. Do you not see how many foolish things they are inventing every day just to titillate the nerves for a moment, and that done, how there comes a reaction? The majority of people are just like a flock of sheep. If the leading sheep falls into a ditch, all the rest follow and break their necks. In the same way, what one leading member of a society does, all the others do without thinking what they are doing.

When a man begins to see the vanity of worldly things, he will feel he ought not to be thus played upon or borne along by nature. That is slavery. If a man has a few kind words said to him, he begins to smile, and when he hears a few harsh words, he begins to weep. He is a slave to a bit of bread, to a breath of air—a slave to dress, a slave to patriotism, to country, to name and fame. He is thus in the midst of slavery, and the real man has become buried within through his bondage. What you call man is a slave. When one realizes all this slavery, then comes the desire to be free; an intense desire comes. If a piece of burning charcoal is placed on a man's head, see how he struggles to throw it off. Similar will be the struggles for freedom of a man who really understands that he is a slave of nature.

The next discipline is also a very difficult one: *nityanitya-viveka*—discriminating between that which is true and that which is untrue, between the eternal and the transitory. God alone is eternal; everything else is transitory. Everything dies. The angels die, men die, animals die, earths die, sun, moon, and stars all die; everything undergoes constant change. The mountains of today were the oceans of yesterday and will be oceans tomorrow. Everything is in a state of flux. The whole universe is a mass of change. But there is One who never changes, and that is God. And the nearer we get to Him, the less will be the change for us, the less will nature be able to work on us, and when we reach Him and stand with Him, we shall conquer nature. We shall be masters of these phenomena of nature, and they will have no effect on us.

Why is this discipline so necessary? Because religion is not attained through the ears, nor through the eyes, nor yet through the brain. No scriptures can make us religious. We may study all the books that are in the world, yet we may not understand a word of religion or of God. We may talk all our lives and yet may not be the better for it. We may be the most intellectual people the world ever saw, and yet we may not come to God at all.

Where is God? Where is the field of religion? It is beyond the senses, beyond consciousness. Consciousness is only one of the many planes in which we work. You will have to transcend the field of consciousness, go beyond the senses, approach nearer and nearer to your own center, and as you do that, you will approach nearer and nearer to God. What is the proof of God? Direct perception, *pratyaksha*. The proof of this wall is that I perceive it. God has been perceived that way by thousands before, and will be perceived by all who want to perceive Him. But this perception is not sense perception at all. It is supersensuous, superconscious, and all this training is needed to take us beyond the senses.

By means of all sorts of past work and attachments we are being dragged downward. These preparations will make us pure and light. Bondages will fall off by themselves, and we shall be buoyed up beyond this plane of sense perception to which we are tied down, and then we shall see and hear and feel things which men in the three ordinary states—waking, dream, and sleep—neither feel nor see nor hear. Then we shall speak a strange language, as it were, and the world will not understand us, because it does not know anything but the senses.

True religion is entirely transcendental. Every being that is in the universe has the potentiality of transcending the senses. Even the little worm will one day transcend the senses and reach God. No life will be a failure; there is no such thing as failure in the universe. A hundred times man will hurt himself, a thousand times he will tumble, but in the end he will realize that he is God. We know there is no progress in a straight line. Every soul moves, as it were, in a circle and will have to complete it, and no soul can go so low but there will come a time when it will have to go upward. No one will be lost. We are all projected from one common center, which is God. The highest as well as the lowest life God ever projected will come back to the Father of all lives. "From whom all beings are projected, in whom all live, and unto whom they all return—that is God."[1] (I. 405-8, 410-12, 415-16)

IN QUEST OF THE SELF

A god and a demon went to learn about the Self from a great sage. They studied with him for a long time. At last the sage told them, "You yourselves are the Being you are seeking." Both of them thought that their bodies were the Self. The demon went back to his people quite satisfied and said: "I have learned everything that was to be learned: Eat, drink, and be merry. We are the Self. There is nothing beyond us." The demon was ignorant by nature, so he never inquired any further, but was perfectly contented with the idea that he was God and that by the Self was meant the body.

The god had a purer nature. He at first committed the mistake of thinking, "I, this body, am Brahman; so let me keep it strong and healthy and well dressed, and give it all sorts of enjoyments." But soon he found out that that could not be the meaning of the sage, their master. There must be something higher. So he came back and said: "Sir, did you teach me that this body was the Self? If so, I see that all bodies die. The Self cannot die." The sage said: "Find it out yourself. Thou art That." Then the god thought that the vital forces which work the body were what the sage meant [by the Self]. But after a time he found that if he ate, these vital forces remained strong, but if he starved, they became weak. The god then went back to the sage and said, "Sir, do you mean that the vital forces are the Self?" The sage said: "Find out for yourself. Thou art That."

The god returned home once more, thinking that it was the mind, perhaps, that was the Self. But in a short while he saw that thoughts were so various—now good, again bad. The mind was too changeable to be the Self. He went back to the sage and said: "Sir, I do not think that the mind is the Self. Did you mean that?" "No," replied the sage. "Thou art That. Find out for yourself." The god went home and at last found that he was the Self, beyond all thought, one, without birth or death, whom the sword cannot pierce or fire burn, whom the air cannot dry or water melt, the beginningless and endless, the immovable, the intangible, the omniscient, the omnipotent Being—that It was neither the body nor the mind, but beyond them all. So he was satisfied. But the poor demon did not get the truth, owing to his fondness for the body.

This world has a good many of these demoniac natures, but there are some gods too. If one proposes to teach any science to increase the power of sense enjoyment, one finds multitudes ready for it. If one undertakes to show the supreme goal, one finds few to listen to him. Very few have the power to grasp the higher—fewer still, the patience to attain it. (I. 140-42)

THOU ART THAT

Upon the same tree there are two birds, one on the top, the other below. The one on the top is calm, silent, and majestic, immersed in his own glory. The one on the lower branches, eating sweet and bitter fruits by turns, hopping from branch to branch, becomes happy and miserable by turns. After a time the lower bird eats an exceptionally bitter fruit and gets disgusted. He then looks up and sees the other bird, that wondrous one of golden plumage, who eats neither sweet nor bitter fruit, who is neither happy nor miserable, but is calm, Self-centered, and sees nothing beyond his Self. The lower bird longs for this condition but soon forgets it and again begins to eat the fruits. In a little while he eats another exceptionally bitter fruit, which makes him feel miserable, and he again looks up and tries to get nearer to the upper bird. Once more he forgets, and after a time he looks up. And so on he goes, again and again, until he comes very near to the beautiful bird and sees the reflection of light from his plumage playing around his own body, and he feels a change and seems to melt away. Still nearer he comes, and everything about him melts away, and at last he understands this wonderful change. The lower bird was, as it were, only a substantial-looking shadow, a reflection of the higher. He himself was, in essence, the upper bird all the time. This eating of fruits, sweet and bitter, and this lower little bird, weeping and happy by turns, were a vain chimera, a dream. All along the real bird was there above, calm and silent, glorious and majestic, beyond grief, beyond sorrow.

The upper bird is God, the Lord of this universe, and the lower bird is the human soul, eating the sweet and bitter fruits of this world. Now and then comes a heavy blow to the soul. For a time he stops the eating and goes toward the unknown

God, and a flood of light comes. He thinks that this world is a vain show. Yet again the senses drag him down, and he begins as before to eat the sweet and bitter fruits of the world. Again an exceptionally hard blow comes. His heart becomes open again to divine light. Thus gradually he approaches God, and as he gets nearer and nearer, he finds his old self melting away. When he has come near enough, he sees that he is no other than God, and he exclaims: "He whom I have described to you as the Life of this universe, as present in the atom and in suns and moons—He is the basis of our own life, the Soul of our soul. Nay, thou art That." (II. 394-96)

Note

1 Taittiriya Upanishad, 3.1.

VIII

BHAKTI YOGA
(The Path of Devotion)

Swami Vivekananda in Madras, February 1897

WHAT IS BHAKTI?

Bhakti yoga is a real, genuine search after the Lord, a search beginning, continuing, and ending in love. One single moment of the madness of extreme love of God brings us eternal freedom. "Bhakti," says Narada in his explanation of the bhakti aphorisms, "is intense love of God." "When a man gets it, he loves all, hates none. He becomes satisfied forever." "This love cannot be reduced to any earthly benefit," because as long as worldly desires last, that kind of love does not come. "Bhakti is greater than karma, greater than yoga," because these are intended for an object in view, while bhakti is its own fruition, "its own means and its own end."

The best definition of bhakti, however, is given by the king of bhaktas, Prahlada: "That deathless love which the ignorant have for the fleeting objects of the senses—as I keep meditating on Thee, may that love not slip away from my heart!"

"Lord, they build high temples in Your name; they make large gifts in Your name; I am poor, I have nothing, so I take this body of mine and place it at Your feet. Do not give me up, O

Lord." Such is the prayer proceeding out of the depths of the bhakta's heart. To him who has experienced it, this eternal sacrifice of the self unto the Beloved Lord is higher by far than all wealth and power, than even all soaring thoughts of renown and enjoyment. The peace of the bhakta's calm resignation is a peace that passeth all understanding and is of incomparable value. His *apratikulya* [self-surrender] is a state of the mind in which it has no interests and naturally knows nothing that is opposed to it. In this state of sublime resignation, everything in the shape of attachment goes away completely, except that one all-absorbing love for Him in whom all things live and move and have their being. This attachment of love for God is indeed one that does not bind the soul but effectively breaks all its bondages.

The Devi Bhagavata gives us the following definition of the higher love (*para-bhakti*): "As oil poured from one vessel to another falls in an unbroken line, so when the mind in an unbroken stream thinks of the Lord, we have what is called para-bhakti, or supreme love." This kind of undisturbed and ever-steady direction of the mind and heart to the Lord, with an inseparable attachment, is indeed the highest manifestation of man's love for God. (III. 31-32, 36, 84-86)

THE MYSTERY OF LOVE

We see love everywhere in nature. Whatever in society is good and great and sublime is the working out of that love. Whatever in society is very bad, nay, diabolical, is also the ill-directed working out of the same emotion of love. It is this same emotion that gives us the pure and holy conjugal love between husband and wife as well as the sort of love that goes to satisfy the lowest forms of animal passion. The emotion is the same, but its manifestation is different in different cases. It is the same feeling of love, well or ill-directed, that impels one man to do good and to give all he has to the poor, while it makes another man cut the throats of his brethren and take away all their possessions. The former loves others as much as the latter loves himself. The direction of the love is bad in the case of the latter, but it is right and proper in the other case. The same fire that cooks a meal for us may burn a child, and it is no fault of the fire if it does so; the difference lies in the way it is used. Therefore, love—the intense longing for association, the strong desire on the part of two to become one, and, it may be after all, of all to become merged in one—is being manifested everywhere in higher or lower forms as the case may be.

Bhakti yoga is the science of higher love. It shows us how to direct it. It shows us how to control it, how to manage it, how to use it, how to give it a new aim, as it were, and from it obtain the highest and most glorious results—that is, how to make it lead us to spiritual blessedness. Bhakti yoga does not say, "Give up." It only says, "Love—love the Highest!" And everything low naturally falls off from him, the object of whose love is the Highest.

"I cannot tell anything about Thee except that Thou art my love. Thou art beautiful! Oh, Thou art beautiful! Thou art beauty itself." What is, after all, really required of us in this yoga is that our thirst after the beautiful should be directed to God. What is the beauty in the human face, in the sky, in the stars, and in the moon? It is only the partial apprehension of the real, all-embracing Divine Beauty. "He shining, everything shines. It is through His light that all things shine." Take this high position of bhakti, which makes you forget at once all your little personalities. Take yourself away from all the world's little selfish clingings. Do not look upon humanity as the center of all your human and higher interests. Stand as a witness, as a student, and observe the phenomena of nature. Have the feeling of personal nonattachment with regard to man, and see how this mighty feeling of love is working itself out in the world. Sometimes a little friction is produced, but that is only in the course of the struggle to attain the higher, real love. Sometimes there is a little fight or a little fall, but it is all only by the way. Stand aside and freely let these frictions come. You feel the frictions only when you are in the current of the world. But when you are outside of it, simply as a witness and as a student, you will be able to see that there are millions and millions of channels in which God is manifesting Himself as Love.

"Wherever there is any bliss, even though in the most sensual of things, there is a spark of that Eternal Bliss which is the Lord Himself." Even in the lowest kinds of attraction there is the germ of divine love. One of the names of the Lord in

Sanskrit is Hari, and this means "He who attracts all things to Himself." His is, in fact, the only attraction worthy of human hearts. Who can really attract a soul? Only He. Do you think dead matter can truly attract the soul? It never did and never will. When you see a man going after a beautiful face, do you think that it is the handful of arranged material molecules which really attracts the man? Not at all. Behind those material particles there must be, and is, the play of divine influence and divine love. The ignorant man does not know it, but yet, consciously or unconsciously, he is attracted by it and it alone. So even the lowest forms of attraction derive their power from God Himself.

The Lord is the great magnet, and we are all like iron filings. We are being constantly attracted by Him, and all of us are struggling to reach Him. All this struggling of ours in this world is surely not intended for selfish ends. Fools do not know what they are doing. The work of their life is, after all, to approach the great magnet. All the tremendous struggling and fighting in life is intended to make us ultimately go to Him and be one with Him. (III. 73-75)

THE RELIGION OF LOVE

One star arises, another bigger one comes, and then a still bigger one; and at last the sun comes and all the lesser lights vanish. That sun is God. The stars are the smaller loves. When that Sun bursts upon a man, he becomes mad—what Emerson calls "a God-intoxicated man." He becomes transfigured into God. Everything is merged in that one ocean of love. Ordinary love is mere animal attraction. Otherwise why is there a distinction between the sexes? If one kneels before an image, it is dreadful idolatry; but if one kneels before husband or wife, it is quite permissible!

We are all babies struggling. Millions of people make a trade of religion. A few men in a century attain to that love of God, and the whole country becomes blessed and hallowed. When a son of God appears a whole country becomes blessed. It is true that few such are born in any one century in the whole world, but all should strive to attain that love of God. Who knows but you or I may be the next to attain it. Let us struggle therefore.

You read in the Sermon on the Mount, "Ask, and it shall be given you; seek, and ye shall find; knock, and it shall be opened unto you." The difficulty is, who seeks, who wants?

Bhakti is a religion. Religion is not for the many. That is impossible. A sort of knee-drill, standing up and sitting down, may be suited for the many, but religion is for the few. There are in every country only a few hundred who can be and will be religious. The others cannot be religious because they will not be awakened, and they do not want to be. The chief thing is to *want* God. We want everything except God, because our ordinary wants are supplied by the external world. It is only when our necessities have gone beyond the external world that we want a supply from the internal, from God.

There is a form of religion which is fashionable. My friend has much furniture in her parlor. It is the fashion to have a Japanese vase, so she must have one even if it costs a thousand dollars. In the same way she will have a little religion and join a church. Bhakti is not for such. That is not *want*. Want is that without which we cannot live.

What do we want? Let us ask ourselves this question every day: Do we want God? You may read all the books in the universe, but this love is not to be had by the power of speech, not by the highest intellect, not by the study of various sciences. He who desires God will get Love. Unto him God gives Himself. Love is always mutual, reflective. You may hate me, and if I want to love you, you repulse me. But if I persist, in a month or a year you are bound to love me. It is a well-known psychological phenomenon. As the loving wife thinks of her departed husband, with the same love we must desire the Lord, and then we will find God. And all books and the various sciences would not be able to teach us anything. By reading books we become parrots; no one becomes learned by reading books. If a man reads but one word of love, he indeed becomes learned. So we want first to get that desire.

We find people going to church and saying: "God, give me such and such. God, heal my disease." They want nice healthy bodies, and because they hear that someone will do this work for them, they go and pray to Him. It is better to be an atheist than to have such an idea of religion. As I have told you, this bhakti is the highest ideal. I don't know whether we shall reach it or not in millions of years to come, but we must make it our highest ideal, make our senses aim at the highest. (IV. 16-21)

THE TRIANGLE OF LOVE

We may represent love as a triangle, each of the angles of which corresponds to one of its inseparable characteristics. There can be no triangle without all its three angles, and there can be no true love without its three following characteristics: The first angle of our triangle of love is that love knows no bargaining. The second angle of the triangle of love is that love knows no fear. The third angle of the love-triangle is that love knows no rival, for in it is always embodied the lover's highest ideal.

Love we hear spoken of everywhere. Everyone says, "Love God." Men do not know what it is to love. If they did, they would not talk so glibly about it. Every man says he can love and then in no time finds out that there is no love in his nature. Every woman says she can love and soon finds out that she cannot. The world is full of the talk of love, but it is hard to love. Where is love? How do you know that there is love? The first test of love is that it knows no bargaining. So long as you see a man love another only to get something from him, you know that that is not love. It is shopkeeping. Wherever there is any question of buying and selling, it is not love. So when a man prays to God, "Give me this, and give me that," it is not love. How can it be? I offer you a prayer and you give me something in return. That is what it is—mere shopkeeping.

A certain great king went to hunt in a forest, and there he happened to meet a sage. He had a little conversation with him and became so pleased with him that he asked him to accept a present from him. "No," said the sage, "I am perfectly satisfied with my condition. These trees give me enough fruit to eat. These beautiful pure streams supply me with all the water I want. I sleep in these caves. What do I care for your presents, though you be an emperor?" The emperor said, "Just to purify me, to gratify me, come with me into the city and take some present." At last the sage consented to go with the emperor, and he was taken into the emperor's palace, where there were gold, jewelry, marble, and most wonderful things.

Wealth and power were manifest everywhere. The emperor asked the sage to wait a minute while he repeated his prayer, and he went into a corner and began to pray, "Lord, give me more wealth, more children, more territory." Meanwhile, the sage got up and began to walk away. The emperor saw him going and went after him. "Stay, sir, You did not take my present and are going away." The sage turned to him and said: "Beggar, I do not beg of beggars. What can you give? You have been begging yourself all the time."

That is not the language of love. What is the difference between love and shopkeeping if you ask God to give you this and give you that? The first test of love is that it knows no bargaining. Love is always the giver and never the taker. Says the child of God: "If God wants, I give Him my everything, but I do not want anything from Him. I want nothing in this universe. I love Him because I want to love Him, and I ask no favor in return. Who cares whether God is almighty or not? I do not want any power from Him nor any manifestation of His power. Sufficient for me that He is the God of love. I ask no more questions."

The second test is that love knows no fear. So long as man thinks of God as a Being sitting above the clouds, with rewards in one hand and punishments in the other, there can be no love. Can you frighten one into love? Does the lamb love the lion? The mouse, the cat? The slave, the master? Slaves sometimes simulate love, but is it love? Where do you ever see love in fear? It is always a sham. With love never comes the idea of fear. Think of a young mother in the street: If a dog barks at her, she flees into the nearest house. The next day she is in the street with her child, and suppose a lion rushes upon the child. Where will be her position? Just at the mouth of the lion, protecting her child. Love conquered all her fear. So also in the love of God.

Who cares whether God is a rewarder or a punisher? That is not the thought of a lover. Think of a judge when he comes home: What does his wife see in him? Not a judge, or a rewarder or punisher, but her husband, her love. What do his children see in him? Their loving father—not the punisher or rewarder. So the children of God never see in Him a punisher or a rewarder. It is only people who have never tasted of love that fear and quake. Cast off all fear—though these horrible ideas of God as a punisher or rewarder may have their use in savage minds. Some men, even the most intellectual, are spiritual savages, and these ideas may help them. But to men who are spiritual, men who are approaching religion, in whom spiritual insight is awakened, such ideas are simply childish, simply foolish. Such men reject all ideas of fear.

The third is a still higher test. Love is always the highest ideal. When one has passed through the first two stages, when one has thrown off all shopkeeping and cast off all fear, one then begins to realize that love is always the highest ideal. How many times in this world we see a beautiful woman loving an ugly man! How many times we see a handsome man loving an ugly woman! What is the attraction? Lookers-on only see the ugly man or the ugly woman, but not so the lover. To the lover the beloved is the most beautiful being that ever existed. How is it? The woman who loves the ugly man takes, as it were, the ideal of beauty that is in her own mind and projects it on this ugly man; and what she worships and loves is not the ugly man, but her own ideal. That man is, as it were, only the suggestion; and upon that suggestion she throws her own ideal and covers it, and it becomes her object of worship. Now this applies in every case where we love.

The highest ideal of every man is called God. Ignorant or wise, saint or sinner, man or woman, educated or uneducated, cultivated or uncultivated—to every human being the highest ideal is God. The synthesis of all the highest ideals of beauty, of sublimity, and of power gives us the most complete conception of the loving and lovable God. (III. 86-89, II. 47-49, III. 89)

THE NEED FOR A TEACHER

Every soul is destined to be perfect, and every being, in the end, will attain to that state. Whatever we are now is the result of whatever we have been or thought in the past, and whatever we shall be in the future will be the result of what we do or think now. But this does not preclude our receiving help from outside. The possibilities of the soul are always quickened by some help from outside—so much so that, in the vast majority of cases in the world, help from outside is almost absolutely necessary. The quickening influence comes from outside, and that works upon our own potentialities; and then the growth begins, spiritual life comes, and man becomes holy and perfect in the end. This quickening impulse that comes from outside cannot be received from books. The soul can receive impulse only from another soul, and from nothing else. We may study books all our lives, we may become very intellectual, but in the end we find we have not developed at all spiritually. It does not follow that a high order of intellectual development always shows an equivalent development of the spiritual side of man. On the other hand, we find cases almost every day where the intellect has become very highly developed at the expense of the spirit.

Now in intellectual development we can get much help from books, but in spiritual development, almost nothing. In studying books, sometimes we are deluded into thinking that we are being spiritually helped. But if we analyze ourselves we shall find that only our intellect has been helped and not the spirit. That is the reason why almost every one of us can speak most wonderfully on spiritual subjects, but when the time of action comes, we find ourselves so woefully deficient. It is because books cannot give us that impulse from outside. To quicken the spirit, that impulse must come from another soul.

That soul from which this impulse comes is called the *guru*, the teacher, and the soul to which the impulse is conveyed is called the *disciple*, the student. In order to convey this impulse, in the first place, the soul from which it comes must possess the power of transmitting it, as it were, to another. And in the second place, the object to which it is transmitted must be fit to receive it. The seed must be a living seed, and the field must be ready ploughed, and when both these conditions are fulfilled, a wonderful growth of religion takes place. "The speaker of religion must be wonderful; so must the hearer be," and when both of these are really wonderful, extraordinary, then alone will splendid spiritual growth come, and not otherwise. These are the real teachers, and these are the real students.

How are we to know a teacher? In the first place, the sun requires no torch to make it visible. We do not light a candle to see the sun. When the sun rises we instinctively become aware of its rising, and when a teacher of men comes to help us, the soul will instinctively know that it has found the truth. Truth stands on its own evidences. It does not require any other testimony to attest it. It is self-effulgent. It penetrates into the inmost recesses of our nature, and the whole universe stands up and says, "This is Truth." These are the very great teachers, but we can get help from the lesser ones also. And as we ourselves are not always sufficiently intuitive to be certain of our judgment of the man from whom we receive, there ought to be certain tests. There are certain conditions necessary in the taught and also in the teacher.

The conditions necessary in the taught are purity, a real thirst after knowledge, and perseverance.

In the teacher we must first see that he knows the secret of the scriptures. The whole world reads scriptures—Bibles, Vedas, Korans, and others—but they are only words, external arrangement, syntax, the etymology, the philology, the dry bones of religion. The teacher may be able to find what the age is of any book, but words are only the external forms in which things come. Those who deal too much in words and let the mind run always in the force of words lose the spirit. So the teacher must be able to know the *spirit* of the scriptures.

The second condition necessary in the teacher is that he must be sinless. The question was once asked me in England by a friend: "Why should we look to the personality of a teacher? We have only to judge what he says and take that up." Not so. If a man wants to teach me something of dynamics or chemistry or any other physical science, he may be of any character. He can still teach dynamics or any other science. For the knowledge that the physical sciences require is simply intellectual and depends on intellectual strength. A man can have, in such a case, a gigantic intellectual power without the least development of his soul. But in the spiritual sciences it is impossible from first to last that there can be any spiritual light in that soul which is impure. What can such a soul teach? It knows nothing. Spiritual truth is purity. "Blessed are the pure in heart, for they shall see God." In that one sentence is the gist of all religions. If you have learned that, all that has been said in the past and all that it is possible to say in the future you have known. You need not look into anything else, for you have all that is necessary in that one sentence. It could save the world, were all the other scriptures lost.

The third condition is motive. We should see that he does not teach with any ulterior motive—for name or fame or anything else—but simply for love, pure love for you. When spiritual forces are transmitted from the teacher to the taught, they can only be conveyed through the medium of love. There is no other medium that can convey them. Any other motive, such as gain or name, would immediately destroy the conveying medium. Therefore all must be done through love. One who has known God can alone be a teacher. When you see in the teacher that these conditions are fulfilled, you are safe. If they are not fulfilled, it is unwise to accept him.

A blind man may come to a museum, but he comes and goes only. If he is to see, his eyes must first be opened. This eye-opener of religion is the teacher. With the teacher, therefore, our relationship is that of ancestor and descendant. The teacher is the spiritual ancestor, and the disciple is the spiritual descendant. It is all very well to talk of liberty and independence, but without humility, submission, veneration, and faith, there will not be any religion. It is a significant fact that where this relation still exists between the teacher and the taught, there alone gigantic spiritual souls grow. But in those who have thrown it off, religion is made into a diversion. In nations and churches where this relation between teacher and taught is not maintained, spirituality is almost an unknown quantity. It never comes without that feeling. There is no one to transmit and no one to be transmitted to, because they are all independent. From whom can they learn? And if they come to learn, they come to *buy* learning. "Give me a dollar's worth of religion. Can I not pay a dollar for it?" Religion cannot be got that way!

You may go and knock your head against the four corners of the world, seek in the Himalayas, the Alps, the Caucasus, the Desert of Gobi or Sahara, or the bottom of the sea, but it will not come until you find a teacher. Find the teacher, serve him as a child, open your heart to his influence, see in him God manifested. (IV. 21-28)

ON PRAYER

God is both Personal and Impersonal as we are personal and impersonal.

Prayer and praise are the first means of growth. Repeating the names of God has wonderful power.

A *mantra* is a special word or sacred text or name of God chosen by the guru for repetition and reflection by the disciple. The disciple must concentrate on a personality for prayer and praise, and that is his *Ishta*.

These words (*mantras*) are not sounds of words but God Himself, and we have them within us. Think of Him, speak of Him. [Have] no desire for the world! Buddha's Sermon on the Mount was, "As thou thinkest, so art thou."

After attaining superconsciousness the bhakta descends again to love and worship.

Pure love has no motive. It has nothing to gain.

After prayer and praise comes meditation. Then comes reflection on the name and on the Ishta of the individual.

Pray that that manifestation which is our Father, our Mother, may cut our bonds.

Pray, "Take us by the hand as a father takes his son, and leave us not."

Pray, "I do not want wealth or beauty, this world or another, but Thee, O God! Lord! I have become weary. Oh, take me by the hand, Lord. I take shelter with Thee. Make me Thy servant. Be Thou my refuge."

Pray, "Thou [art] our Father, our Mother, our dearest Friend! Thou who bearest this universe, help us to bear the little burden of this our life. Leave us not. Let us never be separated from Thee. Let us always dwell in Thee."

When love of God is revealed and is all, this world appears like a drop.

Pass from nonexistence to existence, from darkness to light. (VI. 90-91)

THE SUPREME WORSHIP

It is in love that religion exists and not in ceremony—in the pure and sincere love in the heart. Unless a man is pure in body and mind, his coming into a temple and worshipping Shiva is useless. The prayers of those who are pure in mind and body will be answered by Shiva, and those who are impure and yet try to teach religion to others will fail in the end. External worship is only a symbol of internal worship, but internal worship and purity are the real things. Without them, external worship would be of no avail. Therefore you must all try to remember this.

This is the gist of all worship: to be pure and to do good to others. He who sees Shiva in the poor, in the weak, and in the diseased, really worships Shiva. And if he sees Shiva only in the image, his worship is but preliminary. He who has served and helped one poor man seeing Shiva in him, without thinking of his caste or creed or race or anything, with him Shiva is more pleased than with the man who sees Him only in temples.

A rich man had a garden and two gardeners. One of these gardeners was very lazy and did not work. But when the owner came to the garden the lazy man would get up and fold his arms and say, "How beautiful is the face of my master," and dance before him. The other gardener would not talk much, but would work hard and produce all sorts of fruits and vegetables, which he would carry on his head to his master, who lived a long way off. Of these two gardeners, which would be the more beloved of his master? Shiva is that master and this world is His garden, and there are two sorts of gardeners here—the one who is lazy, hypocritical, and does nothing, only talking about Shiva's beautiful eyes and nose and other features, and the other, who is taking care of Shiva's children, all those who are poor and weak, all animals, and all His creation. Which of these would be the more beloved of Shiva? Certainly he who serves His children. He who wants to serve the father must serve the children first. He who wants to serve Shiva must serve His children—must serve all creatures in this world first. It is said in the shastra [the scriptures] that those who serve the servants of God are His greatest servants. So you will bear this in mind. (III. 141-42)

LOVE, LOVER, AND BELOVED

This external world is only the world of suggestion. All that we see, we project out of our own minds. A grain of sand gets washed into the shell of an oyster and irritates it. The irritation produces in the oyster a secretion that covers the grain of sand, and the beautiful pearl is the result. Similarly, external things furnish us with suggestions over which we project our own ideals and make our objects. The wicked see this world as a perfect hell, and the good, as a perfect heaven. Lovers see this world as full of love, and haters, as full of hatred. Fighters see nothing but strife, and the peaceful, nothing but peace. The perfect man sees nothing but God. So we always worship our highest ideal, and when we have reached the point when we love the ideal as the ideal, all arguments and doubts vanish forever. Who cares whether God can be demonstrated or not? The ideal can never go, because it is a part of my own nature. I shall only question the ideal when I question my own existence, and as I cannot question the one, I cannot question the other. Who cares whether God can be almighty and all-merciful at the same time or not? Who cares whether He is the rewarder of mankind, whether He looks at us with the eyes of a tyrant or with the eyes of a beneficent monarch?

The lover has passed beyond all these things, beyond rewards and punishments, beyond fears and doubts, beyond scientific or any other demonstration. Sufficient unto him is the ideal of love. And is it not self-evident that this universe is but a manifestation of this love? What is it that makes atoms unite with atoms, molecules with molecules, and causes planets to fly toward each other? What is it that attracts man to man, man to woman, woman to man, and animals to animals, drawing the whole universe, as it were, toward one center? It is what is called love. Its manifestation is from the lowest atom to the highest being. Omnipotent, all-pervading, is this love. What manifests itself as attraction in the sentient and the insentient, in the particular and in the universal, is the love of God. It is the one motive power that is in the universe. Under the impetus of that love, Christ gives his life for humanity, Buddha even for an animal, the mother for the child, the husband for the wife. It is under the impetus of the same love that men are ready to give up their lives for their country. And, strange to say, under the impetus of the same love the thief steals, the murderer murders. Even in these cases the spirit is the same, but the manifestation is different. This is the one motive power in the universe. The thief has love for gold. The love is there, but it is misdirected. So in all crimes, as well as in all virtuous actions, behind stands that eternal love. Suppose a man writes a check for a thousand dollars for the poor of New York, and at the same time, in the same room, another man forges the name of a friend. The light by which both of them write is the same, but each one will be responsible for the use he makes of it. It is not the light that is to be praised or blamed. Unattached, yet shining in everything, is love, the motive power of the universe, without which the universe would fall to pieces in a moment. And this love is God.

"None, O beloved, loves the husband for the husband's sake, but for the Self that is in the husband. None, O beloved, ever loves the wife for the wife's sake, but for the Self that is in the wife. None ever loves anything else except for the Self."[1] Even this selfishness, which is so much condemned, is but a manifestation of the same love. Stand aside from this play. Do not mix in it, but see this wonderful panorama, this grand drama, played scene after scene, and hear this wonderful harmony. All are the manifestations of the same love. Even in selfishness, that self will multiply, grow and grow. That one self, the one man, will become two selves when he gets married; several, when he gets children. And thus he grows until he feels the whole world as his Self, the whole universe as his Self. He expands into one mass of universal love, infinite love—the love that is God.

At the beginning it was love for the self, but the claims of the little self made love selfish. At the end came the full blaze of light, when that self had become the Infinite. That God, who at first was a Being somewhere, became resolved, as it were, into Infinite Love. Man himself was also transformed. He was approaching God. He was throwing off all vain desires, of which he was full before. With desires vanished selfishness, and at the apex he found that Love, Lover, and Beloved were One. (II. 49-51, 53)

Note

Brihadaranyaka Upanishad, 2.4.5.

IX

RAJA YOGA
(The Path of Meditation)

In Kashmir, 1898
Left to Right: Miss Josephine MacLeod, Mrs. Ole Bull, Swami Vivekananda, Sister Nivedita

THE SCIENCE OF RAJA YOGA

The teachers of the science of raja yoga declare not only that religion is based upon the experience of ancient times, but that no man can be religious until he has had the same experiences himself. Yoga is the science which teaches us how to get these experiences. It is not much use to talk about religion until one has felt it. If there is a God we must see Him; if there is a soul we must perceive it; otherwise it is better not to believe. It is better to be an outspoken atheist than a hypocrite.

Man wants truth, wants to experience truth for himself. When he has grasped it, realized it, felt it within his heart of hearts, then alone, declare the Vedas, will all doubts vanish, all darkness be scattered, and all crookedness be made straight.

The science of raja yoga proposes to put before humanity a practical and scientifically worked out method of reaching this truth. In the first place, every science must have its own method of investigation. If you want to become an astronomer and sit down and cry, "Astronomy! Astronomy!" it will never come to you. The same with chemistry. A certain method must be followed. You must go to a laboratory, take different substances, mix them up, compound them, experiment with them, and out of that will come a knowledge of chemistry. If you want to be an astronomer you must go to an observatory, take a telescope, study the stars and planets, and then you will become an astronomer. Each science must have its own methods. I could preach to you thousands of sermons, but they would not make you religious until you practiced the method. These are the truths of the sages of all countries, of all ages, of men pure and unselfish, who had no motive but to do good to the world. They all declare that they have found some truth higher than what the senses can bring us, and they invite verification. They ask us to take up the method and practice honestly, and then, if we do not find this higher truth, we will have the right to say that there is no truth in the claim. But before we have done that, we are not rational in denying the truth of their assertions. So we must work faithfully, using the prescribed methods, and light will come.

In acquiring knowledge we make use of generalization, and generalization is based upon observation. We first observe facts, then generalize, and then draw conclusions or principles. The knowledge of the mind, of the internal nature of man, of thought, can never be had until we have first the power of observing the facts that are going on within. It is comparatively easy to observe facts in the external world, for many instruments have been invented for the purpose, but in the internal world we have no instrument to help us. Yet we know we must observe in order to have a real science. Without proper analysis, any science will be hopeless—mere theorizing. And that is why all the psychologists have been quarreling among themselves since the beginning of time, except those few who found the means of observation.

The science of raja yoga proposes, in the first place, to give us such a means of observing the internal states. The instrument is the mind itself. The power of attention, when properly guided and directed toward the internal world, will analyze the mind and illumine facts for us. The powers of the mind are like rays of light dissipated. When they are concentrated they illumine. This is our only means of knowledge.

How has all the knowledge in the world been gained but by the concentration of the powers of the mind? The world is ready to give up its secrets if we only know how to knock, how to give it the necessary blow. The strength and force of the blow come through concentration. There is no limit to the power of the human mind. The more concentrated it is, the more power is brought to bear on one point. That is the secret.

It is easy to concentrate the mind on external things. The mind naturally goes outward. But it is not so in the case of religion or psychology or metaphysics, where the subject and the object are one. The object is internal—the mind itself is the object. It is necessary to study the mind itself—mind studying mind. We know that there is the power of the mind called reflection. I am talking to you. At the same time I am standing aside, as it were, a second person, and knowing and hearing what I am saying. You work and think at the same time, while a portion of your mind stands by and sees what you are thinking. The powers of the mind should be concentrated and turned back upon it. And as the darkest places reveal their secrets before the penetrating rays of the sun, so will this concentrated mind penetrate its own innermost secrets. Thus will we come to the basis of belief, the real, genuine religion. We will perceive for ourselves whether we have souls or not, whether life is of five minutes or of eternity, whether there is a God in the universe or not. It will all be revealed to us.

This is what raja yoga proposes to teach. The goal of all its teaching is how to concentrate the mind; then, how to discover the innermost recesses of our own minds; then, how to generalize their contents and form our own conclusions from them. It never asks what our religion is—whether we are deists or atheists, whether Christians, Jews, or Buddhists. We are human beings—that is sufficient. Every human being has the right and the power to seek religion. Every human being has the right to ask the reason why and to have his question answered by himself—if he only takes the trouble.

So far, then, we see that in the study of this raja yoga no faith or belief is necessary. Believe nothing until you find it out for yourself. That is what it teaches us. Truth requires no prop to make it stand. Do you mean to say that the facts of our awakened state require any dreams or imaginings to prove them? Certainly not. This study of raja yoga takes a long time and constant practice. A part of this practice is physical, but in the main it is mental. (I. 127-32)

THE POWERS OF THE MIND

Have you ever noticed the phenomenon that is called *thought transference*? A man here is thinking something, and that thought is manifested in somebody else, in some other place. With preparations—not by chance—a man wants to send a thought to another mind at a distance, and this other mind knows that a thought is coming, and he receives it exactly as it is sent out. Distance makes no difference. The thought goes and reaches the other man, and he understands it.

This shows that there is a continuity of mind, as the yogis call it. The mind is universal. Your mind, my mind, all these little minds, are fragments of that universal mind—little waves in the ocean. And on account of this continuity, we can convey our thoughts directly to one another.

You see what is happening all around us. The world is one of influence. Part of our energy is used up in the preservation of our own bodies. Beyond that, every particle of our energy is, day and night, being used in influencing others. Our bodies, our virtues, our intellect, and our spirituality, all these are continuously influencing others, and so, conversely, we are being influenced by them. This is going on all around us. Now, to take a concrete example: A man comes. You know he is very learned. His language is beautiful, and he speaks to you by the hour, but he does not make any impression. Another man comes, and he speaks a few words, not well arranged, ungrammatical perhaps—all the same, he makes an immense impression. Many of you have seen that. So it is evident that words alone cannot always produce an impression. Words, even thoughts, contribute only one-third of the influence in making an impression; the man, two-thirds. What you call the personal magnetism of the man—that is what goes out and impresses you.

In our families there are the heads. Some of them are successful, others are not. Why? We complain of others in our failures. The moment I am unsuccessful, I say that so-and-so is the cause of the failure. In failure, one does not like to confess one's own faults and weaknesses. Each person tries to hold himself faultless and lay the blame upon somebody or something else, or even on bad luck. When heads of families fail they should ask themselves why it is that some persons manage a family so well and others do not. Then you will find that the difference is owing to the man—his presence, his personality.

The ideal of all education, all training, should be this man-making. But instead of that, we are always trying to polish up the outside. What use is there in polishing up the outside when there is no inside? The end and aim of all training is to make the man grow. The man who influences, who throws his magic, as it were, upon his fellow beings, is a dynamo of power, and when that man is ready, he can do anything and everything he likes. That personality put upon anything will make it work.

Compare the great teachers of religion with the great philosophers. The philosophers scarcely influenced anybody's inner man, and yet they wrote most marvelous books. The religious teachers, on the other hand, moved countries in their lifetime. The difference was made by personality. In the philosopher it is a faint personality that influences; in the great prophets it is tremendous. In the former we touch the intellect; in the latter we touch life.

The science of raja yoga claims that it has discovered the laws which develop this personality, and by proper attention to those laws and methods, each one can grow and strengthen his personality. This is one of the great practical things, and this is the secret of all education. This has a universal application. In the life of the householder, in the life of the poor, the rich, the man of business, the spiritual man, in everyone's life, it is a great thing, the strengthening of this personality.

We constantly complain that we have no control over our actions, over our thoughts. But how can we have it? If we can get control over the fine movements, if we can get hold of thought at the root, before it has become thought, before it has become action, then it would be possible for us to control the whole. Now, if there is a method by which we can analyze, investigate, understand, and finally grapple with those finer powers, the finer causes, then alone is it possible to have control over ourselves. And the man who has control over his own mind assuredly will have control over every other mind. That is why purity and morality have been always the object of religion. A pure, moral man has control of himself. And all minds are the same—different parts of one Mind. He who knows one lump of clay has known all the clay in the universe.

He who knows and controls his own mind knows the secret of every mind and has power over every mind. (II. 13-17)

HOW TO BE A YOGI

The yogi must always practice. He should try to live alone. The companionship of different sorts of people distracts the mind. He should not speak much, because to speak distracts the mind; not work much, because too much work distracts the mind. The mind cannot be controlled after a whole day's hard work. One observing the above rules becomes a yogi. Such is the power of yoga that even the least of it will bring a great amount of benefit. It will not hurt anyone, but will benefit everyone. First of all, it will tone down nervous excitement, bring calmness, enable us to see things more clearly. The temperament will be better and the health will be better. Sound health will be one of the first signs, and a beautiful voice. Defects in the voice will be changed. This will be among the first of the many effects that will come. Those who practice hard will get many other signs. Sometimes there will be sounds, as a peal of bells heard at a distance, commingling, and falling on the ear as one continuous sound. Sometimes things will be seen—little specks of light floating and becoming bigger and bigger; and when these things come, know that you are progressing fast.

Those who want to be yogis and practice hard, must take care of their diet at first. But for those who want only a little practice for everyday, business sort of life, let them not eat too much; otherwise they may eat whatever they please. For those who want to make rapid progress and to practice hard, a strict diet is absolutely necessary.

When one begins to concentrate, the dropping of a pin will seem like a thunderbolt going through the brain. As the organs get finer, the perceptions get finer. These are the stages through which we have to pass, and all those who persevere will succeed. Give up all argumentation and other distractions. Is there anything in dry, intellectual jargon? It only throws the mind off its balance and disturbs it. The things of the subtler planes have to be realized. Will talking do that? So give up all vain talk. Read only those books written by persons who have had realization.

Those who really want to be yogis must give up, once and for all, this nibbling at things. Take up one idea—make that one idea your life. Think of it, dream of it, live on that idea. Let the brain, muscles, nerves, every part of your body, be full of that idea, and just leave every other idea alone. This is the way to success, and this is the way great spiritual giants are produced. Others are mere talking machines. If we really want to be blessed and make others blessed, we must go deeper.

The first step is not to disturb the mind, not to associate with persons whose ideas are disturbing. All of you know that certain persons, certain places, certain foods, repel you. Avoid them. And those who want to go to the highest, must avoid all company, good or bad. Practice hard. Whether you live or die does not matter. You have to plunge in and work without thinking of the result. If you are brave enough, in six months you will be a perfect yogi. But those who take up just a bit of it and a little of everything else make no progress. It is of no use simply to take a course of lessons. To those who are full of *tamas* [laziness], ignorant, and dull—those whose minds never get fixed on any idea, who only crave for something to amuse them—religion and philosophy are simply objects of entertainment. These are the unpersevering. They hear a talk, think it very nice, and then go home and forget all about it. To succeed you must have tremendous perseverance, tremendous will. "I will drink the ocean," says the persevering soul. "At my will mountains will crumble up." Have that sort of energy, that sort of will, work hard, and you will reach the goal. (I. 175-78)

THE PRACTICE OF YOGA

The body must be properly taken care of. The people who torture their flesh are diabolical. Always keep your mind joyful. If melancholy thoughts come, kick them out. A yogi must not eat too much, but he also must not fast; he must not sleep too much, but he must not go without any sleep. In all things only the man who holds the golden mean can become a yogi.

What is the best time for practice in yoga? The junction time of dawn and twilight, when all nature becomes calm. Take the help of nature. Take the easiest posture in sitting. Hold the three parts straight—the ribs, the shoulders, and the head—leaving the spine free and straight, not leaning backward or forward. Then mentally picture the body as perfect, part by part. Then send a current of love to all the world. Then pray for enlightenment.

The same faculty that we employ in dreams and thoughts—namely, imagination—will also be the means by which we arrive at Truth. When the imagination is very powerful, the object becomes visualized. Take up an idea, devote yourself to it, struggle on in patience, and the sun will rise for you.

The purer the mind, the easier it is to control. Purity of the mind must be insisted upon if you would control it. Do not think covetously about mere mental powers. Let them go. One who seeks the powers of the mind succumbs to them. Almost all who desire powers become ensnared by them.

Every wave of passion restrained is a balance in your favor. It is therefore good *policy* not to return anger for anger, as with all true morality.

Never talk about the faults of others, no matter how bad they may be. Nothing is ever gained by that. You never help one by talking about his faults. You do him an injury and injure yourself as well. You cannot judge a man by his faults. Remember, the wicked are always the same all over the world. The thief and the murderer are the same in Asia and Europe and America. They form a nation by themselves. It is only in the good and the pure and the strong that you find variety. Do not recognize wickedness in others. Wickedness is ignorance, weakness. What is the good of telling people they are weak? Criticism and destruction are of no avail. We must give them something higher. Tell them of their own glorious nature, their birthright.

Never quarrel about religion. All quarrels and disputations concerning religion simply show that spirituality is not present. Religious quarrels are always over the husks. When purity, when spirituality goes, leaving the soul dry, quarrels begin and not before. (VI. 130, 133, 135, 126, 136, 127, 141-42, 127)

SELF-CONTROL

We must assert our godhead in the midst of all difficulties. Nature wants us to react, to return blow for blow, cheating for cheating, lie for lie, to hit back with all our might. It requires a superdivine power not to hit back, to keep control, to be unattached.

It is very difficult, but we can overcome the difficulty by constant practice. We must learn that nothing can happen to us unless we make ourselves susceptible to it. We get only that for which we are fitted. Let us give up our pride and understand this, that never is misery undeserved. There never has been a blow undeserved. There never has been an evil for which I did not pave the way with my own hands. We ought to know that. Analyze yourselves and you will find that every blow you have received came to you because you prepared yourselves for it. You did half and the external world did the other half. That is how the blow came. That will sober us up. At the same time, from this very analysis will come a note of hope, and the note of hope is: "I have no control of the external world, but that which is in me and nearer unto me, my own world, is in my control. If the two together are required to make a failure, if the two together are necessary to give me a blow, I will not contribute the one which is in my control, and how then can the blow come? If I get real control of myself, the blow will never come."

We are all the time, from our childhood, trying to lay the blame upon something outside ourselves. We are always standing up to set other people right and not ourselves. If we are miserable, we say, "Oh, the world is a devil's world." We curse others and say, "What infatuated fools!" But why should we be in such a world if we really are so good? If this is a devil's world, we must be devils also. Why else should we be here? "Oh, the people of the world are so selfish!" True enough. But why should we be found in that company if we are better? Just think of that.

We only get what we deserve. It is a lie when we say that the world is bad and we are good. It can never be so. It is a terrible lie we tell ourselves.

This is the first lesson to learn: Be determined not to curse anything outside, not to lay the blame upon anyone outside, but be a man, stand up, lay the blame on yourself. You will find that that is always true. Get hold of yourself. (II. 6-8)

HOW TO CONTROL EMOTION

The *chitta-vrittis*, the mind-waves, which are gross, we can appreciate and feel. They can be more easily controlled. But what about the finer instincts? How can they be controlled? When I am angry my whole mind becomes a huge wave of anger. I feel it, see it, handle it, can easily manipulate it, can fight with it, but I shall not succeed perfectly in the fight until I can get down below to its causes. A man says something very harsh to me, and I begin to feel that I am getting heated. And he goes on till I am perfectly angry and forget myself and identify myself with anger. When he first began to abuse me, I thought, "I am going to be angry." Anger was one thing and I was another. But when I became angry, I *was* anger. These feelings have to be controlled in the germ, the root, in their fine forms, even before we have become conscious that they are acting on us.

With the vast majority of mankind the fine states of these passions are not even known—the states below consciousness from which they emerge. When a bubble is rising from the bottom of the lake, we do not see it—nor even when it has nearly come to the surface. It is only when it bursts and makes a ripple that we know it is there. We shall only be successful in grappling with the waves when we can get hold of them in their fine forms. And until you can get hold of them and subdue them before they become gross, there is no hope of conquering any passion perfectly. To control our passions we have to control them at their very roots. Then alone shall we be able to burn out their very seeds. As fried seeds thrown into the ground will never come up, so these passions will never arise.

Meditation is one of the great means of controlling the rising of these waves. By meditation you can make the mind subdue these waves. And if you go on practicing meditation for days and months and years—until it has become a habit, until it comes in spite of yourself—anger and hatred will be controlled and checked. (I. 241-43)

CONCENTRATION

Concentration is the essence of all knowledge. Nothing can be done without it. Ninety percent of thought force is wasted by the ordinary human being, and therefore he is constantly committing blunders. The trained man, or mind, never makes a mistake. When the mind is concentrated and turned back on itself, all within us will be our servants, not our masters. The Greeks applied their concentration to the external world, and the result was perfection in art, literature, etc. The Hindus concentrated on the internal world, upon the unseen realms in the Self, and developed the science of yoga. Yoga is controlling the senses, will, and mind. The benefit of its study is that we learn to control instead of being controlled. The mind seems to be layer on layer. Our real goal is to cross all these intervening strata of our being and find God. The end and aim of yoga is to realize God. To do this we must go beyond relative knowledge, go beyond the sense world. The world is awake to the senses. The children of the Lord are asleep on that plane. The world is asleep to the Eternal. The children of the Lord are awake in that realm. These are the sons of God. There is but one way to control the senses—to see Him who is the Reality in the universe. Then and only then can we really conquer our senses.

Concentration is restraining the mind into smaller and smaller limits. There are eight processes for thus restraining the mind: The first is *yama*—controlling the mind by avoiding externals. All morality is included in this. Beget no evil. Injure no living creature. If you injure nothing for twelve years, then even lions and tigers will go down before you. Practice truthfulness. Twelve years of absolute truthfulness in thought, word, and deed gives a man what he wills. Be chaste in thought, word, and action. Chastity is the basis of all religions. Personal purity is imperative. Next is *niyama*—not allowing the mind to wander in any direction. Then *asana*—

posture. There are eighty-four postures, but the best is that most natural to each one—that is, [the one that] can be kept longest with the greatest ease. After this comes *pranayama*—restraint of breath. Then *pratyahara*—drawing in of the organs from their objects. Then *dharana*—concentration. Then *dhyana*—contemplation, or meditation. (This is the kernel of the yoga system.) And last, *samadhi*—superconsciousness.

The purer the body and mind, the quicker the desired result will be obtained. You must be perfectly pure. Do not think of evil things. Such thoughts will surely drag you down. If you are perfectly pure and practice faithfully, your mind can finally be made a searchlight of infinite power. There is no limit to its scope. But there must be constant practice and nonattachment to the world. When a man reaches the superconscious state, all feeling of the body melts away. Then alone does he become free and immortal. To all external appearance, unconsciousness and superconsciousness are the same, but they differ as a lump of clay from a lump of gold. One whose whole soul is given up to God has reached the superconscious plane. (VI. 123-25)

MEDITATION

First, meditation should be of a negative nature. Think away everything. Analyze everything that comes in the mind by the sheer action of the will.

Next, assert what we really are—Existence, Knowledge, and Bliss—Being, Knowing, and Loving.

Meditation is the means of unification of the subject and object. Meditate:

Above, it is full of me; below, it is full of me; in the middle, it is full of me. I am in all beings and all beings are in me. Om Tat Sat. I am It. I am the Existence above mind. I am the one Spirit of the universe. I am neither pleasure nor pain.

The body drinks, eats, and so on. I am not the body. I am not the mind. I am He.

I am the witness. I look on. When health comes I am the witness. When disease comes I am the witness.

I am Existence, Knowledge, Bliss.

I am the essence and nectar of knowledge. Through eternity I change not. I am calm, resplendent, and unchanging. (VI. 91-92)

EQUANIMITY OF THE MIND IS YOGA

There was a great sage in India called Vyasa. This Vyasa is known as the author of the Vedanta aphorisms and was a holy man. His father had tried to become a perfect man and had failed. His grandfather had also tried and failed. His great-grandfather had similarly tried and failed. He himself did not succeed perfectly, but his son, Shuka, was born perfect. Vyasa taught his son wisdom, and after teaching him the knowledge of truth himself, he sent him to the court of King Janaka. Janaka was a great king and was called Janaka Videha. *Videha* means "without a body." Although a king, he had entirely forgotten that he had a body. He felt all the time that he was Spirit. This boy, Shuka, was sent to be taught by him.

The king knew that Vyasa's son was coming to him to learn wisdom, so he made certain arrangements beforehand. When the boy presented himself at the gates of the palace, the guards took no notice of him whatsoever. They only gave him a seat, and he sat there for three days and nights, nobody speaking to him, nobody asking him who he was or whence he came. He was the son of a very great sage. His father was honored by the whole country, and he himself was a most respectable person; yet the low, vulgar guards of the palace would take no notice of him.

After that, suddenly, the ministers of the king and all the big officials came there and received him with the greatest honor. They conducted him in and showed him into splendid rooms, gave him the most fragrant baths and wonderful dress, and for eight days they kept him there in all kinds of luxury. That solemnly serene face of Shuka did not change even to the smallest extent by the change in the treatment accorded to him. He was the same in the midst of this luxury as when waiting at the door.

Then he was brought before the king. The king was on his throne, music was playing, and dancing and other amusements were going on. The king then gave him a cup of milk, full to the brim, and asked him to go seven times round the hall without spilling even a drop. The boy took the cup and proceeded in the midst of the music and the attraction of the beautiful faces. As desired by the king, seven times did he go round, and not a drop of the milk was spilt. The boy's mind could not be attracted by anything in the world unless he allowed it to affect him. And when he brought the cup to the king, the king said to him: "What your father has taught you and what you have learned yourself, I can only repeat. You have known the Truth. Go home."

Thus the man who has practiced control over himself cannot be acted upon by anything outside. There is no more slavery for him. His mind has become free. (I. 90-92)

X

VEDANTA IN PRACTICE

Swami Vivekananda in Pasadena, California, 1900

PREPARATIONS FOR HIGHER LIFE

The first thing necessary is a quiet and peaceable life. If I have to go about the world the whole day to make a living, it is hard for me to attain anything very high in this life. Perhaps in another life I shall be born under more propitious circumstances. But if I am earnest enough, these very circumstances will change even in this birth. The master said, "My child, if you desire after God, God shall come to you." The disciple did not understand his master fully. One day both went to bathe in a river, and the master said, "Plunge in," and the boy did so. In a moment the master was upon him, holding him down. He would not let the boy come up. When the boy struggled and was exhausted, he let him go. "Yes, my child, how did you feel there?" "Oh, the desire for a breath of air!" "Do you have that kind of desire for God?" "No, sir." "Have that kind of desire for God and you shall have God."

If you want to be a yogi you must be free and place yourself in circumstances where you are alone and free from all anxiety. He who desires a comfortable and nice life and at the same time wants to realize the Self is like the fool who, wanting to cross the river, caught hold of a crocodile, mistaking it for a log of wood. "Seek ye first the Kingdom of God and His righteousness, and all these things shall be added unto you." Unto him comes everything, who does not care for anything. Fortune is like a flirt. She cares not for him who wants her, but she is at the feet of him who does not care for her. Money comes and showers itself upon one who does not care for it. So does fame come in abundance until it is a trouble and a burden. They always come to the master. The slave never gets anything. The master is he who can live in spite of them, whose life does not depend upon the little, foolish things of the world. Live for an ideal and that one ideal alone. Let it be so great, so strong, that there may be nothing else left in the mind—no place for anything else, no time for anything else.

How some people give all their energies, time, brain, body, and everything to become rich! They have no time for breakfast! Early in the morning they are out and at work! They die in the attempt—ninety percent of them—and the rest, when they make money, cannot enjoy it. That is grand! I do not say it is bad to try to be rich. It is marvelous, wonderful! Why, what does it show? It shows that one can have the same amount of energy and struggle for freedom as one has for money. We know we have to give up money and all other things when we die, and yet, see the amount of energy we can put forth for them. But we—the same human beings—should we not put forth a thousandfold more strength and energy to acquire that which never fades, but which remains with us forever? For this is the one great friend—our own good deeds, our own spiritual excellence—that follows us beyond the grave. Everything else is left behind here with the body.

That is the one great first step—the real desire for the ideal. In the West the difficulty is that everything is made so easy. It is not truth, but development, that is the great aim. The struggle is the great lesson. Mind you, the great benefit in this life is struggle. It is through that we pass. If there is any road to heaven, it is through hell. Through hell to heaven is always the way. When the soul has wrestled with circumstances and has met death—a thousand times death on the way—but, nothing daunted, has struggled forward again and again and yet again—then the soul comes out as a giant and laughs at the ideal he has been struggling for, because he finds how much greater is he than the ideal. I am the end, my own Self and nothing else. For what is there to compare to my own Self? Can a bag of gold be the ideal of my soul? Certainly not! My soul is the highest ideal that I can have. Realizing my own real nature is the one goal of my life.

There is nothing that is absolutely evil. The devil has a place here as well as God, else he would not be here. Just as I told you, it is through hell that we pass to heaven. Our mistakes have places here. Go on! Do not look back if you think you have done something that is not right. Now, do you believe you could be what you are today had you not made those mistakes before? Bless your mistakes, then. They have been angels unawares. Blessed is torture! Blessed is happiness! Do not care what your lot is. Hold on to the ideal. March on!

And then along with it, there must be meditation. Meditation is the one thing. Meditate! The greatest thing is meditation. It is the nearest approach to spiritual life—the mind meditating. It is the one moment in our daily life that we are not at all material—the soul thinking of itself, free from all matter—this marvelous touch of the soul! (V. 250-53)

HINTS ON PRACTICAL SPIRITUALITY

The task before us is vast; and first and foremost, we must seek to control the vast mass of sunken thoughts that have become automatic with us. The evil deed is, no doubt, on the conscious plane; but the cause that produced the evil deed was far beyond in the realms of the unconscious, unseen and therefore more potent.

Practical psychology first of all directs its energies in controlling the unconscious, and we know that we can do it. Why? Because we know the cause of the unconscious is the conscious. The unconscious thoughts are the millions of our old submerged conscious thoughts—old conscious actions become petrified. We do not look at them, do not know them, have forgotten them. But, mind you, if the power of evil is in the unconscious, so also is the power of good. We have many things stored in us as in a pocket. We have forgotten them; [we]

do not even think of them. And there are many of them, rotting, becoming positively dangerous. They come forth, the unconscious causes that kill humanity. True psychology would, therefore, try to bring them under the control of the conscious. The great task is to revive the whole man, as it were, in order to make him the complete master of himself. Even what we call the automatic action of the organs within our bodies, such as the liver, etc., can be made to obey our commands.

This is the first part of the study—the control of the unconscious. The next is to go beyond the conscious. Just as unconscious work is beneath consciousness, so there is another work that is above consciousness. When this superconscious state is reached, man becomes free and divine. Death becomes immortality, weakness becomes infinite power, and iron bondage becomes liberty. That is the goal, the infinite realm of the superconscious.

Everyone without exception, every one of us, can attain this culmination of yoga. But it is a terrible task. If a person wants to attain this truth, he will have to do something more than listen to lectures and take a few breathing exercises. Everything lies in the preparation. How long does it take to strike a light? Only a second. But how long it takes to make the candle! How long does it take to eat a dinner? Perhaps, half an hour. But hours to prepare the food! We want to strike the light in a second, but we forget that the making of the candle is the chief thing.

Though it is so hard to reach the goal, yet even our smallest attempts are not in vain. We know that nothing is lost. In the Gita, Arjuna asks Krishna, "Those who fail in attaining perfection in yoga in this life, are they destroyed like the clouds of summer?"[1] Krishna replies: "Nothing, my friend, is lost in this world. Whatever one does, that remains as one's own. And if the fruition of yoga does not come in this life, one takes it up again in the next birth."[2] Otherwise, how do you explain the marvelous childhood of Jesus, Buddha, Shankara?

The greatest help to spiritual life is meditation (dhyana). In meditation we divest ourselves of all material conditions and feel our divine nature. We do not depend upon any external help in meditation. The touch of the soul can paint the brightest color even in the dingiest places. It can cast a fragrance over the vilest thing. It can make the wicked divine—and all enmity, all selfishness, is effaced. The less the thought of the body, the better. For it is the body that drags us down. It is attachment, identification, that makes us miserable. That is the secret: to think that I am the Spirit and not the body, and that the whole of this universe, with all its relations, with all its good and all its evil, is but as a series of paintings—scenes on a canvas—of which I am the witness. (II. 34-37)

SPIRITUAL PRACTICE ACCORDING TO VEDANTA

The truth has to be heard, then reflected upon, and then to be constantly asserted. Think always, "I am Brahman." Every other thought must be cast aside as weakening. Cast aside every thought that says that you are men or women. Let body go and mind go and gods go and ghosts go. Let everything go but that One Existence. "Where one hears another, where one sees another, that is small. Where one does not hear another, where one does not see another, that is Infinite."[3] That is the highest when the subject and the object become one. When I am the listener and I am the speaker, when I am the teacher and I am the taught, when I am the creator and I am the created—then alone fear ceases. There is not another to make us afraid. There is nothing but myself. What can frighten me? This is to be heard day after day. Get rid of all other thoughts. Everything else must be thrown aside, and this is to be repeated continually, poured through the ears until it reaches the heart, until every nerve and muscle, every drop of blood, tingles with the idea that I am He, I am He.

Before you begin to practice, clear your mind of all doubts. Fight and reason and argue, and when you have established it in your mind that this and this alone can be the truth and nothing else, do not argue any more. Close your mouth. Hear not argumentation, nor argue yourself. What is the use of any more arguments? You have satisfied yourself. You have decided the question. What remains? The truth has now to be realized. Therefore, why waste valuable time in vain arguments? The truth has now to be meditated upon, and every idea that strengthens you must be taken up, and every thought that weakens you must be rejected. The bhakta [devotee] meditates upon forms and images and all such things and upon God. This is the natural process, but a slower one. The yogi meditates upon various centers in his body and manipulates powers in his mind. The jnani says, "The mind does not exist, nor the body." This idea of the body and of the mind must go, must be driven off. Therefore it is foolish to think of them. It would be like trying to cure one ailment by bringing in another. His meditation therefore is the most difficult one, the negative. He denies everything, and what is left is the Self. This is the most analytical way. The jnani wants to tear away the universe from the Self by the sheer force of analysis. It is very easy to say, "I am a jnani," but very hard to really be one. "The way is long." It is, as it were, like walking on the sharp edge of a razor. Yet despair not. "Awake, arise, and stop not until the goal is reached," say the Vedas.[4]

So what is the meditation of the jnani? He wants to rise above every idea of body or mind, to drive away the idea that he is the body. For instance, when I say, "I, Swami," immediately the idea of the body comes. What must I do then? I must give the mind a hard blow and say: "No, I am not the body. I am the Self." Who cares if disease comes or death in the most horrible form? I am not the body. Why make the body nice? To enjoy the illusion once more? To continue the slavery? Let it go. I am not the body. That is the way of the jnani. The bhakta says, "The Lord has given me this body that I may safely cross the ocean of life, and I must cherish it until the journey is accomplished." The yogi says, "I must be careful of the body, so that I may go on steadily and finally attain liberation." The jnani feels that he cannot wait. He must reach the goal this very moment. He says: "I am free through eternity. I am never bound. I am the God of the universe through all eternity. Who shall make me perfect? I am perfect already." The jnani seeks to tear himself away from this bondage of matter by the force of intellectual conviction. This is the negative way—the *neti, neti*—"not this, not this." (III. 25-28)

REALIZATION AND ITS METHOD

Infinite manifestation dividing itself in portions still remains infinite, and each portion is infinite.[5]

Brahman is the same though appearing in two forms—changeable and unchangeable, expressed and unexpressed. Know that the knower and the known are one. The trinity—the knower, the known, and the knowing—is manifesting as this universe. The God that the yogi sees in meditation, he sees through the power of his own Self.

What we call nature, fate, is simply God's will.

As long as enjoyment is sought, bondage remains. Only the imperfect being can enjoy, because enjoyment is the fulfilling of desire. The human soul enjoys nature. The underlying reality of nature, soul, and God is Brahman, but Brahman is unseen until we bring It out. It may be brought out by *pramantha*, or friction, just as we can produce fire by friction. The body is the lower piece of wood, Om is the pointed piece, and meditation is the friction. Through friction, that is to say, meditation, that light which is the knowledge of Brahman will burst forth in the soul. Seek it through tapas. Holding the body upright, sacrifice the organs of sense in the mind. The sense centers are within, and their organs without. So drive them into the mind and through dharana, concentration, fix the mind in dhyana, meditation.[6] Brahman permeates the universe, as butter permeates milk; but friction makes it manifest in one place. As churning brings out the butter in the milk, so dhyana brings the realization of Brahman in the soul.

Brahman is without action. Atman is Brahman, and we are Atman—knowledge like this takes away all error. This must be heard, apprehended intellectually, and finally realized. Reflection is applying reason and establishing this knowledge in ourselves by reason. Realizing is making it a part of our lives by constant thinking of it. This constant thought, dhyana, is like the unbroken flow of oil as it is poured from vessel to vessel. Dhyana holds the mind in this thought day and night and so helps us to attain liberation. Think always "Soham, Soham" [I am He, I am He]. This is almost as good as liberation. Say it day and night. Realization will come as the result of this continuous cogitation. (VII. 35-38)

PRACTICAL VEDANTA—I

I will ask you to understand that Vedanta, though it is intensely practical, is always so in the sense of the ideal. It does not preach an impossible ideal, however high it be, and it is high enough for an ideal. In one word, this ideal is that you are divine. "Thou art That." This is the essence of Vedanta. After all its ramifications and intellectual gymnastics, you know the human soul to be pure and omniscient. You see that such superstitions as birth and death would be entire nonsense when spoken of in connection with the soul. The soul was never born and will never die, and all these ideas that we are going to die and are afraid to die are mere superstitions. And all such ideas as that we can do this or cannot do that are superstitions. We can do everything.

Vedanta teaches men to have faith in themselves first. As certain religions of the world say that a man who does not believe in a Personal God outside of himself is an atheist, so Vedanta says that a man who does not believe in himself is an atheist. Not believing in the glory of our own soul is what Vedanta calls atheism. To many this is, no doubt, a terrible idea; and most of us think that this ideal can never be reached. But Vedanta insists that it can be realized by everyone. One may be either man or woman or child; one may belong to any race—nothing will stand as a bar to the realization of this ideal, because, as Vedanta shows, it is realized already; it is already there.

Vedanta recognizes no sin. It recognizes only error. And the greatest error, says Vedanta, is to think that you are weak, that you are a sinner, a miserable creature, and that you have no power and you cannot do this and that. Every time you think in that way, you rivet, as it were, one more link in the chain that binds you down. You add one more layer of hypnotism on to your own soul. Therefore, whosoever thinks he is weak is wrong; whosoever thinks he is impure is wrong and is throwing a bad thought into the world.

We must always bear in mind that in Vedanta there is no attempt at reconciling the present life—the hypnotized life, this false life which we have assumed—with the ideal. But this false life must go, and the real life, which is always existing, must manifest itself, must shine out. No man becomes purer and purer. It is a matter of greater manifestation. The veil drops away, and the native purity of the soul begins to manifest itself. Everything is ours already—infinite purity, freedom, love, and power.

The central ideal of Vedanta is oneness. We must not look down with contempt on others. All of us are going toward the same goal. The difference between weakness and strength is one of degree. The difference between virtue and vice is one of degree. The difference between heaven and hell is one of degree. The difference between life and death is one of degree. All differences in this world are of degree and not of kind, because oneness is the secret of everything. All is One, which manifests Itself either as thought or life or soul or body, and the difference is only in degree. As such, we have no right to look down with contempt upon those who are not developed exactly in the same degree as we are. Condemn none. If you can stretch out a helping hand, do so. If you cannot, fold your hands, bless your brothers, and let them go their own way. Dragging down and condemning is not the way to work. Never is work accomplished in that way. We spend our energies in condemning others. Criticism and condemnation are a vain way of spending our energies, for in the long run we come to learn that all are seeing the same thing, are more or less approaching the same ideal, and that most of our differences are merely differences of expression.

There may be weakness, says Vedanta, but never mind; we want to grow. The remedy for weakness is not brooding over weakness, but thinking of strength. Teach men of the strength that is already within them. Never say no; never say, "I cannot"; for you are infinite. Even time and space are as nothing compared with your nature. You can do anything and everything. You are almighty.

"This Atman is first to be heard of." Hear day and night that you are that Soul. Repeat it to yourselves day and night till it enters into your very veins, till it tingles in every drop of blood, till it is in your flesh and bone. Let the whole body be full of that one ideal: "I am the birthless, the deathless, the blissful, the omniscient, the omnipotent, ever-glorious Soul." Think of it day and night. Think of it till it becomes part and parcel of your life. Meditate upon it, and out of that will come work. "Out of the fullness of the heart the mouth speaketh," and out of the fullness of the heart the hand worketh also. Action will come. Fill yourselves with the ideal. Whatever you do, think well on it. All your actions will be magnified, transformed, deified, by the very power of this thought.

Tell it to men who are weak, and persist in telling it: "You are the Pure One. Awake and arise, O mighty one! This sleep does not become you. Awake and arise. It does not befit you. Think not that you are weak and miserable. Almighty one, arise and awake, and manifest your true nature. It is not fitting that you think yourself a sinner. It is not fitting that you think yourself weak." Say that to the world, say it to yourselves, and see what a practical result comes. See how with an electric flash the truth is manifested, how everything is changed. Tell that to mankind and show them their power. Then we shall learn how to apply it in our daily lives.

To be able to use what we call *viveka*, discrimination, to learn how, in every moment of our lives, in every one of our actions, to discriminate between what is right and wrong, true and false, we shall have to know the test of truth, which is purity, oneness. Everything that makes for oneness is truth. Love is truth and hatred is false, because hatred makes for multiplicity. It is hatred that separates man from man; therefore it is wrong and false. It is a disintegrating power. It separates and destroys. (II. 294-97, 299-300, 302-4)

PRACTICAL VEDANTA—II

In various Upanishads we find that this Vedanta philosophy is not the outcome of meditation in the forests only, but that the very best parts of it were thought out and expressed by brains which were busiest in the everyday affairs of life. We cannot conceive of any man busier than an absolute monarch, a man who is ruling over millions of people, and yet some of these rulers were deep thinkers.

Everything goes to show that this philosophy must be very practical. Later on, when we come to the Bhagavad Gita—most of you, perhaps, have read it; it is the best commentary we have on the Vedanta philosophy—curiously enough, the scene is laid on a battlefield, where Krishna teaches this philosophy to Arjuna. And the doctrine that stands out luminously on every page of the Gita is that of intense activity, but in the midst of it, eternal calmness.

This is the secret of work, to attain which is the goal of Vedanta. Inactivity, as we understand it in the sense of *passivity*, certainly cannot be the goal. Were it so, then the walls around us would be the wisest of things. They are inactive. Clods of earth, stumps of trees, would be the greatest sages in the world. They are inactive. Nor does inactivity become activity when it is combined with passion. Real activity, which is the goal of Vedanta, is combined with eternal calmness, the calmness that cannot be ruffled, the balance of mind that is never disturbed, whatever happens. And we all know from our experience in life that that is the best attitude for work.

I have been asked many times how we can work if we do not have the passion which we generally feel for work. I also thought in that way years ago. But as I am growing older, getting more experience, I find it is not true. The less passion there is, the better we work. The calmer we are, the better for us and the more the amount of work we can do. When we let loose our feelings we waste so much energy, shatter our nerves, disturb our minds, and accomplish very little work. The energy that ought to have gone out as work is spent as mere feeling, which counts for nothing. It is only when the mind is very calm and collected that the whole of its energy is spent in doing good work. And if you read the lives of the great workers the world has produced, you will find that they were wonderfully calm men. Nothing, as it were, could throw them off their balance. That is why the man who becomes angry never does a great amount of work, and the man whom nothing can make angry accomplishes so much. The man who gives way to anger or hatred or any other passion cannot work. He only breaks himself to pieces and does nothing practical. It is the calm, forgiving, equable, well-balanced mind that does the greatest amount of work.

Vedanta says that this can be realized not only in the depths of forests or in caves, but by men in all possible conditions of life. We have seen that the people who discovered these truths were neither living in caves or forests nor following the ordinary vocations of life, but were men who, we have every reason to believe, led the busiest of lives, men who had to command armies, to sit on thrones and look to the welfare of millions—and all these in the days of absolute monarchy, and not, as in these days, when a king is to a great extent a mere figurehead. Yet they could find time to think out all these thoughts, to realize them, and to teach them to humanity.

These conceptions of Vedanta must come out, must not remain only in the forest or only in the cave, but they must come out to work at the bar and the bench, in the pulpit, and in the cottage of the poor man, with the fishermen who are catching fish, and with the students who are studying. They call to every man, woman, and child, whatever be their occupation, wherever they may be. And what is there to fear? How can the fishermen and all these carry out the ideals of the Upanishads? The way has been shown. It is infinite; religion is infinite. None can go beyond it. And whatever you do sincerely is good for you. Even the least thing well done brings marvelous results. Therefore let everyone do what little he can. If the fisherman thinks that he is the Spirit, he will be a better fisherman. If the student thinks he is the Spirit, he will be a better student. If the lawyer thinks that he is the Spirit, he will be a better lawyer, and so on. (II. 292-93, 296, III. 245)

ENJOY THROUGH RENUNCIATION

There is evil in the world; give up the world—that is the great teaching, and no doubt, the only teaching. Give up the world. There cannot be two opinions that to understand the truth every one of us has to give up error. There cannot be two opinions that every one of us, in order to have good, must give up evil. There cannot be two opinions that every one of us to have life must give up what is death. And yet, what remains to us if this theory involves giving up the life of the senses, life as we know it? And what else do we mean by *life*? If we give this up, what remains?

We shall understand this better when, later on, we come to the more philosophical portions of Vedanta. But for the present I beg to state that in Vedanta alone we find a rational solution to the problem. Here I can only lay before you what Vedanta seeks to teach, and that is the deification of the world.

Vedanta does not, in reality, denounce the world. The ideal of renunciation nowhere attains such a height as in the teachings of Vedanta. But at the same time, dry suicidal advice is not intended. It really means deification of the world—giving up the world as we think of it, as we know it, as it appears to us, and knowing what it really is. Deify it. It is God alone.

We read at the commencement of one of the oldest of the Upanishads, "Whatever exists in this universe is to be covered with the Lord." We have to cover everything with the Lord Himself, not by a false sort of optimism, not by blinding our eyes to the evil, but by really seeing God in everything. Thus we have to give up the world. And when the world is given up, what remains? God. What is meant? You can have your wife. It does not mean that you are to abandon her, but that you are to see God in the wife. Give up your children—what does that mean? To turn them out of doors, as some human brutes do in every country? Certainly not. That is diabolism. It is not religion. But see God in your children. So in everything. In life and in death, in happiness and in misery, the Lord is equally present. The whole world is full of the Lord. Open your eyes and see Him.

This is what Vedanta teaches. Give up the world which you have conjectured, because your conjecture was based upon a very partial experience, upon very poor reasoning, and upon your own weakness. Give it up. The world we have been thinking of so long, the world we have been clinging to so long, is a false world of our own creation. Give that up. Open your eyes and see that, as such, it never existed. It was a dream, maya. What existed was the Lord Himself. It is He who is in the child, in the wife, and in the husband. It is He who is in the good and in the bad. He is in the sin and in the sinner. He is in life and in death.

A tremendous assertion indeed! Yet that is the theme Vedanta wants to demonstrate, to teach, and to preach.

Who enjoys the picture—the seller or the seer? The seller is busy with his accounts, computing what his gain will be, how much profit he will realize on the picture. His brain is full of that. He is looking at the hammer and watching the bids. He is intent on hearing how fast the bids are rising. That man is enjoying the picture who has gone there without any intention of buying or selling. He looks at the picture and enjoys it. So this whole universe is a picture. When these desires have vanished, men will enjoy the world, and then this buying and selling and these foolish ideas of possession will be ended. The moneylender gone, the buyer gone, the seller gone, this world remains a picture, a beautiful painting.

I never read of any more beautiful conception of God than the following: "He is the Great Poet, the Ancient Poet. The whole universe is His poem, coming in verses and rhymes and rhythms, written in infinite bliss." When we have given up desires, then alone shall we be able to read and enjoy this universe of God. Then everything will become deified. Nooks and corners, byways and shady places, that we thought dark and unholy, will all be deified. They will all reveal their true nature, and we shall smile at ourselves and think that all this weeping and crying has been but child's play, and we were only standing by, watching.

So do your work, says Vedanta. It first advises us how to work: by giving up—giving up the apparent, illusive world. What is meant by that? Seeing God everywhere. Thus do you work. Desire to live a hundred years. Have all earthly desires if you wish, only deify them, convert them into heaven. Have the desire to live a long life of helpfulness, of blissfulness and activity, on this earth. Thus working, you will find the way out. There is no other way. (II. 145-47, 149-50)

GOD SPEAKS THROUGH THE HEART

It is one of the evils of your Western civilization that you are after intellectual education alone, and take no care of the heart. It only makes men ten times more selfish, and that will be your destruction. When there is a conflict between the heart and the brain, let the heart be followed, because intellect has only one state, reason, and within that, intellect works and cannot get beyond. It is the heart that takes one to the highest plane, which intellect can never reach. It goes beyond intellect and reaches what is called inspiration. The intellect can never become inspired. Only the heart, when it is enlightened, becomes inspired. An intellectual, heartless man never becomes an inspired man. It is always the heart that speaks in the man of love. It discovers a greater instrument than intellect can give you—the instrument of inspiration. Just as the intellect is the instrument of knowledge, so the heart is the instrument of inspiration. In a lower state it is a much weaker instrument than the intellect. An ignorant man knows nothing, but he is a little emotional by nature. Compare him with a great professor —what wonderful power the latter possesses! But the professor is bound by his intellect, and he can be a devil and an intellectual man at the same time. The man of heart can never be a devil. No man with emotion was ever a devil. Properly cultivated, the heart can be changed and will go beyond intellect; it will function through inspiration. Man will have to go beyond intellect in the end. The knowledge of man, his powers of perception, of reasoning and intellect and heart, all are busy churning this milk of the world. Out of long churning comes butter, and this butter is God. Men of heart get the butter, and the buttermilk is left for the intellectual.

These are all preparations for the heart—for that love, for that intense sympathy appertaining to the heart. It is not at all necessary to be educated or learned to get to God. A sage once told me: "To kill others one must be equipped with swords and shields, but to commit suicide a needle is sufficient. So to teach others, much intellect and learning are necessary, but not so for your own self-illumination." Are you pure? If you are pure you will reach God. "Blessed are the pure in heart, for they shall see God." If you are not pure, and you know all the sciences in the world, that will not help you at all. You may be buried in all the books you read, but that will not be of much use. It is the heart that reaches the goal. Follow the heart. A pure heart sees beyond the intellect. It gets inspired. It knows things that reason can never know. Whenever there is conflict between the pure heart and the intellect, always side with the pure heart, even if you think what your heart is doing is unreasonable. When it is desirous of doing good to others, your brain may tell you that it is not politic to do so, but follow your heart and you will find that you make fewer mistakes than by following your intellect. The pure heart is the best mirror for the reflection of truth, so all these disciplines are for the purification of the heart. And as soon as it is pure, all truths flash upon it in a minute. All truth in the universe will manifest in your heart if you are sufficiently pure.

Through the intellect is not the way to solve the problem of misery, but through the heart. If all this vast amount of effort had been spent in making men purer, gentler, more forbearing, this world would have a thousandfold more happiness than it has today. Always cultivate the heart. Through the heart the Lord speaks, and through the intellect you yourself speak. (I. 412-15)

HOW TO OVERCOME WEAKNESS

This is the one question I put to every man, woman, or child when they are in physical, mental, or spiritual training: "Are you strong? Do you feel strength?"—for I know it is Truth alone that gives strength. I know that Truth alone gives life, and nothing but going toward Reality will make us strong, and none will reach Truth until he is strong. Every system, therefore, that weakens the mind makes one superstitious, makes one mope, makes one desire all sorts of wild impossibilities, mysteries, and superstitions, I do not like, because its effect is dangerous. Such systems never bring any good. Such things create morbidity in the mind, make it weak—so weak that in course of time, it will be almost impossible to receive Truth or live up to It.

Strength, therefore, is the one thing needful. Strength is the medicine for the world's disease. Strength is the medicine the poor must have when tyrannized over by the rich. Strength is the medicine the ignorant must have when oppressed by the learned, and it is the medicine sinners must have when tyrannized over by other sinners. And nothing gives such strength as this idea of monism. Nothing makes us so moral as this idea of monism. Nothing makes us work so well, at our best and highest, as when all the responsibility is thrown upon ourselves. If the whole responsibility is thrown upon our own shoulders, we shall be at our highest and best. When we have nobody to grope toward, no devil to lay our blame upon, no Personal God to carry our burdens, when we alone are responsible, then we shall rise to our highest and best. "I am responsible for my fate. I am the bringer of good unto myself. I am the bringer of evil. I am the Pure and Blessed One." We must reject all thoughts that assert the contrary. "I have neither death nor fear; I have neither caste nor creed; I have neither father nor mother nor brother, neither friend nor foe—for I am Existence, Knowledge, and Bliss Absolute. I am the Blissful One, I am the Blissful One. I am not bound either by virtue or by vice, by happiness or by misery. Pilgrimages and books and ceremonials can never bind me. I have neither hunger nor thirst. The body is not mine, nor am I subject to the superstitions and decay that come to the body. I am Existence, Knowledge, and Bliss Absolute. I am the Blissful One, I am the Blissful One."

This, says Vedanta, is the only prayer that we should have. This is the only way to reach the goal—to tell ourselves and to tell everybody else that we are divine. And as we go on repeating this, strength comes. He who falters at first will get stronger and stronger, and the voice will increase in volume until Truth takes possession of our hearts and courses through our veins and permeates our bodies. Delusion will vanish as the light becomes more and more effulgent, load after load of ignorance will vanish, and then will come a time when all else has disappeared and the Sun alone shines. (II. 201-2)

THE OPEN SECRET

None can die. None can be degraded forever. Life is but a playground, however gross the play may be. However we may receive blows and however knocked about we may be, the Soul is there and is never injured. We are that Infinite.

Thus sang a Vedantist: "I never had fear or doubt. Death never came to me. I never had a father or mother, for I was never born. Where are my foes?—for I am All. I am Existence, Knowledge, Bliss Absolute. I am It. I am It. Anger and lust and jealousy, evil thoughts and all these things, never came to me, for I am Existence, Knowledge, Bliss Absolute. I am It. I am It."[7]

That is the remedy for all disease, the nectar that cures death. Here we are in this world, and our nature rebels against it. But let us repeat: "I am It. I am It. I have no fear or doubt or death. I have no sex or creed or color. What creed can I have? What sect is there to which I should belong? What sect can hold me? I am in every sect."

However much the body rebels, however much the mind rebels, in the midst of uttermost darkness, in the midst of agonizing tortures, in uttermost despair, repeat this once, twice, thrice, evermore. Light comes gently, slowly, but surely it comes.

Many times I have been in the jaws of death, starving, footsore, and weary. For days and days I had no food, and often could walk no farther. I would sink down under a tree, and life would seem to be ebbing away. I could not speak. I could scarcely think. But at last the mind reverted to the idea: "I have no fear or death. I never hunger or thirst. I am It! I am It! The whole of nature cannot crush me—it is my servant. Assert thy strength, thou Lord of lords and God of gods! Regain thy lost empire! Arise and walk and stop not!" And I would rise up, reinvigorated, and here am I, living, today. Thus, whenever darkness comes, assert the reality and everything adverse must vanish. For, after all, it is but a dream. Mountain high though the difficulties appear, terrible and gloomy though all things seem, they are but maya. Fear not—it is banished. Crush it and it vanishes. Stamp upon it and it dies. Be not afraid. Think not how many times you fail. Never mind—time is infinite. Go forward. Assert yourself again and again, and light must come.

You may pray to everyone that was ever born, but who will come to help you? And what of the way of death from which none knows escape? "Help thyself by thyself. None else can help thee, friend. For thou alone art thy greatest enemy; thou alone art thy greatest friend."[8] Get hold of the Self, then. Stand up. Don't be afraid. In the midst of all miseries and all weakness let the Self come out, faint and imperceptible though it be at first. You will gain courage, and at last like a lion you will roar out: "I am It! I am It! I am neither a man nor a woman nor a god nor a demon, no, nor any of the animals, plants, or trees. I am neither poor nor rich, neither learned nor ignorant. All these things are very little compared with what I am, for I am It! I am It! Behold the sun and the moon and the stars. I am the light that is shining in them! I am the beauty of the fire! I am the power in the universe! For I am It! I am It!

"My real pleasure was never in earthly things—in husband, wife, children, and other things. For I am like the infinite blue sky: Clouds of many colors pass over it and play for a second;

they move off, and there is the same unchangeable blue. Happiness and misery, good and evil, may envelop me for a moment, veiling the Self, but I am still there. They pass away because they are changeable. I shine because I am unchangeable. If misery comes, I know it is finite; therefore it must die. If evil comes, I know it is finite. It must go. I alone am infinite and untouched by anything. For I am the Infinite, that eternal, changeless Self."—So sings one of our poets.[9]

Let us drink of this cup—this cup that leads to everything that is immortal, everything that is unchangeable. Fear not. Believe not that we are evil, that we are finite, that we can ever die. It is not true.

"This is to be heard of, then to be thought about, and then to be meditated upon."[10] When the hands work, the mind should repeat, "I am It. I am It." Think of it, dream of it, until it becomes the bone of your bones and the flesh of your flesh, until all the hideous dreams of littleness, of weakness, of misery, and of evil have entirely vanished, and no more then can the Truth be hidden from you, even for a moment. (II. 402-5)

Notes

1 Bhagavad Gita, 6.38.

2 Bhagavad Gita, 6.40.

3 Chandogya Upanishad, 7.24.1.

4 Katha Upanishad, 1.3.14.

5 Infinity is one, without a second, ever indivisible, and unmanifested. By "infinite manifestation" the Swami means the universe, both visible and invisible. Although it is made up of countless forms that are limited by their very nature, still as a whole it is always infinite; nay, even a portion of it is infinite, as each such portion is inseparably united with it.

6 When the thought current is interrupted, it is called *concentration*; when the flow is uninterrupted, it is called *meditation*.

7 Shankara, "Nirvanashatkam," adapted.

8 Bhagavad Gita, 6.5.

9 Dattatreya Avadhuta in the Avadhuta Gita.

10 Brihadaranyaka Upanishad, 4.5.6.

XI

THE GOAL OF VEDANTA

Swami Vivekananda in San Francisco, 1900

IS HEAVEN THE GOAL?

We have seen that the oldest idea in the *Samhita* portion of the Vedas was only about heaven, where people had bright bodies and lived with the fathers. Gradually other ideas came, but they were not satisfying. There was still need for something higher. Living in heaven would not be very different from life in this world. At best it would only be a very healthy rich-man's life, with plenty of sense enjoyments and a sound body which knows no disease. It would be this material world, only a little more refined. And we have seen the difficulty: The external, material world can never solve the problem. So also no heaven can solve it. If this world cannot solve the problem, no multiplication of this world can do so, because, we must always remember, matter is only an infinitesimal part of the phenomena of nature.

The vast part of the phenomena we actually see is not matter. For instance, in every moment of our lives, what a great part is played by thought and feeling, compared with the material phenomena outside! How vast is this internal world with its tremendous activity! The sense phenomena are very small compared with it. The heaven solution commits this mistake: It insists that the whole of phenomena is only in touch, taste, sight, etc. So this idea of heaven did not give full satisfaction to all.

The sages realized Him through the power of introspection and got beyond both joy and misery, beyond what we call virtue and vice, beyond good and bad deeds, beyond being and nonbeing. He who has seen Him has seen the Reality. But what then about heaven? Heaven is the idea of happiness minus unhappiness. That is to say, what we want is the joys of this life minus its sorrows. This is a very good idea, no doubt—it comes naturally—but it is a mistake throughout, because there is no such thing as absolute good, nor [is there] any such thing as absolute evil. You have all heard of that rich man in Rome who learned one day that he had only about a million pounds of his property left. He said, "What shall I do tomorrow?" and forthwith committed suicide. A million pounds was poverty to him.

What is joy and what is sorrow? They are vanishing entities, continually vanishing. When I was a child I thought if I could be a cabman it would be the very acme of happiness for me to drive about. I do not think so now. To what joy will you cling? This is the one point we must all try to understand, and it is one of the last superstitions to leave us. Everyone's idea of pleasure is different. I have seen a man who is not happy unless he swallows a lump of opium every day. He may dream of a heaven where the land is made of opium. That would be a very bad heaven for me. Again and again in Arabian poetry we read of a heaven with beautiful gardens through which rivers run. I lived much of my life in a country where there is too much water. Many villages are flooded and thousands of lives are sacrificed every year. So my heaven would not have gardens through which rivers flow. I would have a land where very little rain falls. Our pleasures are always changing. If a young man dreams of heaven, he dreams of a heaven where he will have a beautiful wife. When that same man becomes old he does not want a wife. Our necessities make our heaven, and the heaven changes with the change of our necessities. If we had a heaven like the one desired by those to whom sense enjoyment is the very end of existence, then we would not progress. That would be the most terrible curse we could pronounce on the soul.

Is this all we can come to—a little weeping and dancing, and then to die like a dog? What a curse you pronounce on the head of humanity when you long for these things! That is what you do when you cry after the joys of this world, for you do not know what true joy is. What philosophy insists on is, not to give up joys, but to know what joy really is. The old Norwegian heaven was a tremendous fighting place where all sat before Odin. They had a wild boar hunt, and then they went to war and slashed each other to pieces. But in some way or other, after a few hours of such fighting, the wounds all healed up, and they went into a hall where the boar had been roasted, and had a carousal. And then the wild boar took form again, ready to be hunted the next day. That is much the same thing as our heaven—not a whit worse; only our ideas may be a little more refined. We want to hunt wild boars and get to a place where all our enjoyments will continue, just as the Norwegian imagined that the wild boar was hunted and eaten every day and recovered the next day.

Now, philosophy insists that there is a joy which is absolute, which never changes. That joy cannot be the joys and pleasures we have in this life, and yet Vedanta shows that everything that is joyful in this life is but a particle of that real joy, because that is the only joy there is. Every moment, really, we are enjoying the Absolute Bliss, though it is covered up, misunderstood, and caricatured. (II. 158-59, 165-67)

THE EXPERIENCE OF COSMIC CONSCIOUSNESS

Disciple: Sir, is there any such statement in the Upanishads that Ishvara [God] is an all-powerful Person? People generally believe in such an Ishvara.

Swami Vivekananda: The highest principle, the Lord of all, cannot be a Person. The *jiva* is an individual and the sum total of all jivas is Ishvara. In the jiva, *avidya*, or nescience, is predominant, but Ishvara controls maya, composed of avidya and *vidya* [knowledge], and independently projects this world of movable and immovable things out of Himself. But Brahman transcends both the individual and collective aspects, the jiva and Ishvara. In Brahman there is no part. It is for the sake of easy comprehension that parts have been imagined in It. That part of Brahman in which there is the superimposition of creation, maintenance, and dissolution of the universe has been spoken of as *Ishvara* in the scriptures, while the other unchangeable portion, with reference to which there is no thought of duality, is indicated as Brahman. But do not, on that account, think that Brahman is a distinct and separate substance from the jivas and the universe. The Qualified Monists hold that it is Brahman that has transformed Itself into the jivas and the universe. The Advaitists, on the contrary, maintain that the jivas and the universe have been merely superimposed on Brahman. But in reality there has been no modification in Brahman. The Advaitist says that the universe consists only of name and form. It endures only so long as there are name and form. When, through meditation and other practices, name and form are dissolved, then only the transcendent Brahman remains. Then the separate reality of the jivas and the universe is felt no longer. Then it is realized that that One is the eternal, pure Essence of Intelligence, or Brahman. The real nature of the jiva is Brahman. When the veil of name and form vanishes through meditation, etc., then that idea is simply realized. This is the substance of pure Advaita. The Vedas, the Vedanta, and all other scriptures only explain this idea in different ways.

Disciple: How then is it true that Ishvara is an almighty Person?

Swamiji: Man is man in so far as he is qualified by the limiting adjunct of mind. Through the mind he has to understand and grasp everything, and therefore whatever he thinks must be limited by the mind. Hence, it is the natural tendency of man to imagine the personality of Ishvara [God] based on his own personality. Man can only think of his ideal as a human being. When, buffeted by sorrows in this world of disease and death, he is driven to desperation and helplessness, then he seeks refuge with someone, [with] whom he may feel safe. But where is that refuge to be found? The omnipresent Atman, which depends on nothing else to support it, is the only Refuge. At first man does not find that. When discrimination and dispassion arise, in the course of meditation and spiritual practices, he comes to know it. In whatever way he may progress on the path of spirituality, he is unconsciously awakening Brahman within himself. But the means may be different in different cases. Those who have faith in the Personal God have to undergo spiritual practices holding on to that idea. If there is sincerity, through that will come the awakening of the lion of Brahman within. The knowledge of Brahman is the one goal of all beings, but the various ideas are the various paths to it. Although the real nature of the jiva is Brahman, still, as he has identification with the qualifying adjunct of the mind, he suffers from all sorts of doubts and difficulties, pleasure and pain. But everyone from Brahma [the creator] down to a blade of grass is advancing toward the realization of his real nature. And none can escape the round of births and deaths until he realizes his identity with Brahman. When a person attains these three—a human birth, a strong desire for liberation, and the grace of an illumined soul—then his longing for Self-knowledge becomes intensified. Otherwise the minds of men, given to lust and greed, never incline that way. How could the desire to know Brahman arise in one who has the hankering in his mind for the pleasures of family life, for wealth, and for fame? He, who is prepared to renounce all, who amid the strong current of the duality of good and evil, happiness and misery, is calm, steady, balanced, and awake to his ideal, alone endeavors to attain Self-knowledge. He alone, by the might of his own power, tears asunder the net of the world. "Breaking the barriers of maya, he emerges like a mighty lion."

Disciple: Well then, is it true that without *sannyasa* [renunciation] there can be no knowledge of Brahman?

Swamiji: That is true, a thousand times. Without dispassion for the world, without renunciation, without giving up the desire for enjoyment, absolutely nothing can be accomplished in spiritual life. "It is not like a sweetmeat in the hands of a child which you can snatch by a trick."

Disciple: But, sir, in the course of spiritual practices that renunciation may come.

Swamiji: Let those to whom it will come gradually have it in that way. But why should you sit and wait for that? At once begin to dig the channel that will bring the waters of spirituality to your life. Sri Ramakrishna used to deprecate lukewarmness in spiritual attainments as, for instance, saying that religion would come gradually, and that there was no hurry for it. When one is thirsty, can one sit idle? Does he not run about for water? Because your thirst for spirituality has not come, you are sitting idly. The desire for knowledge has not grown strong. Therefore you are satisfied with the little pleasures of family life.

Disciple: Really I do not understand why I don't get that idea of renouncing everything. Do make some way for that, please.

Swamiji: The end and the means are all in your hands. I can only stimulate them. You have read so many scriptures and are serving and associating with such *sadhus* [monks] who have known Brahman; if even this does not bring the idea of renunciation, then your life is in vain. But it will not be altogether in vain. The effects of this will manifest some way or other in time.

The disciple was much dejected and again said to Swamiji: Sir, I have come under your refuge. Do open the path of *mukti* [liberation] for me—that I may realize the Truth in this body.

Swamiji: What fear is there? Always discriminate—your body, your house, these jivas, and the world are all absolutely unreal like a dream. Always think that this body is only an inert instrument. And the self-contained *Purusha* [Self] within is your real nature. The adjunct of mind is His first subtle covering. Then there is this body, which is His gross, outer covering. The indivisible, changeless, self-effulgent Purusha is lying hidden under these delusive veils. Therefore your real nature is unknown to you. The direction of the mind, which always runs after the senses, has to be turned within. The mind has to be killed. The body is but gross—it dies and dissolves into the five elements. But the bundle of mental impressions, which is the mind, does not die soon. It remains for some time in seed form and then sprouts and grows in the form of a tree. It takes on another physical body and goes the round of birth and death, until Self-knowledge arises. Therefore I say, by meditation and concentration and by the power of philosophical discrimination, plunge this mind in the Ocean of Existence-Knowledge-Bliss Absolute. When the mind dies, all limiting adjuncts vanish and you are established in Brahman.

Disciple: Sir, it is so difficult to direct this uncontrollable mind toward Brahman.

Swamiji: Is there anything difficult for the hero? Only men of faint hearts speak so. "Mukti is easy of attainment only to the hero—but not to cowards." Says the Gita, "By renunciation and by practice is the mind brought under control, O Arjuna." The *chitta*, or mind-stuff, is like a transparent lake, and the waves that rise in it by the impact of sense impressions constitute *manas*, or the mind. Therefore the mind consists of a succession of thought waves. From these mental waves arises desire. Then that desire transforms itself into will and works through its gross instrument, the body. Again, as work is endless, so its fruits also are endless. Hence the mind is always being tossed by myriads of waves—the fruits of work. This mind has to be divested of all modifications [*vrittis*] and reconverted into the transparent lake so that there remains not a single wave of modification in it. Then will Brahman manifest Itself. The scriptures give a glimpse of this state in such passages as: "Then all the knots of the heart are cut asunder,"[1] etc. Do you understand?

Disciple: Yes, sir, but meditation must base itself on some object.

Swamiji: You yourself will be the object of your meditation. Think and meditate that you are the omnipresent Atman. "I am neither the body nor the mind nor the *buddhi* [determinative faculty], neither the gross nor the subtle body"[2]—by this process of elimination, immerse your mind in the transcendent knowledge, which is your real nature. Kill the mind by thus plunging it repeatedly in this. Then only you will realize the Essence of Intelligence, or be established in your real nature. Knower and known, meditator and the object meditated upon, will then become one, and the cessation of all phenomenal superimpositions will follow. This is styled in the shastras as the transcendence of the triad of relative knowledge [*triputibheda*]. There is no relative or conditioned knowledge in this state. When the Atman is the only knower, by what means can you possibly know It? The Atman is Knowledge, the Atman is Intelligence, the Atman is *Satchidananda*. It is through the inscrutable power of maya, which cannot be indicated as either existent or nonexistent, that the relative consciousness has come upon the jiva, who is none other than Brahman. This is generally known as the conscious state. And the state in which this duality of relative existence becomes one in the pure Brahman is called in the scriptures the superconscious state, and described in such words as, "It is like an ocean perfectly at rest and without a name."[3]

Swamiji spoke these words as if from the profound depths of his realization of Brahman.

Swamiji: All philosophy and scriptures have come from the plane of relative knowledge of subject and object. But no thought or language of the human mind can fully express the Reality, which lies beyond the plane of relative knowledge. Science, philosophy, etc., are only partial truths. So they can never be adequate channels of expression for the transcendent Reality. Hence, viewed from the transcendent standpoint, everything appears to be unreal—religious creeds and works, I and thou and the universe—everything is unreal! Then only it is perceived: I am the only reality. I am the all-pervading Atman, and I am the proof of my own existence. Where is the room for a separate proof to establish the reality of my existence? I am, as the scriptures say, "Always known to myself as the eternal subject."[4] I have seen that state, realized it. You also see and realize it and preach this truth of Brahman to all. Then only will you attain peace.

While speaking these words Swamiji's face wore a serious expression and he was lost in thought. After some time he continued: Realize in your own life this knowledge of Brahman, which harmonizes all theories and is the rationale of all truths, and preach it to the world. This will conduce to your own good and the good of others as well. I have told you today the essence of all truths. There is nothing higher than this.

Disciple: Sir, now you are speaking of jnana, but sometimes you proclaim the superiority of bhakti, sometimes of karma, and sometimes of yoga. This confuses our understanding.

Swamiji: Well, the truth is this: The knowledge of Brahman is the ultimate goal—the highest destiny of man. But man cannot remain absorbed in Brahman all the time. When he comes out of It, he must have something to engage himself. At that time he should do such work as will contribute to the real well-being of people. Therefore do I urge you in the service of the jivas in a spirit of oneness. But, my son, such are the intricacies of work that even great saints are caught in them and become attached. Therefore work has to be done without any desire for results. This is the teaching of the Gita. But know that in the knowledge of Brahman there is no touch of any relation to work. Good works, at the most, purify the mind. Therefore has the commentator Shankara so sharply criticized the doctrine of the combination of jnana and karma. Some attain to the knowledge of Brahman by means of unselfish work. This is also a means, but the end is the realization of Brahman. Know this thoroughly that the goal of the path of discrimination and of all other modes of practice is the realization of Brahman.

Disciple: Now, sir, please tell me about the utility of raja yoga and bhakti yoga.

Swamiji: Striving in these paths also, some attain the realization of Brahman. The path of bhakti, or devotion to God, is a slow process, but is easy to practice. In the path of yoga there are many obstacles. Perhaps the mind runs after psychic powers and thus draws you away from attaining your real nature. Only the path of jnana is of quick fruition and the rationale of all other creeds. Hence it is equally esteemed in all countries and all ages. But even in the path of discrimination there is the chance that the mind will get stuck in the interminable net of vain argumentation. Therefore, along with it, meditation should be practiced. By means of discrimination and meditation, the goal, or Brahman, has to be reached. One is sure to reach the goal by practicing in this way. This, in my opinion, is the easy path, ensuring quick success.

Disciple: Now please tell me something about the doctrine of the Incarnation of God.

Swamiji: You want to master everything in a day, it seems!

Disciple: Sir, if the doubts and difficulties of the mind be solved in one day, then I shall not have to trouble you time and again.

Swamiji: Those by whose grace the knowledge of the Atman, which is extolled so much in the scriptures, is attained in a minute are the moving *tirthas* [holy places]—the Incarnations. From their very birth they are knowers of Brahman, and between Brahman and the knower of Brahman there is not the least difference. "He who knows Brahman becomes Brahman."[5] The Atman cannot be known by the mind, for it is itself the Knower—this I have already said. Therefore man's relative knowledge reaches up to the *avataras*—those who are always established in the Atman. The highest ideal of Ishvara that the human mind can grasp is the avatara. Beyond this there is no relative knowledge. Such knowers of Brahman are rarely born in the world. And very few people can understand them. They alone are the proof of the truths of the scriptures—the towers of light in the ocean of the world. Through the company of such avataras and by their grace, the darkness of the mind disappears in a trice and realization flashes immediately in the heart. Why or by what process it comes cannot be ascertained. But it does come. I have seen it happen like that. Sri Krishna spoke the Gita, establishing Himself in the Atman. Those passages of the Gita where He speaks with the word "I," invariably indicate the Atman: "Take refuge in Me alone" means, "Be established in the Atman." This knowledge of the Atman is the highest aim of the Gita. The references to yoga, etc., are but incidental to this realization of the Atman. Those who have not this knowledge of the Atman are "suicides." "They kill themselves by the clinging to the unreal."[6] They lose their life in the noose of sense pleasures. You are also men, and can't you ignore this trash of sensual enjoyment that won't last for two days? Should you also swell the ranks of those who are born and die in utter ignorance? Accept the *beneficial* and discard the *pleasant*. Speak of this Atman to all, even to the lowest. By continued speaking, your own intelligence also will clear up. And always repeat the great mantras—"Thou art That," "I am That," "All this is verily Brahman"—and have the courage of a lion in the heart. What is there to fear? Fear is death—fear is the greatest sin.

Disciple: Sir, can a man do work even after realization?

Swamiji: After realization, what is ordinarily called work does not persist. It changes its character. The work the jnani does only conduces to the well-being of the world. Whatever a man of realization says or does contributes to the welfare of all. (VII. 191-200)

THE MYSTERY OF BIRTH AND DEATH

The Atman never comes nor goes, is never born nor dies. It is nature that moves before the Atman, and the reflection of this motion is on the Atman, and the Atman ignorantly thinks *it* is moving and not nature. When the Atman thinks that, it is in bondage, but when it comes to find it never moves, that it is omnipresent, then freedom comes. The Atman in bondage is called *jiva*. Thus you see that when it is said that the Atman comes and goes, it is said only for facility of understanding, just as for convenience in studying astronomy you are asked to suppose that the sun moves round the earth, though such is not the case. So the jiva, the soul, comes to higher or lower states. This is the well-known law of reincarnation, and this law binds all creation.

People in this country [America] think it too horrible that man should come up from an animal. Why? What will be the end of these millions of animals? Are they nothing? If we have a soul, so have they, and if they have none, neither have we. It is absurd to say that man alone has a soul and the animals none. I have seen men worse than animals.

The human soul has sojourned in lower and higher forms, migrating from one to another, according to the *samskaras*, or impressions. But it is only in the highest form, as man, that it attains freedom.

This going from birth to death, this traveling, is what is called *samsara* in Sanskrit—literally, the round of birth and death. All creation, passing through this round, will sooner or later become free.

Every form, let us say, beginning from the little worm and ending in man, is like one of the cars of the Ferris wheel. The car is in motion all the time, but the occupants change. A man goes into a car, moves with the wheel, and comes out. The wheel goes on and on. A soul enters one form, resides in it for a time, then leaves it and goes into another and quits that again for a third. Thus the round goes on till it comes out of the wheel and becomes free.

What then becomes of all this threefold eschatology of the dualist, that when a man dies he goes to heaven or goes to this or that sphere, and that the wicked persons become ghosts and become animals, and so forth? None comes and none goes, says the nondualist. How can you come and go? You are infinite. Where is the place for you to go?

In a certain school a number of little children were being examined. The examiner had foolishly put all sorts of difficult questions to the little children. Among others there was this question: "Why does the earth not fall?" His intention was to bring out the idea of gravitation or some other intricate scientific truth from these children. Most of them could not even understand the question, and so they gave all sorts of wrong answers. But one bright little girl answered it with another question: "Where shall it fall?" The very question of the examiner was nonsense on the face of it. There is no up and down in the universe—the idea is only relative. So it is with regard to the soul. The very question of birth and death in regard to it is utter nonsense. Who goes and who comes? Where are you not? Where is the heaven that you are not in already? Omnipresent is the Self of man. Where is it to go? Where is it not to go? It is everywhere. So all this childish dream, this puerile illusion of birth and death, of heavens and higher heavens, and of lower worlds, all vanishes immediately for the perfect. For the nearly perfect it vanishes after showing them the several scenes up to Brahmaloka. It continues for the ignorant.

How is it that the whole world believes in going to heaven and in dying and being born? I am studying a book; page after page is being read and turned over. Another page comes and is turned over. Who changes? Who comes and goes? Not I, but the book. This whole nature is a book before the soul. Chapter after chapter is being read and turned over, and every now and then a scene opens. That is read and turned over. A fresh one comes, but the soul is ever the same—eternal. It is nature that is changing, not the soul of man. This never changes. Birth and death are in nature, not in you. Yet the ignorant are deluded. Just as we, under delusion, think that the sun is moving, and not the earth, in exactly the same way we think that *we* are dying, and not nature. These are, therefore, all hallucinations. Just as it is a hallucination when we think that the fields are moving and not the railway train, exactly in the same manner is the hallucination of birth and death. (II. 257-61, 276-78)

REINCARNATION: THE JOURNEY TOWARD THE GOAL

The human being is composed first of this external covering, the body; secondly, of the fine [subtle] body, consisting of mind, intellect, and ego. Behind them is the real soul of man. We have seen that all the powers of the gross body are borrowed from the mind; and the mind, the fine body, borrows its powers and luminosity from the soul standing behind. A great many questions now arise about the nature of the soul. If the existence of the soul is admitted on the basis of the argument that it is self-luminous, that knowledge, existence, and blessedness are its essence, it naturally follows that this soul cannot have been created from nothing. A self-luminous existence, independent of any other existence, could never have nonexistence for its cause. We have seen that even the physical universe cannot have come from nothing, not to speak of the soul. It always existed.

Here comes a very interesting question, that question which is generally known as the reincarnation of the soul. Sometimes people get frightened at the idea; and superstition is so strong that even thinking men believe that they are the outcome of nothing, and then, with the grandest logic, [they] try to deduce the theory that although they have come out of zero, they will be eternal ever afterward. Those that come out of zero will certainly have to go back to zero. Neither you nor I nor anyone present has come out of zero nor will go back to zero. We have been existing eternally, and will exist, and there is no power under the sun, or above the sun, that can undo your or my existence or send us back to zero. Now, this idea of reincarnation is not only not a frightening idea, but most essential for the moral well-being of the human race. It is the only logical conclusion that thoughtful men can arrive at. If you are going to exist in eternity hereafter, it must be that you have existed through eternity in the past; it cannot be otherwise.

I will try to answer a few objections that are generally brought against the theory. The first objection is: Why do we not remember our past? But do we remember all our past in this life? How many of you remember what you did when you were babies? None of you remembers your babyhood; and if upon memory depends your existence, then this argument proves that you did not exist as babies because you do not remember your babyhood. It is simply unmitigated nonsense to say that our existence depends on our remembering it. How can we remember our past life? That brain is gone, broken into pieces, and a new brain has been manufactured. What has come to this brain is the resultant, the sum total, of the impressions acquired in our past; with [these impressions] the mind has come to inhabit the new body. I, as I stand here, am the effect, the result, of all the infinite past that is tacked on to me.

Such is the power of superstition that many of those who deny the doctrine of reincarnation believe that we are descended from monkeys. But they do not have the courage to ask why we do not remember our monkey life! When a great ancient sage, a seer or a prophet of old who came face to face with Truth, says something, these modern men stand up and say, "Oh, he was a fool!" But just use another name—Huxley or Tyndall—then it must be true, and they take it for granted. In place of ancient superstitions they have erected modern superstitions; in place of the old popes of religion they have installed modern popes of science.

So we see that this objection as to memory is not valid; and that is about the only serious objection raised against this theory.

Although we have seen that it is not necessary for the acceptance of this theory that there should be the memory of past lives, yet at the same time we are in a position to assert that there are instances which show that this memory does come, and that each one of us will get back this memory at the time of liberation, when we shall find that this world is but a dream. Then alone will you realize in the soul of your soul that you are but actors and the world is a stage; then alone will the idea of nonattachment come to you with the power of thunder; then all this thirst for enjoyment, this clinging to life and this world, will vanish forever; then the mind will see as clear as daylight how many times all these existed for you—how many millions of times you had fathers and mothers, sons and daughters, husbands and wives, relatives and friends, wealth and power. They came and went. How many times you were on the topmost crest of the wave, and how many times you were down at the bottom of despair! When memory brings all these to you, then alone will you stand as a hero and smile when the world frowns upon you. Then alone will you stand up and say: "I care not even for thee, O Death! What terrors hast thou for me?" This will come to all.

Are there any arguments, any rational proofs, for the reincarnation of the soul? So far we have been giving the negative side, showing that the opposite arguments to disprove it are invalid. Are there any positive proofs? There are—and most valid ones, too. No other theory except that of reincarnation accounts for the wide divergence that we find between man and man in their power to acquire knowledge. First let us consider the process by which knowledge is acquired. Suppose I go into the street and see a dog. How do I know it is a dog? I refer it to my mind, and in my mind are groups of all my past experiences, arranged and pigeonholed, as it were. As soon as a new impression comes, I take it up and refer it to some of the old pigeonholes, and as soon as I find a group of the same impressions already existing, I place it in that group and I am satisfied. I know it is a dog because it coincides with impressions already there. And when I do not find the cognates of a new experience inside, I become dissatisfied. When, not finding the cognates of an impression, we become dissatisfied, this state of mind is called ignorance; but when, finding the cognates of an impression already existing, we become satisfied, this is called knowledge. When one apple fell, men became dissatisfied. Then gradually they found a series of the same impressions, forming, as it were, a chain. What was the chain they found? That all apples fell. They called this gravitation.

Now, we see that without a fund of already existing experiences any new experience would be impossible, for there would be nothing to which to refer the new impression. So if, as some of the European philosophers think, a child came into the world with what they call a *tabula rasa*, such a child would never attain to any degree of intellectual power, because he would have nothing to which to refer his new experiences. We see that the power of acquiring knowledge varies in each individual, and this shows that each one of us has come with his own fund of knowledge. Knowledge can only be got in one way, the way of experience; there is no other way to know. If we have not had the experience in this life, we must have had it in other lives.

How is it that the fear of death is everywhere? A little chicken is just out of the egg and an eagle comes, and the chicken flies in fear to its mother. There is an old explanation (I should hardly dignify it by such a name)—it is called instinct. What makes that little chicken just out of the egg afraid to die? How is it that as soon as a duckling hatched by a hen comes near water, it jumps into it and swims? It never swam before nor saw anything swim. People call it instinct. It is a big word, but it leaves us where we were before.

Let us study this phenomenon of instinct. A child begins to play on the piano. At first she must pay attention to every key she is fingering, and as she goes on and on for months and years, the playing becomes almost involuntary, instinctive. What was first done with conscious will does not require later on an effort of the will. This is not yet a complete proof. One half remains, and that is [the fact] that almost all the actions which are now instinctive can be brought under the control of the will. Each muscle of the body can be brought under control. This is perfectly well known. So the proof is complete, by this double method, that what we now call instinct is the degeneration of voluntary actions. Therefore, if the analogy applies to the whole creation, if all nature is uniform, then what is instinct in lower animals, as well as in men, must be the degeneration of will.

From the study of the macrocosm, we discovered that each evolution presupposes an involution, and each involution an evolution. How is instinct explained in the light of this knowledge? What we call instinct is the result of voluntary action. Instinct in men or animals must therefore have been created by their previous voluntary actions. When we speak of voluntary actions, we admit previous experience. This previous experience thus creates instinct. The little chicken's fear of death, the duckling's taking to the water, and all the involuntary actions in the human being, which are the result of past experiences, have now become instinctive.

So far we have proceeded very clearly, and so far the latest science is with us. The latest scientific men[7] are coming back to the ancient sages, and, as far as they have done so, there is no difficulty. They admit that each man and each animal is born with a fund of experience, and that all the instincts in the mind are the result of past experience. "But what," they ask, "is the use of saying that that experience belongs to the soul? Why not say it belongs to the body, and the body alone? Why not say it is hereditary transmission?" This is the last question. Why not say that all the experience with which I am born is the resultant of all the past experience of my ancestors? The sum total of the experience from the little protoplasm up to the highest human being is in me, but it has come from body to body in the course of hereditary transmission. Where will the difficulty be?

This question is very nice, and we admit some part of this hereditary transmission. How far? As far as furnishing the material of the body. We, by our past actions, are born in a certain body, and the suitable material for that body comes from the parents who have made themselves fit to have our soul as their offspring. But the simple hereditary theory takes for granted, without any proof, the most astonishing proposition: that mental experience can be recorded in matter, that mental experience can be involved in matter.

When I look at you, in the lake of my mind there is a wave. That wave subsides, but it remains in fine form, as an impression. We understand a physical impression's remaining in the body. But what proof is there for assuming that the mental impression can remain in the body, since the body goes to pieces? What carries it? Even granting that it is possible for each mental impression to remain in the body—that every impression, beginning from the first man down to my father, was in my father's body—how could it be transmitted to me? Through the bioplasmic cell? How could that happen? The father's body does not come to the child *in toto*. The same parents may have a number of children. Then, from this theory of hereditary transmission, where the impression and the impressed are one, because both are material, it rigorously follows that, by the birth of every child, the parents must lose a part of their own impressions, or, if the parents should transmit the whole of their impressions, then, after the birth of the first child, their minds would be a vacuum.

Again, if in the bioplasmic cell the infinite amount of impressions from all time have entered, where and how can they exist there? This is a most impossible position, and until these physiologists can prove how and where those impressions live in that cell, and what they mean by a mental impression's sleeping in the physical cell, their position cannot be taken for granted.

So far it is clear, then, that these impressions are in the mind, that the mind comes to take birth after birth and uses the material most proper for it, and that the mind which has made itself fit for only a particular kind of body will have to wait until it gets that material. This we understand. The theory then comes to this: There is hereditary transmission so far as furnishing the material to the soul is concerned. But the soul migrates and manufactures body after body; and each thought we think and each deed we do is stored in it in fine forms, ready to spring up again and take a new shape. When I look at you, a wave rises in my mind. It goes down, as it were, and becomes finer and finer, but it does not die. It is ready to start up again as a wave in the shape of memory. So all these impressions are in my mind, and when I die, the resultant force of them will be upon me. A ball is here, and each one of us takes a mallet in his hands and strikes the ball from all sides; the ball goes from point to point in the room, and when it reaches the door it flies out. What carries it out? The resultant of all these blows. That will give it its direction. So what directs the soul when the body dies? The resultant, the sum total, of all the works it has done, of all the thoughts it has thought. If the resultant is such that it has to manufacture a new body for further experience, it will go to those parents who are ready to supply it with suitable material for that body.

Thus from body to body it will go, sometimes to a heaven, and back again to earth, becoming a man or some lower animal. In this way it will go on until it has finished its experience and completed the circle. It then knows its own nature, knows what it is, and its ignorance vanishes. Its powers become manifest; it becomes perfect. No more is there any necessity for the soul to work through physical bodies, nor is there any necessity for it to work through fine or mental bodies. It shines in its own light and is free—no more to be born, no more to die.

We shall not go now into the particulars of this. But I shall bring before you one more point with regard to this theory of reincarnation. It is the theory that advances the freedom of the human soul. It is the one theory that does not lay the blame of all our weakness upon somebody else, which is a common human failing. We do not look at our own faults. The eyes do not see themselves; they see the eyes of everybody else. We human beings are very slow to recognize our own weakness, our own faults, as long as we can lay the blame upon somebody else. Men in general lay all the blame on their fellowmen, or, failing that, on God; or they conjure up a ghost called fate.

Where is fate and what is fate? We reap what we sow. We are the makers of our own fate. None else has the blame, none else the praise. The wind is blowing; those vessels whose sails are unfurled catch it and go forward on their way, but those that have their sails furled do not catch the wind. Is that the fault of the wind? Is it thc fault of the merciful Father, whose wind of mercy is blowing without ceasing, day and night, whose mercy knows no decay—is it His fault that some of us are happy and some unhappy?

Those who blame others—and alas! their number is increasing every day—are generally miserable souls, with helpless brains, who have brought themselves to that pass through their own mistakes. Though they blame others, this does not alter their position. It does not serve them in any way. This attempt to throw the blame upon others only weakens them the more. Therefore blame none for your own faults; stand upon your own feet and take the whole responsibility upon yourselves. Say: "This misery that I am suffering is of my own doing, and that very thing proves that it will have to be undone by me alone. That which I created, I can demolish; that which is created by someone else, I shall never be able to destroy." Therefore stand up, be bold, be strong. Take the whole responsibility on your own shoulders and know that you are the creator of your own destiny.

All the strength and succor you want is within yourselves. Therefore make your own future. Let the dead past bury its dead. The infinite future is before you, and you must always remember that each word, thought, and deed lays up a store for you, and that as the bad thoughts and bad works are ready to spring upon you like tigers, so also there is the inspiring hope that the good thoughts and good deeds are ready with the power of a hundred thousand angels to defend you always and forever. (II. 216-25)

INSPIRED TALKS

Good is near Truth but is not yet Truth. After learning not to be disturbed by evil, we have to learn not to be made happy by good. We must find that we are beyond both evil and good. We must study their adjustment and see that they are both necessary.

Really good and evil are one and are in our mind. When the mind is self-poised, neither good nor bad affects it. Be perfectly free—then neither can affect you, and you will enjoy freedom and bliss. Evil is the iron chain, good is the gold one. Both are chains. The thorn of evil is in our flesh. Take another thorn from the same bush and extract the first thorn, then throw away both and be free.

There is only one Power, whether manifesting as evil or good. God and the devil are the same river with the water flowing in opposite directions. (VII. 4, 5, 22)

In the world, take always the position of the giver. Give everything and look for no return. Give love, give help, give service, give any little thing you can, but keep out barter. Make no conditions, and none will be imposed. Let us give out of our own bounty, just as God gives to us. (VII. 5)

Be brave and be sincere, then follow any path with devotion, and you must reach the Lord. Lay hold of one link of the chain, and the whole chain must come by degrees. Water the roots of the tree—that is, reach the Lord—and the whole tree is watered. Getting the Lord, we get all.

One-sidedness is the bane of the world. The more sides you can develop the more souls you have, and you can see the universe through all souls. Determine your own nature and stick to it. *Nishtha* [devotion to one ideal] is the only method for the beginner, but with devotion and sincerity it will lead to all. Churches, doctrines, forms, are the hedges to protect the tender plant, but they must later be broken down that the plant may become a tree. So the various religions, Bibles, Vedas, dogmas—all are just tubs for the little plant, but it must get out of the tub. (VII. 6-7)

Give up all evil company, especially at the beginning. Avoid worldly company—that will distract your mind. Give up all thought of "me and mine." To him who has nothing in the universe, the Lord comes. Cut the bondage of all worldly affections. Go beyond laziness and also beyond all worry as to what will become of you. Never turn back to see the result of what you have done. Give all to the Lord and go on and think not of it. When the whole soul pours in a continuous current to God, when there is no time to seek money or name or fame, no time to think of anything but God, then will come into your hearts that infinite, wonderful bliss of love. All desires are but beads of glass. (VII. 10)

My Master [Sri Ramakrishna] used to say: "All is God, but tiger-God is to be shunned. All water is water, but we avoid dirty water for drinking."

The whole sky is the censer of God, and the sun and moon are the lamps. What other temple is needed? All eyes are Thine, yet Thou hast not an eye. All hands are Thine, yet Thou hast not a hand. (VII. 13-14)

Neither seek nor avoid. Take what comes. It is liberty to be affected by nothing. Do not merely endure—be unattached. Remember the story of the bull. A mosquito sat long on the horn of a certain bull. Then his conscience troubled him and he said: "Mr. Bull, I have been sitting here a long time. Perhaps I annoy you. I am sorry. I will go away." But the bull replied: "Oh no, not at all! Bring your whole family and live on my horn. What can you do to me?" (VII. 14)

The Lord has hidden Himself best, and His work is best, so he who hides himself best accomplishes most. Conquer yourself and the whole universe is yours. (VII. 15)

In the state of sattva we see the very nature of things; we go beyond the senses and beyond reason. The adamantine wall that shuts us in is egotism. We refer everything to ourselves, thinking I do this, that, or the other. Get rid of this puny "I." Kill this diabolism in us. "Not I, but Thou"—say it, feel it, live it. Until we give up the world manufactured by the ego, never can we enter the kingdom of heaven. None ever did, none ever will. To give up the world is to forget the ego, to know it not at all—living *in* the body, but not *of* it. This rascal ego must be obliterated. Bless men when they revile you. Think how much good they are doing you. They can only hurt themselves. Go where people hate you. Let them thrash the ego out of you and you will get nearer to the Lord. (VII. 15)

Materialism says: The voice of freedom is a delusion. Idealism says: The voice that tells of bondage is delusion. Vedanta says: You are free and not free at the same time—never free on the earthly plane, but ever free on the spiritual. (VII. 32)

Religion without philosophy runs into superstition. Philosophy without religion becomes dry atheism. (VII. 36)

Religion, the great milch cow, has given many kicks, but never mind—it also gives a great deal of milk. The milkman does not mind the kick of the cow which gives much milk. (VII. 44.)

Even if there be no God, still hold fast to love. It is better to die seeking God than to live as a dog, seeking only carrion. Choose the highest ideal and give your life up to that. "Death being so certain, it is the highest thing to give up life for a great purpose."[8] (VII. 45)

Religion gives you nothing new. It only takes off obstacles and lets you see your Self. (VII. 62)

Ishvara [God] is the Atman as seen or grasped by the mind. His highest name is Om. So repeat it, meditate on it, and think of all its wonderful nature and attributes. Repeating Om continually is the only true worship. It is not a word—it is God Himself. (VII. 62)

The Vedas cannot show you Brahman—you are That already. They can only help to take away the veil that hides the truth from your eyes. The first veil to vanish is ignorance, and when that is gone, sin goes. Next, desire ceases, selfishness ends, and all misery disappears. This cessation of ignorance can only come when I know that God and I are one. In other words, identify yourself with the Atman, not with human limitations. Disidentify yourself with the body, and all pain will cease. This is the secret of healing. The universe is a case of hypnotization. Dehypnotize yourself and cease to suffer. (VII. 46)

In order to be free we have to pass through vice to virtue, and then get rid of both. Tamas [inertia] is to be conquered by rajas [activity]; both are to be submerged in sattva [goodness]. Then go beyond the three qualities. Reach a state where your very breathing is a prayer. (VII. 46)

With all powers comes further misery, so kill desire. Getting any desire is like putting a stick into a nest of hornets. *Vairagya* [renunciation] is finding out that desires are but gilded balls of poison. (VII. 46)

Everything in the universe is struggling to complete a circle, to return to its source, to return to its only real Source, the Atman. The search for happiness is a struggle to find the balance, to restore the equilibrium. The happiest moments we ever know are when we entirely forget ourselves. (VII. 48-49)

The whole secret of existence is to have no fear. Never fear what will become of you. Depend on no one. Only the moment you reject all help are you free. The full sponge can absorb no more. (VII. 49)

Vedanta and modern science both posit a self-evolving Cause. In It exist all subsidiary causes. Take, for example, the potter shaping a pot. The potter is the primal cause, the clay, the material cause, and the wheel, the instrumental cause. But the Atman is all three. The Atman is cause and manifestation too. The Vedantist says that the universe is not real; it is only apparent. Nature is God seen through nescience. The pantheists say that God has become nature or this world. The Advaitists affirm that God is appearing as this world, but He is not this world. (VII. 50)

A blind man cannot see color, so how can we see evil unless it is in us? We compare what we see outside with what we find in ourselves and pronounce judgment accordingly. If we are pure, we cannot see impurity. It may exist, but not for us. See only God in every man, woman, and child. See it by the *antarjyotis*, the inner light, and seeing that, we can see naught else. Do not want this world, because what you desire you get. Seek the Lord and the Lord only. (VII. 63-64)

Eat the mangoes and let the rest quarrel over the basket. See Christ—then you will be a Christian. All else is talk. The less talking the better.

Learn until the glory of the Lord shines through your face. (VII. 65)

Truth must have no compromise. Teach truth and make no apology for any superstition; neither drag truth down to the level of the listener. (VII. 70)

Employ all powers—philosophy, work, prayer, meditation. Crowd on all sails, put on full steam, and reach the goal. The sooner, the better. (VII. 71)

"Truth alone triumphs, not untruth."[9] Stand upon Truth and you have got God. (VII. 72)

Give up hope completely—that is the highest state. What is there to hope for? Burst asunder the bonds of hope, stand on your Self, and be at rest. Never mind what you do. Give up all to God, but have no hypocrisy about it. (VII. 82)

"That day is indeed a bad day when we do not speak of the Lord—not a stormy day." (VII. 82)

He who wants to enter the realm of light must make a bundle of all shopkeeping religion and cast it away before he can pass the gates. It is not that you do not get what you pray for. You get everything, but it is low, vulgar—a beggar's religion. "A fool indeed is he who, living on the banks of the Ganga, digs a little well for water. A fool indeed is the man who, coming to a mine of diamonds, begins to search for glass beads." These prayers for health and wealth and material prosperity are not bhakti [devotion]. (VII. 83-84)

Never lose faith in yourself—you can do anything in this universe. Never weaken. All power is yours. (VII. 85)

"Drinking the cup of desire, the world becomes mad." As day and night never come together, so desire and the Lord can never come together. Give up desire. (VII. 91)

Do not cling to old superstitions. Be ever ready for new truths. "Fools are they who would drink brackish water from a well that their forefathers have dug and would not drink pure water from a well that others have dug." Until we realize God for ourselves we can know nothing about Him. How can we understand that Moses saw God unless we too see Him? If God ever came to anyone He will come to me. I will go to God direct. Let Him talk to me. I cannot take belief as a basis—that is atheism and blasphemy. If God spoke to a man in the deserts of Arabia two thousand years ago, He can also speak to me today, else how can I know that He has not died? (VII. 96-97)

Think day and night: "This universe is zero. Only God is." Have intense desire to get free. Say, "Soham, Soham" [I am He, I am He], whatever comes. Let the body die. This idea of the body is but a worn-out fable. Be still and know that you are God. (VII. 92)

Let a few stand out and live for God alone and save religion for the world. Sacrifice on God's altar earth's purest and best. He who struggles is better than he who never attempts. Even to look on one who has given up has a purifying effect. Stand up for God. Let the world go. Have no compromise. (VII. 100-101)

SIX STANZAS ON NIRVANA[10]

I am neither the mind nor the intellect nor the ego nor the mind-stuff;
I am neither the body nor the changes of the body;
I am neither the senses of hearing, taste, smell, or sight,
Nor am I the ether, the earth, the fire, the air;
I am Existence Absolute, Knowledge Absolute, Bliss Absolute—
I am He, I am He (Shivoham, Shivoham).

I am neither the prana nor the five vital airs;
I am neither the materials of the body nor the five sheaths;
Neither am I the organs of action nor the object of the senses;
I am Existence Absolute, Knowledge Absolute, Bliss Absolute—
I am He, I am He (Shivoham, Shivoham).

I have neither aversion nor attachment, neither greed nor
delusion;
Neither egotism nor envy, neither dharma nor moksha;
I am neither desire nor the objects of desire;
I am Existence Absolute, Knowledge Absolute, Bliss Absolute—
I am He, I am He (Shivoham, Shivoham).

I am neither sin nor virtue, neither pleasure nor pain,
Nor temple nor worship nor pilgrimage nor scriptures,
Neither the act of enjoying, the enjoyable, nor the enjoyer;
I am Existence Absolute, Knowledge Absolute, Bliss Absolute—
I am He, I am He (Shivoham, Shivoham).

I have neither death nor fear of death nor caste;
Nor was I ever born, nor had I parents, friends, and relations;
I have neither guru nor disciple;
I am Existence Absolute, Knowledge Absolute, Bliss Absolute—
I am He, I am He (Shivoham, Shivoham).

I am untouched by the senses; I am neither mukti nor
knowable;
I am without form, without limit, beyond space, beyond
time;
I am in everything; I am the basis of the universe; everywhere
am I.
I am Existence Absolute, Knowledge Absolute, Bliss Absolute—
I am He, I am He (Shivoham, Shivoham).
(IV. 391-92)

Notes

1 Mundaka Upanishad, 2.2.8.
2 Shankara, "Nirvanashatkam," 1.
3 Shankara, *Vivekachudamani*, 410.
4 Shankara, *Vivekachudamani*, 409.
5 Mundaka Upanishad, 3.2.9.
6 Isha Upanishad, 3.
7 Most probably Swami Vivekananda was referring to Charles Darwin (1809-1882), Thomas Huxley (1825-1895), and Herbert Spencer (1820-1903). According to many Western scholars, the struggle for existence, survival of the fittest, natural selection, and so forth, are the causes of elevating a lower species to a higher. On the other hand, according to Patanjali, an ancient Indian evolutionist, the trans-

formation of one species into another is effected by the "in-filling of nature." That is, as the overflowing water floods a field by breaking down the barriers in its way, so the divine nature of each being continually pushes it toward perfection by removing the obstructions in its evolutionary journey. Evolution takes place in the realm of matter, but matter is insentient. It needs the direct or indirect help of a conscious principle. Without that no evolution can take place. Moreover, evolution presupposes involution. For example, if an amoeba evolves into a highly developed man, then that man must have been involved in the amoeba. If consciousness or intelligence evolves from matter, it must be implicit in that matter.

In 1859 Darwin's *Origin of Species* created a stir among the thinking humanity. After that many scientists, philosophers, psychologists, and theologians debated on his theory. Here are a few more recent views: Sir Julian Huxley wrote, "It [evolutionary truth] shows up mind enthroned above matter, quantity subordinate to quality" (*Evolution After Darwin* [Chicago: The University of Chicago, 1960], Vol. III, 260-61). Pierre Teilhard de Chardin mentioned, "Consciousness transcends by far the ridiculously narrow limits within which our eyes can directly perceive it" (*The Phenomenon of Man* [New York: Harper & Bros., 1961], 300). According to L.S. Berg, "Evolution is to a considerable degree *predetermined*, an *unfolding or manifestation of pre-existing rudiments*" (*Nomogenesis* [Cambridge: The M.I.T. Press, 1969], 403).

8 From the *Hitopadesha*.

9 Mundaka Upanishad, 3.1.6.

10 Shankara's hymn, "Nirvanashatkam," translated by Swami Vivekananda.

XII

THE UNIVERSALITY OF VEDANTA

Swami Vivekananda in San Francisco, 1900

HOW VEDANTA VIEWS OTHER FAITHS

Are all the religions of the world really contradictory? I do not mean the external forms in which great thoughts are clad. I do not mean the different buildings, languages, rituals, books, etc., employed in various religions, but I mean the internal soul of every religion. Every religion has a soul behind it, and that soul may differ from the soul of another religion. But are they contradictory? Do they contradict or supplement each other?—that is the question.

I took up the question when I was quite a boy and have been studying it all my life. Thinking that my conclusion may be of some help to you, I place it before you. I believe that they are not contradictory—they are supplementary. Each religion takes up, as it were, one part of the great universal truth and spends its whole force in embodying and typifying that part of the great truth. It is, therefore, addition, not exclusion. That is the idea. System after system arises, each one embodying a great idea, and ideals must be added to ideals. And this is the march of humanity. Man never progresses from error to truth, but from truth to truth—from lesser truth to higher truth—but never from error to truth.

Then again, we also know that there may be almost contradictory points of view of a thing, but they will all indicate the same thing. Suppose a man is journeying toward the sun, and as he advances he takes a photograph of the sun at every stage. When he comes back he has many photographs of the sun, which he places before us. We see that not two are alike, and yet who will deny that all these are photographs of the same sun from different standpoints? Take four photographs of this church from different corners. How different they would look, and yet they would all represent this church. In the same way, we are all looking at truth from different standpoints, which vary according to our birth, education, surroundings, and so on.

My idea, therefore, is that all these religions are different forces in the economy of God, working for the good of mankind, and that not one can become dead, not one can be killed. Just as you cannot kill any force in nature, so you cannot kill any one of these spiritual forces.

And that universal religion about which philosophers and others have dreamed in every country already exists. It is here. As the universal brotherhood of man is already existing, so also is universal religion.

The greater the number of sects, the more chance of people getting religion. In the hotel, where there are all sorts of food, everyone has a chance to get his appetite satisfied. So I want sects to multiply in every country, that more people may have a chance to be spiritual. Do not think that people do not like religion. I do not believe that. The preachers cannot give them what they need. The same man that may have been branded as an atheist, as a materialist, or what not, may meet a man who gives him the truth needed by him, and he may turn out to be the most spiritual man in the community.

Each nation has a mission of its own to perform in this harmony of races, and so long as that nation keeps to that ideal, nothing can kill that nation. But if that nation gives up its mission in life and goes after something else, its life becomes short and it vanishes.

And so with religions. The fact that all these old religions are living today proves that they must have kept that mission intact. In spite of all their mistakes, in spite of all difficulties, in spite of all quarrels, in spite of all the incrustation of forms and figures, the heart of every one of them is sound—it is a throbbing, beating, living heart. They have not lost, any one of them, the great mission they came for. And it is splendid to study that mission. Take Mohammedanism, for instance. Islam makes its followers all equal. What Mohammedanism comes to preach to the world is this practical brotherhood of all belonging to their faith. That is the essential part of the Mohammedan religion.

With the Hindus you will find one national idea: spirituality. In no other religion, in no other sacred books of the world, will you find so much energy spent in defining the idea of God. They tried to define the idea of the soul so that no earthly touch might mar it. Renunciation and spirituality are the two great ideas of India, and it is because India clings to these ideas that all her mistakes count for so little.

With the Christians, the central idea that has been preached by them is the same: "Watch and pray, for the kingdom of heaven is at hand"—which means, purify your minds and be ready! And that spirit never dies. You recollect that the Christians are, even in the darkest days, even in the most superstitious Christian countries, always trying to prepare themselves for the coming of the Lord by trying to help others, building hospitals, and so on. So long as the Christians keep to that ideal, their religion lives.

Our watchword, then, will be acceptance and not exclusion. Not only toleration, for so-called toleration is often blasphemy and I do not believe in it. I believe in acceptance. Why should I tolerate? Toleration means that I think that you are wrong and I am just allowing you to live. Is it not a blasphemy to think that you and I are allowing others to live? I accept all religions that were in the past, and worship with them all. I worship God with every one of them, in whatever form they worship Him. I shall go to the mosque of the Mohammedan; I shall enter the Christian's church and kneel before the crucifix; I shall enter the Buddhistic temple, where I shall take refuge in Buddha and in his Law. I shall go into the forest and sit down in meditation with the Hindu, who is trying to see the Light which enlightens the heart of everyone.

Not only shall I do all these, but I shall keep my heart open for all that may come in the future. Is God's book finished? Or is revelation still going on? It is a marvelous book—these spiritual revelations of the world. The Bible, the Vedas, the Koran, and all other sacred books are but so many pages, and an infinite number of pages remain yet to be unfolded. I would leave my heart open for all of them. We stand in the present, but open ourselves to the infinite future. We take in all that has been in the past, enjoy the light of the present, and open every window of the heart for all that will come in the future. Salutations to all the prophets of the past, to all the great ones of the present, and to all that are to come in the future! (II. 365-68, 371-74)

VEDANTA AND THE GREAT TEACHERS OF THE WORLD

The universe, according to the theory of the Hindus, is moving in cycles of wave forms. It rises, reaches it zenith, then falls and remains in the hollow, as it were, for some time, once more to rise, and so on, in wave after wave and fall after fall. What is true of the universe is true of every part of it. The march of human affairs is like that. The history of nations is like that: they rise and they fall. After the rise comes a fall. Again, out of the fall comes a rise, with greater power. This motion is always going on.

In the religious world the same movement exists. In every nation's spiritual life there is a fall as well as a rise. The nation goes down and everything seems to go to pieces. Then again it gains strength and rises. A huge wave comes—sometimes a tidal wave—and always on the topmost crest of the wave is a shining soul, a Messenger. Creator and created by turns, he is the impetus that makes the wave rise, the nation rise. At the same time, he is created by the same forces which make the wave, acting and interacting by turns. He puts forth his tremendous power upon society, and society makes him what he is. These are the great world thinkers. These are the Prophets of the world, the Messengers of life, the Incarnations of God.

Man has an idea that there can be only one religion, that there can be only one Prophet, that there can be only one

Incarnation, but that idea is not true. By studying the lives of all these great Messengers, we find that each was destined to play a part, as it were, and a part only—that the harmony consists in the sum total, and not in one note. It is the same in the life of races—no race is born to alone enjoy the world. None dare say so. Each race has a part to play in this divine harmony of nations. Each race has its mission to perform, its duty to fulfill. The sum total is the great harmony.

So not any one of these Prophets is born to rule the world forever. None has yet succeeded and none is going to be the ruler forever. Each only contributes a part, and, as to that part, it is true that in the long run every Prophet will govern the world and its destinies.

These great Messengers and Prophets are great and true. Why? Because each one has come to preach a great idea. We take, first, Krishna. You who have read the Gita know that the one idea all through the book is nonattachment. Remain unattached. The heart's love is due to only One. To whom? To Him who never changes. Who is that One? He is God. Do not make the mistake of giving the heart to anything that is changing, because that is misery. You may give it to a man, but if he dies, misery is the result. You may give it to a friend, but tomorrow he may become your enemy. If you give it to your husband, he may one day quarrel with you. You may give it to your wife, and she may die the day after tomorrow. Now this is the way the world is going on. So says Krishna in the Gita. The Lord is the only one who never changes. His love never fails. Wherever we are and whatever we do, He is ever and ever the same merciful, the same loving heart.

Listen to Buddha's message—a tremendous message. It has a place in our heart. Says Buddha: "Root out selfishness and everything that makes you selfish. Have neither wife, child, nor family. Be not of the world. Become perfectly unselfish."

Behold another Messenger, He of Nazareth. He teaches, "Be ready, for the kingdom of heaven is at hand." I have pondered over the message of Krishna and am trying to work without attachment, but sometimes I forget. Then suddenly comes to me the message of Buddha: "Take care, for everything in the world is evanescent, and there is always misery in this life." I listen to that and I am uncertain which to accept. Then again comes, like a thunderbolt, the message: "Be ready, for the kingdom of heaven is at hand." Do not delay a moment. Leave nothing for tomorrow. Get ready for the final event, which may overtake you immediately, even now. That message also has a place, and we acknowledge it. We salute the Messenger. We salute the Lord.

And then comes Mohammed, the Messenger of equality. Mohammed by his life showed that among Mohammedans there should be perfect equality and brotherhood. There was no question of race, caste, creed, color, or sex.

So we see that each Prophet, each Messenger, has a particular message. When you first listen to that message and then look at his life, you see his whole life stands explained, radiant.

If two men quarrel about religion, just ask them the question: "Have you seen God? Have you seen these things?" One man says that Christ is the only Prophet. Well, has he seen Christ? "Has your father seen Him?" "No, sir." "Has your grandfather seen Him?" "No, sir." "Have you seen Him?" "No, sir." "Then what are you quarreling for? The fruits have fallen into the ditch and you are quarreling over the basket!" Sensible men and women should be ashamed to go on quarreling in that way!

So when each man stands and says "My Prophet is the only true Prophet," he is not correct—he knows not the alpha of religion. Religion is neither talk nor theory nor intellectual consent. It is realization in the heart of our hearts. It is touching God. It is feeling, realizing that I am a spirit in relation to the Universal Spirit and all Its great manifestations. If you have really entered the house of the Father, how can you have seen His children and not known them? And if you do not recognize them, you have not entered the house of the Father. The mother recognizes her child in any dress and knows him however disguised. Recognize all the great spiritual men and women in every age and country, and see that they are not really at variance with one another. (IV. 120-21, 125-26, 128-29, 131-33)

WHY WE DISAGREE

I will tell you a little story. You have heard the eloquent speaker who has just finished say, "Let us cease from abusing each other," and he was very sorry that there should always be so much variance. But I think I should tell you a story that would illustrate the cause of this variance.

A frog lived in a well. It had lived there for a long time. It was born there and brought up there, and yet was a little, small frog. Of course the evolutionists were not there then to tell us whether the frog lost its eyes or not, but for our story's sake we must take it for granted that it had its eyes and that it every day cleansed the water of all the worms and bacilli that lived in it, with an energy that would do credit to our modern bacteriologists. In this way it went on and became a little sleek and fat. Well, one day another frog that lived in the sea came and fell into the well.

"Where are you from?"

"I am from the sea."

"The sea! How big is that? Is it as big as my well?" And he took a leap from one side of the well to the other.

"My friend," said the frog of the sea, "how do you compare the sea with your little well?"

Then the frog took another leap and asked, "Is your sea so big?"

"What nonsense you speak, to compare the sea with your well!"

"Well, then," said the frog of the well, "nothing can be bigger than my well. There can be nothing bigger than this. This fellow is a liar, so turn him out."

That has been the difficulty all the while.

I am a Hindu. I am sitting in my own little well and thinking that the whole world is my little well. The Christian sits in his little well and thinks the whole world is his well. The Mohammedan sits in his little well and thinks that is the whole world. I have to thank you of America for the great attempt [the Parliament of Religions, Chicago, 1893] you are making to break down the barriers of this little world of ours, and hope that in the future the Lord will help you to accomplish your purpose. (I. 4-5)

THE IDEAL OF A UNIVERSAL RELIGION

Hundreds of attempts have been made in India, in Alexandria, in Europe, in China, in Japan, in Tibet, and lastly in America, to formulate a harmonious religious creed, to make all religions come together in love. They have all failed, because they did not adopt any practical plan. Many have admitted that all the religions of the world are right, but they show no practical way of bringing them together so as to enable each of them to maintain its own individuality in the conflux. That plan alone is practical which does not destroy the individuality of any man in religion and at the same time shows him a point of union with all others.

I have also my little plan. I do not know whether it will work or not, and I want to present it to you for discussion. What is my plan? In the first place, I would ask mankind to recognize this maxim, "Do not destroy." Iconoclastic reformers do no good to the world. Break not, pull not anything down, but build. Help, if you can. If you cannot, fold your hands and stand by and see things go on. Do not injure if you cannot render help. Say not a word against any man's convictions so far as they are sincere. Secondly, take man where he stands and from there give him a lift. If it is true that God is the center of all religions and that each of us is moving toward Him along one of these radii, then it is certain that all of us must reach that center. And at the center, where all the radii meet, all our differences will cease. But until we reach there, differences there must be. All these radii converge to the same center. One, according to his nature, travels along one of these lines, and another, along another. And if we all push onward along our own lines, we shall surely come to the center, because "all roads lead to Rome."

What can you and I do? Do you think you can teach even a child? You cannot. The child teaches himself. Your duty is to afford opportunities and to remove obstacles. A plant grows. Do *you* make the plant grow? Your duty is to put a hedge round it and see that no animal eats up the plant, and there your duty ends. The plant grows of itself. So it is in regard to the spiritual growth of every man. None can teach you. None can make a spiritual man of you. You have to teach yourself. Your growth must come from inside. What can an external teacher do? He can remove the obstructions a little, and there his duty ends. Therefore help, if you can, but do not destroy. Give up all ideas that *you* can make men spiritual. It is impossible. There is no other teacher to you than your own soul. Recognize this.

What comes of it? In society we see so many different natures. There are thousands and thousands of varieties of minds and inclinations. A thorough generalization of them is impossible, but for our practical purpose it is sufficient to have them characterized into four classes. First, there is the active man, the worker. He wants to work, and there is tremendous energy in his muscles and his nerves. His aim is to work—to build hospitals, do charitable deeds, make streets, to plan and to organize. Then there is the emotional man, who loves the sublime and the beautiful to an excessive degree. He loves to think of the beautiful, to enjoy the aesthetic side of nature, and to adore Love and the God of Love. He loves with his whole heart the great souls of all times, the prophets of religions, and the Incarnations of God on earth. He does not care whether reason can or cannot prove that Christ or Buddha existed. He does not care for the exact date when the Sermon on the Mount was preached, or for the exact moment of Krishna's birth. What he cares for is their personalities, their lovable figures. Such is his ideal. This is the nature of the lover, the emotional man. Then there is the mystic, whose mind wants to analyze its own self, to understand the workings of the human mind—what the forces are that are working inside, and how to know, manipulate, and obtain control over them. This is the mystical mind. Then there is the philosopher, who wants to weigh everything and use his intellect even beyond the possibilities of all human thinking.

Now, a religion, to satisfy the largest proportion of mankind, must be able to supply food for all these various types of minds. And where this capability is wanting, the existing sects all become one-sided.

What I want to propagate is a religion that will be equally acceptable to all minds. It must be equally philosophic, equally emotional, equally mystical, and equally conducive to action. If professors from the colleges come—scientific men and physicists—they will court reason. Let them have it as much as they want. There will be a point beyond which they will think they cannot go without breaking with reason. They will say: "These ideas of God and salvation are superstitions. Give them up!" I shall say: "Mr. Philosopher, this body of yours is a bigger superstition. Give *it* up. Don't go home to dinner or to your philosophic chair. Give up the body, and if you cannot, cry quarter and sit down." For religion must be able to show us how to realize the philosophy that teaches that this world is one, that there is but one Existence in the universe. Similarly, if the mystic comes, we must welcome him, be ready to give him the science of mental analysis, and practically demonstrate it before him. And if emotional people come, we must sit, laugh, and weep with them in the name of the Lord. We must "drink the cup of love and become mad." If the energetic worker comes, we must work with him with all the energy that we have. And this combination will be the ideal of the nearest approach to a universal religion.

Would to God that all men were so constituted that in their minds all these elements—of philosophy, mysticism, emotion, and of work—were equally present in full! That is the ideal, my ideal of a perfect man. Everyone who has only one or two of these elements of character I consider one-sided. This world is almost full of such one-sided men, who possess knowledge of that one road only in which they move, and to whom anything else is dangerous and horrible. To become harmoniously balanced in all these four directions is *my* ideal of religion. And this religion is attained by what we in India call yoga—union. To the worker, it is union between himself and the whole of humanity; to the mystic, between his lower self and Higher Self; to the lover, union between himself and the God of Love; and to the philosopher, it is the union of all existence. This is what is meant by yoga. (II. 384-88)

VEDANTA AND PRIVILEGE

The idea of privilege is the bane of human life. Two forces, as it were, are constantly at work—one making caste and the other breaking caste; in other words, the one making for privilege, the other breaking down privilege. And whenever privilege is broken down, more and more light and progress come to a race. This struggle we see all around us. Of course there is first the brutal idea of privilege—that of the strong over the weak. There is the privilege of wealth. If a man has more money than another, he wants a little privilege over those who have less. There is the still subtler and more powerful privilege of intellect. Because one man knows more than others he claims more privilege. And the last of all, and the worst, because the most tyrannical, is the privilege of spirituality. If some persons think they know more of spirituality, of God, they claim a superior privilege over everyone else. They say: "Come down and worship us, ye common herds. We are the messengers of God, and you have to worship us."

None can be Vedantists and at the same time admit of privilege to anyone, either mental, physical, or spiritual—absolutely no privilege for anyone. The same power is in every man, the one manifesting more, the other less. The same potentiality is in everyone. Where is the claim to privilege? All knowledge is in every soul, even in the most ignorant. He has not manifested it, but perhaps he has not had the opportunity—the environments were not, perhaps, suitable to him. When he gets the opportunity he will manifest it. The idea that one man is born superior to another has no meaning in Vedanta. (I. 423)

VEDANTA AND SCIENCE

Advaita was never allowed to come to the people. At first some monks got hold of it and took it to the forests, and so it came to be called the "forest philosophy." By the mercy of the Lord, Buddha came and preached it to the masses, and the whole nation became Buddhists. Long after that, when atheists and agnostics had destroyed the nation again, it was found out that Advaita was the only way to save India from materialism.

Then Shankaracharya arose and once more revivified the Vedanta philosophy. He made it a rationalistic philosophy. In the Upanishads the arguments are often very obscure. Buddha laid stress upon the moral side of the philosophy, and Shankaracharya, upon the intellectual. He worked out, rationalized, and placed before men the wonderful, coherent system of Advaita.

Materialism prevails in Europe today. You may pray for the salvation of the modern skeptics, but they do not yield. They want reason. The salvation of Europe depends on a rationalistic religion, and Advaita—nonduality, oneness, the idea of the Impersonal God—is the only religion that can have any hold on any intellectual people. It comes whenever religion seems to disappear and irreligion seems to prevail, and that is why it has taken ground in Europe and America.

I would say one thing more in connection with this philosophy. In the old Upanishads we find sublime poetry. Their authors were poets. Plato says that inspiration comes to people through poetry, and it seems as if these ancient rishis, seers of truth, were raised above humanity to show these truths through poetry. They never preached or philosophized or wrote. Music came out of their hearts. In Buddha we had the great, universal heart and infinite patience, making religion practical and bringing it to everyone's door. In Shankaracharya we saw tremendous intellectual power, throwing the scorching light of reason upon everything. We want today that bright sun of intellectuality joined with the heart of Buddha, the wonderful, infinite heart of love and mercy. This union will give us the highest philosophy. Science and religion will meet and shake hands. Poetry and philosophy will become friends. This will be the religion of the future, and if we can work it out, we may be sure that it will be for all times and peoples.

This is the one way that will prove acceptable to modern science, for it has almost come to it. When the scientific teacher asserts that all things are the manifestation of one force, does it not remind you of the God of whom you hear in the Upanishads? "As the one fire entering into the universe expresses itself in various forms, even so that one Soul is expressing Itself in every soul and yet is infinitely more besides."[1] Do you not see whither science is tending? The Hindu nation proceeded through the study of the mind, through metaphysics and logic. The European nations start from external nature, and now they too are coming to the same results. We find that, searching through the mind, we at last come to that Oneness, that Universal One, the Internal Soul of everything, the Essence and Reality of everything, the Ever-Free, the Ever-

Blissful, the Ever-Existing. Through material science we come to the same oneness. Science today is telling us that all things are but the manifestation of one energy, which is the sum total of everything that exists, and the trend of humanity is toward freedom and not toward bondage. (II. 138-41)

EAST AND WEST MUST MEET

"Whenever virtue subsides and vice prevails, I come down to help mankind," declares Krishna in the Bhagavad Gita. Whenever this world of ours, on account of growth, on account of added circumstances, requires a new adjustment, a wave of power comes, and as a man is acting on two planes, the spiritual and the material, waves of adjustment come on both planes. On the one side, of the adjustment on the material plane, Europe has mainly been the basis during modern times, and on the other side, on the spiritual plane, Asia has been the basis of the adjustment throughout the history of the world. Today man requires one more adjustment on the spiritual plane. Today, when material ideas are at the height of their glory and power, today, when man is likely to forget his divine nature through his growing dependence on matter, and is likely to be reduced to a mere money-making machine, an adjustment is necessary. And the voice has spoken. The power is coming to drive away the clouds of gathering materialism. The power has been set in motion which, at no distant date, will bring unto mankind once more the memory of its real nature. And again the place from which this power has started is Asia.

This world of ours is on the plan of the division of labor. It is vain to say that one man shall possess everything. Yet how childish we are! The baby in its ignorance thinks that its doll is the only possession that is to be coveted in this whole universe. So a nation which is great in the possession of material power thinks that this is all that is to be coveted, that this is all that is meant by progress, that this is all that is meant by civilization; and if there are other nations which do not care for possession, and do not possess that power, they are not fit to live; their whole existence is useless. On the other hand, another nation may think that mere material civilization is utterly useless. From the Orient came the voice that once told the world that if a man possesses everything under the sun and does not possess spirituality, what avails it? This is the Oriental type; the other is the Occidental type.

Each of these types has its grandeur, each has its glory. The present adjustment will be the harmonizing, the mingling, of these two ideals. To the Oriental, the world of the Spirit is as real as to the Occidental is the world of the senses. In the spiritual, the Oriental finds everything he wants or hopes for. In it he finds all that makes life real to him. To the Occidental he is a dreamer. To the Oriental, the Occidental is a dreamer, playing with ephemeral toys, and he laughs to think that grown-up men and women should make so much of a handful of matter which they will have to leave sooner or later. Each calls the other a dreamer. But the Oriental ideal is as necessary for the progress of the human race as the Occidental, and I think it is more necessary. Machines never made mankind happy, and never will. He who tries to make us believe this, claims that happiness is in the machine. But it is always in the mind. That man alone who is lord of his mind can become happy, and none else.

And what, after all, is this power of machinery? Why should a man who can send a current of electricity through a wire be called a very great man and a very intelligent man? Does not nature do a million times more than that every moment? Why not then fall down and worship nature? What avails it if you have power over the whole of the world, if you have mastered every atom in the universe? That will not make you happy unless you have the power of happiness in yourself, until you have conquered yourself. Man is born to conquer nature, it is true, but the Occidental means by "nature" only the physical or external nature. It is true that external nature is majestic, with its mountains and oceans and rivers, and with its infinite power and variety. Yet there is a more majestic, internal nature of man, higher than the sun, moon, and stars, higher than this earth of ours, higher than the physical universe, transcending these little lives of ours, and it affords another field of study. There the Orientals excel, just as the Occidentals excel in the other. Therefore it is fitting that, whenever there is a spiritual adjustment, it should come from the Orient. It is also fitting that, when the Oriental wants to learn about machine-making, he should sit at the feet of the Occidental and learn from him. When the Occident wants to learn about the Spirit, about God, about the soul, about the meaning and the mystery of this universe, he must sit at the feet of the Orient. (IV. 154-56)

EASTERN AND WESTERN VIEWS

You will generally hear that this Vedanta philosophy and other Eastern systems look only to something beyond, letting go the enjoyments and struggle of this life. This idea is entirely wrong. It is only ignorant people who do not know anything of Eastern thought and never had brain enough to understand anything of its real teaching who tell you so. On the contrary, we read in our scriptures that our philosophers do not want to go to other worlds, but deprecate them as places where people weep and laugh for a little while only, and then die. As long as we are weak we shall have to go through these experiences, but whatever is true is here, and that is the human soul. And this also is insisted upon, that by committing suicide we cannot escape the inevitable. We cannot evade it. But the right path is hard to find. The Hindu is just as practical as the westerner, only they differ in their views of life. The one says, "Build a good house, have good clothes and food, intellectual culture, and so on, for this is the whole of life," and in that he is immensely practical. But the Hindu says, "True knowledge of the world means knowledge of the soul, metaphysics," and he wants to enjoy that life.

In America there was a great agnostic,[2] a very noble man, a very good man, and a very fine speaker. He lectured on religion, which he said was of no use—why bother our heads about other worlds? He employed this metaphor: "We have an orange here, and we want to squeeze all the juice out of it." I met him once and said: "I agree with you entirely. I have some fruit and I too want to squeeze out the juice. Our difference lies in the choice of the fruit. You want an orange, and I prefer a mango. You think it is enough to live here and eat and drink and have a little scientific knowledge, but you have no right to say that that will suit all tastes. Such a conception is nothing to me. If I had only to learn how an apple falls to the ground or how an electric current shakes my nerves, I would commit suicide. I want to understand the heart of things, the very kernel itself. Your study is the manifestation of life. Mine is life itself. My philosophy says you must know *that* and drive out from your mind all thoughts of heaven and hell and all other superstitions, even though they exist in the same sense that this world exists. I must know the heart of this life, its very essence, what it is—not merely how it works and what are its manifestations. I want the *why* of everything. I leave the *how* to children."

I am practical, very practical, in my own way. So your idea that only the West is practical is nonsense. You are practical in one way, and I in another. There are different types of men and minds. If in the East a man is told that he will find out the truth by standing on one leg all his life, he will pursue that method. If in the West men hear that there is a gold mine somewhere in an uncivilized country, thousands will face the dangers there in the hope of getting the gold, and perhaps only one succeeds. The same men have heard that they have souls but are content to leave the care of them to the church. The easterner will not go near the savages. He says it may be dangerous. But if we tell him that on the top of a high mountain lives a wonderful sage who can give him knowledge of the soul, he tries to climb up to him, even though he may be killed in the attempt. Both types of men are practical, but the mistake lies in regarding this world as the whole of life. Yours is the vanishing point of enjoyment of the senses—there is nothing permanent in it. It only brings more and more misery. But mine brings eternal peace.

I do not say your view is wrong. You are welcome to it. Great good and blessing come out of it. But do not, therefore, condemn my view. Mine also is practical in its own way. Let us all work on our own plans. Would to God all of us were equally practical on both sides! I have seen some scientists who are equally practical as scientists and as spiritual men, and it is my great hope that in course of time the whole of humanity will be efficient in the same manner.

When a kettle of water is coming to the boil, if you watch the phenomenon you find first one bubble rising and then another, and so on, until at last they all join and a tremendous commotion takes place. This world is very similar. Each individual is like a bubble, and the nations resemble many bubbles. Gradually these nations are joining, and I am sure the day will come when separation will vanish and that Oneness to which we are all going will become manifest. A time must come when every man will be as intensely practical in the scientific world as in the spiritual, and then that Oneness, the harmony of Oneness, will pervade the whole world. The whole of mankind will become *jivanmuktas*—free while living. We are all struggling toward that one end through our jealousies and hatreds, through our love and cooperation. A tremendous stream is flowing toward the ocean, carrying us all along with it. And though, like straws and scraps of paper, we may at times float aimlessly about, in the long run we are sure to join the Ocean of Life and Bliss. (II.185-88)

THE FUTURE OF VEDANTA

At the start, I may tell you that I do not know whether it [Vedanta] will ever be the religion of the vast majority of men. Will it ever be able to take hold of one whole nation such as the United States of America? Possibly it may. However, that is the question we want to discuss this afternoon.

I shall begin by telling you what Vedanta is not, and then I shall tell you what it is. But you must remember that, with all its emphasis on impersonal principles, Vedanta is not antagonistic to anything, though it does not compromise or give up the truths which it considers fundamental.

You all know that certain things are necessary to make a religion. First of all there is the book. The power of the book is simply marvelous! Whatever it be, the book is the center round which human allegiance gathers. Not one religion is living today but has a book. With all its rationalism and tall talk, humanity still clings to the books. In your country every attempt to start a religion without a book has failed. In India sects rise with great success, but within a few years they die down because there is no book behind them. So in every other country.

Study the rise and fall of the Unitarian movement. It represents the best thought of your nation. Why should it not have spread like the Methodist, Baptist, and other Christian denominations? Because there was no book. On the other hand, think of the Jews. A handful of men, driven from one country to another, still hold together because they have a book. Think of the Parsees—only a hundred thousand in the world. And do you know that these handfuls of Parsees and Jains still keep on just because of their books? The religions that are living at the present day—every one of them has a book.

The second requisite to make a religion is veneration for some person. He is worshipped either as the Lord of the world or as the great Teacher. Men must worship some embodied man. They must have the Incarnation or the prophet or the great leader. You find it in every religion today. Hindus and Christians—they have Incarnations. Buddhists, Mohammedans, and Jews have prophets. But it is all about the same—all their veneration twines round some person or persons.

The third requisite seems to be that a religion, to be strong and sure of itself, must believe that it alone is the truth—otherwise it cannot influence people. Liberalism dies because it is dry, because it cannot rouse fanaticism in the human mind, because it cannot bring out hatred for everything except itself. That is why liberalism is bound to go down again and again. It can influence only small numbers of people. The reason is not hard to see. Liberalism tries to make us unselfish. But we do not want to be unselfish. We see no immediate gain in unselfishness—we gain more by being selfish. We accept liberalism as long as we are poor, have nothing. The moment we acquire money and power, we turn very conservative. The poor man is a democrat. When he becomes rich, he becomes an aristocrat. In religion, too, human nature acts in the same way.

A prophet arises, promises all kinds of rewards to those who will follow him and eternal doom to those who will not. Thus he makes his ideas spread. All existent religions that are spreading are tremendously fanatic. The more a sect hates other sects, the greater is its success and the more people it draws into its fold. My conclusion, after traveling over a good part of the world and living with many races, and in view of the conditions prevailing in the world, is that the present state of things is going to continue, in spite of much talk of universal brotherhood.

Vedanta does not believe in any of these teachings. First, it does not believe in a book—that is the difficulty to start with. It denies the authority of any book over any other book. It denies emphatically that any one book can contain all the truths about God, soul, the ultimate reality. Those of you who have read the Upanishads remember that they say again and again, "Not by the reading of books can we realize the Self."

Second, it finds veneration for some particular person still more difficult to uphold. Those of you who are students of Vedanta—by Vedanta is always meant the Upanishads—know that this is the only religion that does not cling to any person. Not one man or woman has ever become the object of worship among the Vedantists. It cannot be. A man is no more worthy of worship than any bird, any worm. We are all brothers. The difference is only in degree. I am exactly the same as the lowest worm. You see how very little room there is in Vedanta for any man to stand ahead of us and for us to go and worship him—he dragging us on and we being saved by him. Vedanta does not give you that. No book, no man to worship, nothing.

A still greater difficulty is about God. You want to be democratic in this country. It is the democratic God that Vedanta teaches.

You have a government, but the government is impersonal. Yours is not an autocratic government, and yet it is more powerful than any monarchy in the world. Nobody seems to understand that the real power, the real life, the real strength, is in the unseen, the impersonal, the nobody. As a mere person separated from others, you are nothing, but as an impersonal unit of the nation that rules itself, you are tremendous. You are all one in the government—you are a tremendous power. But where exactly is the power? Each man is the power. There is no king. I see everybody equally the same. I have not to take off my hat and bow low to anyone. Yet there is a tremendous power in each man.

Vedanta is just that. Its God is not the monarch sitting on a throne, entirely apart. There are those who like their God that way—a God to be feared and propitiated. They burn candles and crawl in the dust before Him. They want a king to rule them—they believe in a king in heaven to rule them all. The king is gone from this country at least. Where is the king of heaven now? Just where the earthly king is. In this country the king has entered every one of you. You are all kings in this country. So with the religion of Vedanta. You are all Gods. One God is not sufficient. You are all Gods, says Vedanta.

What is the idea of God in heaven? Materialism. The Vedantic idea is the infinite principle of God embodied in every one of us. God sitting up on a cloud! Think of the utter blasphemy of it! It is materialism—downright materialism. When babies think this way, it may be all right, but when grown-up men try to teach such things, it is downright disgusting—that is what it is. It is all matter, all body idea, the gross idea, the sense idea. Every bit of it is clay and nothing but clay. Is that religion? God is Spirit and He should be worshipped in Spirit and in Truth. Does Spirit live only in heaven? What is Spirit? We are all Spirit. Why is it we do not realize it? What makes you different from me? The body and nothing else. Forget the body, and all is Spirit.

These are what Vedanta has not to give. No book. No man to be singled out from the rest of mankind—"You are worms, and we are the Lord God!"—none of that. If you are the Lord God, I also am the Lord God. So Vedanta knows no sin. There are mistakes but no sin, and in the long run everything is going to be all right. No Satan—none of this nonsense. Vedanta believes in only one sin, only one in the world, and it is this: The moment you think you are a sinner, or anybody else is a sinner, that is sin. From that follows every other mistake, or what is usually called sin. There have been many mistakes in our lives. But we are going on. Glory be unto us that we have made mistakes! Take a long look at your past life. If your present condition is good, it has been caused by all the past mistakes as well as successes. Glory be unto success! Glory be unto mistakes! Do not look back upon what has been done. Go ahead!

You see, Vedanta proposes no sin nor sinner. No God to be afraid of. He is the one being of whom we shall never be afraid, because He is our own Self. There is only one being of whom you cannot possibly be afraid—He is that. Then is not he really the most superstitious person who has fear of God? There may be someone who is afraid of his shadow, but even he is not afraid of himself. God is man's very Self. He is that one being whom you can never possibly fear. What is all this nonsense, the fear of the Lord entering into a man, making him tremble and so on? Lord bless us that we are not all in the lunatic asylum! But if most of us are not lunatics, why should we invent such ideas as fear of God? Lord Buddha said that the whole human race is lunatic, more or less. It is perfectly true, it seems.

No book, no person, no Personal God. All these must go. Again, the senses must go. We cannot be bound to the senses. At present we are tied down—like persons dying of cold in the glaciers. They feel such a strong desire to sleep, and when their friends try to wake them, warning them of death, they say, "Let me die, I want to sleep." We all cling to the little things of the senses, even if we are ruined thereby; we forget there are much greater things.

There is a Hindu legend that the Lord was once incarnated on earth as a pig. He had a pig mate and in course of time several little pigs were born to Him. He was very happy with His family, living in the mire, squealing with joy, forgetting His divine glory and lordship. The gods became exceedingly concerned and came to the earth to beg Him to give up the pig body and return to heaven. But the Lord would have none of that. He drove them away. He said He was very happy and did not want to be disturbed. Seeing no other course, the gods destroyed the pig body of the Lord. At once He regained His divine majesty and was astonished that He could have found any joy in being a pig.

People behave in the same way. Whenever they hear of the Impersonal God, they say, "What will become of my individuality?—my individuality will go!" The next time that thought comes, remember the pig, and then think what an infinite mine of happiness you have, each one of you. How pleased you are with your present condition. But when you realize what you truly are, you will be astonished that you were unwilling to give up your sense life. What is there in your personality? Is it any better than that pig life? And this you do not want to give up! Lord bless us all!

Vedanta formulates, not universal brotherhood, but universal oneness. I am the same as any other man, as any animal—good, bad, anything. It is one body, one mind, one soul throughout. The Spirit never dies. There is no death anywhere, not even for the body. Not even the mind dies. How can even the body die? One leaf may fall—does the tree die? The universe is my body. See how it continues. All minds are mine. With all feet I walk. Through all mouths I speak. In every body I reside.

Why can I not feel it? Because of that individuality, that piggishness. You have become bound up with this mind and can only be here, not there. What is immortality? How few reply, "It is this very existence of ours!" Most people think this is all mortal and dead—that God is not here, that they will become immortal by going to heaven. They imagine that they will see God after death. But if they do not see Him here and now, they will not see Him after death. Though they all believe in immortality, they do not know that immortality is not gained by dying and going to heaven, but by giving up this piggish individuality, by not tying ourselves down to one little body. Immortality is knowing ourselves as one with all, living in all bodies, perceiving through all minds. We are bound to feel in other bodies than this one. We are bound to feel in other bodies. What is sympathy? Is there any limit to this sympathy, this feeling in our bodies? It is quite possible that the time will come when I shall feel through the whole universe.

What is the gain? The pig body is hard to give up. We are sorry to lose the enjoyment of our one little pig body! Vedanta does not say, "Give it up." It says, "Transcend it." No need of asceticism—better would be the enjoyment of two bodies, better three, living in more bodies than one! When I can enjoy through the whole universe, the whole universe is my body.

There are many who feel horrified when they hear these teachings. They do not like to be told that they are not just little pig bodies, created by a tyrant God. I tell them, "Come up!" They say they are born in sin—they cannot come up except through someone's grace. I say, "You are Divine!" They answer: "You blasphemer, how dare you speak so? How can a miserable creature be God? We are sinners!" I get very much discouraged at times, you know. Hundreds of men and women tell me, "If there is no hell, how can there be any religion?" If these people go to hell of their own will, who can prevent them?

Whatever you dream and think of, you create. If it is hell, you die and see hell. If it is evil and Satan, you get a Satan. If ghosts, you get ghosts. Whatever you think, that you become. If you have to think, think good thoughts, great thoughts. This taking for granted that you are weak little worms! By declaring we are weak, we become weak—we do not become better. Suppose we put out the light, close the windows, and call the room dark. Think of the nonsense! What good does it do me to say I am a sinner? If I am in the dark, let me light a lamp. The whole thing is gone. Yet how curious is the nature of men! Though always conscious that the universal mind is behind their life, they think more of Satan, of darkness and lies. You tell them the truth, they do not see it. They like darkness better.

This forms the one great question asked by Vedanta: Why are people so afraid? The answer is that they have made themselves helpless and dependent on others. We are so lazy, we do not want to do anything for ourselves. We want a Personal God, a savior, or a prophet to do everything for us. The very rich man never walks; he always goes in a carriage. But in the course of years, he wakes up one day paralyzed all over. Then he begins to feel that the way he had lived was not good after all. No man can walk for me. Every time one did, it was to my injury. If everything is done for a man by another, he will lose the use of his own limbs. Anything we do ourselves, that is the only thing we do. Anything that is done for us by another never can be ours. You cannot learn spiritual truths from my lectures. If you have learned anything, I was only the spark that brought it out, made it flash. That is all the prophets and teachers can do. All this running after help is foolishness.

You know, there are bullock carts in India. Usually two bulls are harnessed to a cart, and sometimes a sheaf of straw is dangled at the tip of the pole, a little in front of the animals but beyond their reach. The bulls try continually to feed upon the straw but never succeed. This is exactly how we are helped! We think we are going to get security, strength, wisdom, happiness, from the outside. We always hope but never realize our hope. Never does any help come from the outside.

There is no help for man. None ever was, none is, and none will be. Why should there be? Are you not men and women? Are the lords of the earth to be helped by others? Are you not ashamed? You will be helped when you are reduced to dust. But you are Spirit. Pull yourself out of difficulties by yourself! Save yourself by yourself! There is none to help you—never was. To think that there is, is sweet delusion. It comes to no good.

What is the God of Vedanta? He is principle, not person. You and I are all Personal Gods. The absolute God of the universe, the creator, preserver, and destroyer of the universe, is impersonal principle. You and I, the cat, rat, devil, and ghost, all these are Its persons—all are Personal Gods. You want to worship Personal Gods. It is the worship of your own Self. If you take my advice, you will never enter any church. Come out and go and wash off. Wash yourself again and again until you are cleansed of all the superstitions that have clung to you through the ages.

I have been asked many times, "Why do you laugh so much and make so many jokes?" I become serious sometimes—when I have a stomachache! The Lord is all blissfulness. He is the reality behind all that exists. He is the goodness, the truth, in everything. You are His incarnations. That is what is glorious. The nearer you are to Him, the less you will have occasions to cry or weep. The further we are from Him, the more will long faces come. The more we know of Him, the more misery vanishes. If one who lives in the Lord becomes miserable, what is the use of living in Him? What is the use of such a God? Throw Him overboard into the Pacific Ocean! We do not want Him!

Unity is knowledge; diversity is ignorance. This knowledge is your birthright. I have not to teach it to you. There never were different religions in the world. We are all destined to have salvation, whether we will it or not. You have to attain it in the long run and become free, because it is your nature to be free. We are already free, only we do not know it, and we do not know what we have been doing. Throughout all religious systems and ideals is the same morality. One thing only is preached: "Be unselfish. Love others." One says, "Because Jehovah commanded." "Allah," shouted Mohammed. Another cries, "Jesus." If it were only the command of Jehovah, how could it come to those who never knew Jehovah? If it were Jesus alone who gave this command, how could anyone who never knew Jesus get it? If only Vishnu, how could the Jews get it, who never were acquainted with that gentleman? There is another source, greater than all of them. Where is it? In the eternal temple of God, in the souls of all beings, from the lowest to the highest. It is there—that infinite unselfishness, infinite sacrifice, infinite compulsion, to go back to unity.

We have seemingly been divided, limited, because of our

ignorance, and we have become, as it were, the little Mrs. so-and-so and Mr. so-and-so. But all nature is giving this delusion the lie every moment. I am not that little man or little woman cut off from all else. I am the one universal existence. The soul in its own majesty is rising up every moment and declaring its own intrinsic divinity.

This Vedanta is everywhere, only you must become conscious of it. These masses of foolish beliefs and superstitions hinder us in our progress. If we can, let us throw them off and understand that God is Spirit, to be worshipped in Spirit and in Truth. Try to be materialists no more! Throw away all matter! The conception of God must be truly spiritual. All the different ideas of God that are more or less materialistic must go. As man becomes more and more spiritual, he has to throw off all these ideas and leave them behind. As a matter of fact, in every country there have always been a few who have been strong enough to throw away all matter and stand out in the shining light, worshipping the Spirit by the spirit.

If Vedanta—this conscious knowledge that all is one Spirit—spreads, the whole of humanity will become spiritual. But is it possible? I do not know. Not within thousands of years. The old superstitions must run out. You are all interested in how to perpetuate all your superstitions. Then there are the ideas of the family brother, the caste brother, the national brother. All these are barriers to the realization of Vedanta. Religion has been religion to very few.

Most of those who have worked in the field of religion all over the world have really been political workers. That has been the history of human beings. They have rarely tried to live up uncompromisingly to the truth. They have always worshipped the god called society. They have been mostly concerned with upholding what the masses believe—their superstitions, their weakness. They do not try to conquer nature but to fit into nature, nothing else. Go to India and preach a new creed—they will not listen to it. But if you tell them it is from the Vedas, "That is good!" they will say. Here I can preach this doctrine, and you—how many of you take me seriously? But the truth is all here, and I must tell you the truth.

There is another side to the question. Everyone says that the highest, the pure, truth cannot be realized all at once by all, that men have to be led to it gradually through worship, prayer, and other kinds of prevalent religious practices. I am not sure whether that is the right method or not. In India I work both ways.

In Calcutta, I have all these images and temples—in the name of God and the Vedas, of the Bible and Christ and Buddha. Let it be tried. But on the heights of the Himalayas I have a place where I am determined nothing shall enter except pure truth. There I want to work out this idea about which I have spoken to you today. The purpose is to train seekers of truth, and to bring up children without fear and without superstition. They shall not hear about Christs and Buddhas and Shivas and Vishnus—none of these. They shall learn from the start to stand upon their own feet. They shall learn from their childhood that God is the Spirit and should be worshipped in Spirit and in Truth. Everyone must be looked upon as Spirit. That is the ideal. I do not know what success will come of it. Today I am preaching the thing I like. I wish I had been brought up entirely on that, without all the dualistic superstitions.

Sometimes I agree that there is some good in the dualistic method—it helps many who are weak. If a man wants you to show him the polar star, you first point out to him a bright star near it, then a less bright star, then a dim star, and then the polar star. This process makes it easy for him to see it. All the various practices and trainings, Bibles and Gods, are but the rudiments of religion, the kindergartens of religion.

But then I think of the other side. How long will the world have to wait to reach the truth if it follows this slow, gradual process? How long? And where is the surety that it will ever succeed to any appreciable degree? It has not so far. After all, gradual or not gradual, easy or not easy to the weak, is not the dualistic method based on falsehood? Are not all the prevalent religious practices often weakening and therefore wrong? They are based on a wrong idea, a wrong view of man. Would two wrongs make one right? Would the lie become truth? Would darkness become light?

Christ said, "I and my Father are one," and you repeat it. Yet it has not helped mankind. For nineteen hundred years men have not understood that saying. They make Christ the savior of men. He is God and we are worms! Similarly in India. In every country, this sort of belief is the backbone of every sect. For thousands of years millions and millions all over the world have been taught to worship the Lord of the world, the Incarnations, the saviors, the prophets. They have been taught to consider themselves helpless, miserable creatures and to depend upon the mercy of some person or persons for salvation. There are no doubt many marvelous things in such beliefs. But even at their best, they are but kindergartens of religion, and they have helped but little. Men are still hypnotized into abject degradation. However, there are some strong souls who get over that illusion. The hour comes when great men shall arise and cast off these kindergartens of religion and shall make vivid and powerful the true religion, the worship of the Spirit by the Spirit. (VIII. 122-34, 138-41)

Notes

1 Katha Upanishad, 2.2.9.

2 Robert Ingersoll (1833-1899).

Swami Vivekananda's Temple, Belur Monastery
"My ideal, indeed, can be put into a few words, and that is: to preach unto mankind their divinity, and how to make it manifest in every movement of life."—Swami Vivekananda

GLOSSARY

Advaita—nonduality. Also, the name of a school of Vedanta philosophy which teaches the oneness of God, the soul, and the universe. The main exponents of Advaita Vedanta were Gaudapada and Shankara.

Ahriman—the name of the devil in the Zoroastrian religion, who is responsible for everything bad in the world.

Ahura Mazda—the name of God in the Zoroastrian religion, who is responsible for everything good in the world.

Arjuna—one of the five Pandava princes and a great hero of the Indian epic, the *Mahabharata*. The teachings of the Bhagavad Gita were given by Sri Krishna to Arjuna on the battlefield, just before the war of Kurukshetra.

Asana—posture.

Atman—the Self, or the soul. Also denotes the Supreme Soul, which, according to Advaita Vedanta, is identical with the individual soul.

Avatara—an Incarnation of God.

Avidya—ignorance, cosmic or individual, which is responsible for the nonperception of Reality.

Belur—the village in which the headquarters of the Ramakrishna Math and Mission is located. It is about four miles north and across the Ganga from Calcutta.

Bhagavad Gita—lit., the "Song of God." One of the most important scriptures of the Vedanta philosophy, the Bhagavad Gita, or Gita for short, consists of the teachings of Sri Krishna to Arjuna on how to realize God while carrying on the duties of life. The eighteen chapters of this work are actually a part of the Indian epic, the *Mahabharata*.

Bhakti—devotion to God.

Bhakti yoga—the path of devotion. One of the four main yogas, or paths to union with God.

Bhartrihari—a king of ancient India, who renounced his throne for the monastic life. He became a well-known Sanskrit poet and philosopher.

Bhishma—one of the great heroes of the Indian epic, the *Mahabharata*. He was renowned for his devotion to truth.

Brahma—God in his aspect as the Creator of the Universe. The First Person of the Hindu Trinity, the other two being Vishnu and Shiva.

Brahma Sutras—an authoritative treatise on the Vedanta philosophy, ascribed to Vyasa. The Brahma Sutras interpret the spiritual experiences described in the Upanishads through reasoning.

Brahmaloka—the region of Brahma, roughly corresponding to the highest heaven of the dualistic religions, where spiritually evolved souls go after death.

Brahman—the Absolute. The supreme reality of Advaita Vedanta.

Brahmin—a member of the priestly caste, the highest caste in Hindu society.

Brahmo Samaj—a socio-religious reform movement of India, founded by Raja Rammohan Roy (1774-1833).

Buddha—lit., "the Enlightened One." The word refers specifically to Gautama Buddha, ca. 6th century B.C. Born as Prince Siddhartha in what is now Nepal, he renounced the world to become one of the greatest spiritual teachers of all time and the founder of Buddhism.

Buddhi—the determinative faculty of the mind, which makes

decisions. It is sometimes translated as the "intellect."

Chitta—the mind-stuff. That part of the inner organ which is the storehouse of memory or which seeks for pleasurable objects.

Chitta-vrittis—thought-waves of the mind caused by desires.

Dakshineswar—a village on the Ganga, about five miles north of Calcutta. Sri Ramakrishna lived in Dakshineswar for most of his life.

Dama—restraining of the sense organs from all sense objects.

Demoniac nature—men of demoniac nature are impure, immoral, untruthful, lustful, self-honored, haughty, and full of hypocrisy, pride, and arrogance. For details, see the sixteenth chapter of the Bhagavad Gita.

Devas—the gods of Hindu mythology.

Dharana—concentration. The sixth of the eight steps of raja yoga, and a stage in the process of meditation. It is the stage of fixing the mind on a point or object.

Dhyana—meditation, or deepened concentration. Dhyana, the seventh of the eight steps of raja yoga, is defined by Patanjali as "an unbroken flow of thought toward the object of concentration."

Drona—a hero of the Indian epic, the *Mahabharata*. He was a great instructor of the military arts.

Duryodhana—the eldest of the Kaurava princes, who attempted to acquire by deceit the kingdom which rightfully belonged to their cousins, the Pandavas. The story of their feud and the resulting war has been narrated in the great Indian epic, the *Mahabharata*.

Ganapatya—a worshipper of Ganapati, i.e., God in his aspect as the remover of all obstacles.

Gita—*see* Bhagavad Gita.

Guru—the spiritual teacher. *Gu* means darkness, and *ru* means destroyer. He who destroys the darkness, or ignorance, of the disciple is a guru.

Ishta—the Chosen Deity. That aspect of the Personal God which a devotee meditates on in order to attain illumination.

Ishvara—God with attributes. The Personal God.

Janaka, King—an ideal king of Hindu mythology, who was established in the knowledge of Brahman yet remained in the world, carrying on his royal duties.

Jiva—lit., a "living being." The individual soul, which is in essence one with the Universal Soul.

Jivanmukta—one who has attained liberation while living in the body.

Jivanmukti—the state of liberation while living in the body.

Jnana kanda—the philosophical or knowledge portion of the Vedas. Refers specifically to the Upanishads.

Jnana yoga—the path of knowledge and discrimination. One of the four main yogas, or paths to union with God.

Karma—action which yields results to the doer, or which is the effect of his previous deeds. Also, the sacrificial actions ordained by the scriptures.

Karma yoga—the path of selfless work. One of the four main yogas, or paths to union with God.

Krishna—one of the most widely worshipped Incarnations of God in Hinduism. Sri Krishna delivered the message of the Bhagavad Gita to his friend Arjuna on the battlefield of Kurukshetra.

Manas—the faculty of doubt and volition. Sometimes translated as "mind."

Mantra—a sacred word, verse, or Vedic hymn. Also, the name of God which a guru gives to a disciple at the time of initiation.

Mantra-drashta—lit., a "seer of mantras." Refers specifically to the rishis of ancient India, to whom the hymns and prayers of the Vedas were revealed in their meditations.

Maya—a term of the Vedanta philosophy denoting ignorance obscuring the vision of Reality. Also, the cosmic illusion on account of which the one appears as the many, the Absolute as the relative. The word is also used to denote attachment.

Mayavadin—a person who believes that the world is a play of illusory maya and that one should not be attached to it.

Mayavati—a Vedanta center in the Himalayas started in 1899 under the inspiration of Swami Vivekananda. It is the headquarters of Advaita Ashrama, a branch of the Ramakrishna Order, and the editorial office of the journal, *Prabuddha Bharata*.

Moksha—same as Mukti.

Mukti—liberation from karma and the cycle of birth, death, and rebirth through union with God or knowledge of the ultimate reality. Mukti is the goal of spiritual practice.

Mumukshutva—the intense desire for liberation.

Narada—a great sage and lover of God mentioned in the Hindu scriptures.

Nirvana—final absorption in Brahman, or the All-pervading Reality, through the annihilation of the individual ego, desire, and passion. It also means liberation.

Nirvikalpa samadhi—the highest state of samadhi, in which the aspirant realizes his total oneness with Brahman.

Nishtha—steadfast, unswerving devotion to God or to an ideal.

Nityanitya-viveka—discrimination between the real and the unreal, such as Brahman alone is real and all other things in this world are unreal.

Nivedita, Sister—Margaret Noble (1867-1911). An Irish disciple of Swami Vivekananda, who dedicated her life to work for the welfare of India.

Niyama—restraint of the mind. The second of the eight steps of raja yoga.

Om—sometimes written Aum. The most sacred word of the Vedas. It is a symbol of both the Personal God and the Absolute.

Para-bhakti—supreme love of God, characterized by complete selflessness.

Patanjali—the author of the *Yoga Sutras* and the founder of the Yoga system, one of the six systems of orthodox Hindu philosophy, which deals with control of the mind, concentration, meditation, etc.

Personal God—God with attributes, as opposed to the Impersonal Absolute. God as the Creator, Preserver, and Destroyer of the Universe, who is worshipped and adored by the devotees.

Prahlada—the son of a demon king, Hiranyakashipu, and a great devotee of Vishnu, whose life is described in Hindu mythology. In spite of repeated tortures by his father for his piety, Prahlada remained steadfast in his love for Vishnu. Vishnu appeared in the form of a man-lion and killed the father.

Prana—the vital breath, which sustains life in a physical body. Also, the primal energy or force, of which other physical forces are manifestations.

Pranayama—control of the vital energy through the practice

of breathing exercises. The fourth of the eight steps in raja yoga.

Pratyahara—withdrawal of the mind from the sense objects. The fifth of the eight steps of raja yoga.

Pratyaksha—direct perception or realization.

Purusha—lit., "person." A term of the Sankhya philosophy denoting the individual conscious principle. In Vedanta the word denotes the Self, or Atman.

Qualified Advaitist—*see* Qualified Monist.

Qualified Monist—a follower of Qualified Monism, a school of Vedanta founded by Ramanuja. According to this school, the soul and nature are modes of Brahman, and the individual soul is a part of Brahman.

Raja yoga—one of the four main yogas, or paths to union with the Divine. Raja yoga was propounded by Patanjali in the *Yoga Sutras* and stresses control of the mind concentration, and meditation, leading to samadhi.

Rajas—the principle of activity or restlessness. One of three qualities which comprise the universe of mind and matter. *See also* Sattva and Tamas.

Rajasika—one whose nature is characterized by the quality of rajas.

Ramakrishna, Sri—1836-1886. A God-man of India, whose life inspired the modern renaissance of Vedanta. After practicing intense spiritual disciplines and realizing his union with God through various paths within Hinduism, as well as through Christianity and Islam, Sri Ramakrishna proclaimed, "As many faiths, so many paths."

Ramakrishna Math and Mission—a twin institution established in the name of Sri Ramakrishna (1836-1886). The nucleus of the Math (lit., "monastery") was formed by Sri Ramakrishna himself, and the Mission (philanthropic activities) was started by Swami Vivekananda in 1897. There are hundreds of branches of the Ramakrishna Order all over the world, including 12 in the U.S.A.

Rig Veda—one of the four Vedas. The Vedas are the most sacred scriptures of the Hindus and the ultimate authority of the Hindu religion and philosophy. The other three Vedas are the Yajur Veda, the Sama Veda, and the Atharva Veda.

Rishi—a seer of Truth to whom the wisdom of the Vedas was revealed. Also, a general name for a saint or ascetic.

Samadhana—constant concentration of the mind on the Self.

Samadhi—the superconscious state, in which man experiences his identity with the ultimate reality. According to Patanjali, it is a state in which "the true nature of the object shines forth, not distorted by the mind of the perceiver."

Samhita—the section of the Vedas that contains the hymns and prayers used in the sacrifices.

Samsara—the relative world. Also, the relentless cycle of birth, death, and rebirth to which a person is subject as long as he remains ignorant of his identity with Brahman.

Samskara—an impression or tendency created in the mind of a person as the result of an action or thought. The sum total of a person's samskaras, including those from previous births, forms his character.

Sanatana dharma—lit., the "eternal religion." The religion of the Hindus, formulated by the rishis of the Vedas.

Sankhya—one of the six systems of Hindu philosophy, attributed to the sage Kapila. The cosmology of Sankhya is very scientific. It explains how creation evolves from the union of Purusha (Consciousness) and Prakriti (matter).

Sannyasa—the monastic life.

Sannyasin—a monk. One who has taken the vows of sannyasa.

Sat-Chit-Ananda—*see* Satchidananda.

Satchidananda, also Sat-Chit-Ananda—Absolute Existence, Absolute Consciousness, and Absolute Bliss. A term used to describe Brahman, the ultimate reality.

Sattva—the principle of calmness and purity. One of the three qualities which comprise the universe of mind and matter. *See also* Rajas and Tamas.

Sattvika—one whose nature is characterized by the quality of sattva.

Saura—a worshipper of Surya, God as represented by the sun.

Shaivite—a worshipper of Shiva.

Shakta—a worshipper of Shakti, God as the Mother of the Universe.

Shama—a discipline of the mind that keeps it from pursuing worldly pleasures.

Shankara, also Shankaracharya—688-720. One of the greatest saints and philosophers of India and the foremost exponent of Advaita Vedanta.

Shankaracharya—*see* Shankara.
Shastra—a scripture, a sacred book, or a code of law.
Shiva—God in his aspect as the Destroyer of the Universe. The Third Person of the Hindu Trinity, the other two being Brahma and Vishnu. He is also worshipped as the supreme reality.
Shivoham—lit., "I am Shiva." A word repeated by followers of Advaita Vedanta to remind themselves of their identity with Brahman.
Shraddha—faith in the truths of the scriptures and the teachings of the guru.
Shramana—a Buddhist monk.
Shruti—the knowledge which has been learned through hearing, i.e., the Vedas.
Shuka—the son of Vyasa and the narrator of the Srimad Bhagavatam. He is regarded as an ideal monk of India.
Soham—lit., "I am He." A word repeated by followers of Advaita Vedanta to remind themselves of their identity with Brahman.
Swami—a title of address of a Hindu monk.
Tamas—the principle of inertia or dullness. One of the three qualities which comprise the universe of mind and matter. *See also* Rajas and Sattva.
Tamasika—one whose nature is characterized by the quality of tamas.
Tapas—austerity or spiritual discipline.
Tat Tvam Asi—lit., "Thou art That." A sacred utterance of the Vedas denoting the identity of the individual self and the Supreme Self.
Titiksha—the endurance of heat and cold, pleasure and pain, gain and loss, and other pairs of opposites.
Triputibheda—three divisions, i.e., knower-knowledge-knowable or meditator-meditation-object of meditation, which become unified at the time of nirvikalpa samadhi.
Turiyananda, Swami—1863-1922. A monastic disciple of Sri Ramakrishna. He came to the United States in 1899 along with Swami Vivekananda and soon after established the Shanti Ashrama, a retreat in the San Antonio Valley of northern California. He returned to India in 1902.
Upanishads—the sacred scriptures which contain the philosophical aspect of the Vedas. The Upanishads mainly deal with the knowledge of God and record the spiritual expe-

riences of the sages of ancient India. There are about one hundred and eight in number, of which eleven are considered major.

Uparati—the function of the mind that keeps the restrained organs from drifting back again to the objects of the senses.

Vairagya—renunciation, dispassion for the world.

Vaishnavite—a worshipper of Vishnu, especially in one of his Incarnations as Rama, Krishna, or Chaitanya.

Varanasi—a sacred city on the Ganga in the north central part of India. It is believed that anyone who dies there is immediately granted liberation and does not have to be reborn. The city is also known as Benaras, Benares, or Kashi.

Vedanta—lit., the "end of the Vedas." One of the six systems of orthodox Hindu philosophy, based mainly on the teachings of the Upanishads, the Bhagavad Gita, and the Brahma Sutras.

Vedas—the most sacred scriptures of the Hindus and the ultimate authority of the Hindu religion and philosophy. The four Vedas are the Rig Veda, the Sama Veda, the Yajur Veda, and the Atharva Veda.

Vidya—knowledge. Also, knowledge leading to the realization of the ultimate reality.

Vireshwar Shiva—an aspect of Shiva worshipped in Varanasi. Vireshwar literally means "god of the heroes."

Vishnu—God in his aspect as the Preserver of the Universe. The Second Person of the Hindu Trinity, the other two being Brahma and Shiva. He is also worshipped as the supreme reality.

Vivartavada—the appearance of an object as something else without its having undergone any change, as a rope gives rise to the illusion of a snake in darkness.

Viveka—discrimination between the real and the unreal.

Vritti—a thought-wave in the mind.

Vyasa—a celebrated sage, who arranged the Vedas in their present form. He is also the author of the *Mahabharata*, the Brahma Sutras, the Srimad Bhagavatam, and other puranas.

Yama—the god of death in Hindu mythology.

—l.c., lit., "self-control." The first of the eight steps of raja yoga.

Yoga—the union of the individual soul with the Supreme

Soul. Also, the discipline by which such union is effected. The Yoga system of philosophy, ascribed to Patanjali, is one of the six systems of orthodox Hindu philosophy and deals with the realization of Truth through concentration, meditation, etc.

Yudhishthira—the eldest of the five Pandava princes, whose kingdom was deceitfully taken from them by their cousins, the Kauravas. The story of their feud and the resulting war has been narrated in the great Indian epic, the *Mahabharata*.

SUGGESTIONS FOR FURTHER READING

Burke, Marie Louise. *Swami Vivekananda in the West: New Discoveries*. Calcutta: Advaita Ashrama, 1983-85. Vols. I-III.

Chetanananda, Swami, ed. *Meditation and Its Methods: According to Swami Vivekananda*. Hollywood, Calif.: Vedanta Press, 1978.

Chetanananda, Swami. *Swami Adbhutananda: Teachings and Reminiscences*. St. Louis: The Vedanta Society, 1980.

Dattatreya Avadhuta. *Avadhuta Gita: The Song of the Ever-Free*. Translated by Swami Chetanananda. Calcutta: Advaita Ashrama, 1984.

Gambhirananda, Swami, trans. *Brahma-Sutra Bhashya of Shankaracharya*. Calcutta: Advaita Ashrama, 1965.

His Eastern and Western Disciples. *The Life of Swami Vivekananda*. Calcutta: Advaita Ashrama, 1979-81. Vols. I-II.

Isherwood, Christopher. *Ramakrishna and His Disciples*. Hollywood, Calif.: Vedanta Press, 1965.

Isherwood, Christopher, ed. *Vedanta for the Western World*. Hollywood, Calif: Vedanta Press, 1945.

Nikhilananda, Swami, trans. *The Bhagavad Gita*. New York: Ramakrishna-Vivekananda Center, 1978.

Nikhilananda, Swami, trans. *The Gospel of Sri Ramakrishna*. New York: Ramakrishna-Vivekananda Center, 1977.

Nikhilananda, Swami, trans. *The Upanishads*. New York: Ramakrishna-Vivekananda Center, 1977. Vols. I-IV.

Nikhilananda, Swami, ed. *Vivekananda: The Yogas and Other Works*. New York: Ramakrishna-Vivekananda Center, 1953.

Nivedita, Sister. *The Master As I Saw Him*. Calcutta: Udbodhan Office, 1977.

Prabhavananda, Swami, and Christopher Isherwood, trans. *Bhagavad-Gita: The Song of God*. Hollywood, Calif.: Vedanta Press, 1972

Prabhavananda, Swami, and Frederick Manchester, trans. *The Upanishads: Breath of the Eternal*. Hollywood, Calif.: Vedanta Press, 1975.

Rolland, Romain. *The Life of Ramakrishna*. Calcutta: Advaita Ashrama, 1979.

Rolland, Romain. *The Life of Vivekananda and the Universal Gospel*. Calcutta: Advaita Ashrama, 1979.

Saradananda, Swami. *Sri Ramakrishna, the Great Master*. Madras: Sri Ramakrishna Math, 1978-79. Vols. I-II.

Satprakashananda, Swami. *The Goal and the Way*. St. Louis: The Vedanta Society, 1977.

Satprakashananda, Swami. *The Universe, God, and God-Realization*. St. Louis: The Vedanta Society, 1977.

Shankara. *Crest-Jewel of Discrimination (Viveka-Chudamani)*. Translated by Swami Prabhavananda and Christopher Isherwood. Hollywood, Calif.: Vedanta Press, 1975.

Smaranananda, Swami, and Swami Chetanananda. *Sri Ramakrishna: A Biography in Pictures*. Calcutta: Advaita Ashrama, 1981.

Vireshwarananda, Swami, trans. *Brahma-Sutras*. Calcutta: Advaita Ashrama, 1982.

Vivekananda, Swami. *The Complete Works of Swami Vivekananda*. Calcutta: Advaita Ashrama, 1971-72. Vols. I-VIII.

INDEX